SCRIBE

KEZ WICKHAM ST GEORGE

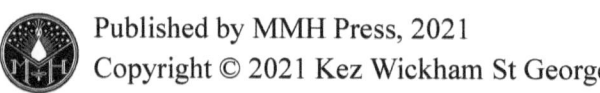 Published by MMH Press, 2021
Copyright © 2021 Kez Wickham St George

All rights reserved. No part of this book may be used or reproduced by any means, graphic, electronic, or mechanical, including photocopying, recording, taping or by any information storage retrieval system without the written permission of the copyright owner except in the case of brief quotations embodied in critical articles and reviews.

This is a work of fiction. Names, characters, businesses, places, events and incidents are either the products of the author/s' imagination or used in a fictitious manner. Any resemblance to actual persons, living or dead, or actual events is purely coincidental.

Because of the dynamic nature of the Internet, any web addresses or links contained in this book may have changed since publication and may no longer be valid. The views expressed in this work are solely those of the authors and do not necessarily reflect the views of the publisher and the publisher hereby disclaims any responsibility for them.

Cover Design: Dylan Ingram
Interior Design: Eleanor Narey & Chelsea Wilcox

National Library of Australia
Cataloguing-in-Publication data:
Scribe/Kez Wickham St George

ISBN: 978-0-6453359-6-5 (paperback)
978-0-6453359-7-2 (ebook)

Dedication

To my Nana Rose, my maternal grandmother. I did not know you well, and your story was never told; all I have of you is memories, a cut crystal drop earring plus a sepia photo of you holding me as a babe. However, what I do know is you were my Nana, that we had a connection, even though it was forbidden because of your beliefs, I am part of you as you are part of me. Thank you. Your granddaughter.

And to Suzanne Fielder, a cousin and friend I truly admired. I loved your humour and zany creative flair for life, our time in Brisbane together was one holiday I will never forget. May your spirit fly high, Suzanne.

KEZ

PROLOGUE

Breathing was the hardest thing to do. As she dragged her sodden body up onto shore, sharp stones cut into her hands as she clawed her way forwards.; her chest was screaming with raw pain as she sucked in each lungful of air, then coughing, before retching the sea water out. The force of it caused her small body to double over, then start the process again, with each breath only managing to grab a tiny lungful of air. Her heart pounded in her ears: *live, breathe, live.* As she knelt exhausted in the sand and foam, she was tormented by the screams of her fellow passengers as the boat exploded on rocks and tore apart in the violent storm. Her mind was spinning as she remembered pale hands grabbing onto her, pulling, clinging, as her own body was pummelled under Neptune's deep roar, drowning out any calls for help.

The dumping of her body onto a small stretch of stony beach was her salvation from a watery grave. Fingers of foam greedily stretched out to her, wanting to suck her back into the turmoil. Using every ounce of muscle she owned, she pulled herself away, looking for an anchor to hang onto. She heard someone else crawling up after her, retching sea water as she had done. Her efforts to save herself had sapped all her strength; she could not move, not yet, except for her eyes, which took in the young man, registering the pain he was in as he held his chest. Blood dripped from a large open gash where a pale cream bone poked through the skin. His T shirt tinged pink as it mixed with the crimson blood and sea water. Somehow, they had both survived. They lay on the rocky beach, hacking up snotty sea water, hoping that more survivors would crawl out of the water. No-one came. Daybreak showed as a thin crack of light against a dirty grey sky. Big fat-bellied rain clouds still rumbled above them, ready to release a watery burden at any moment onto the helpless pair, their only refuge a rock somewhere in the vast Pacific Ocean.

They watched helplessly as their footsteps, the only evidence of their survival, were washed away. Although the ocean still rolled and heaved in an oily swell, the loud crashing of waves onto the surrounding rocks had almost ceased. Two seagulls far above stretched white wings to catch the biting cold wind that swept around her. Rose shivered, her teeth chattering, her mind too numb to realise hypothermia was setting in; fear grabbed her guts as she took in her surroundings. At either side and behind her stood one massive, towering rock, to the front of her, the ocean. She was trapped; as this thought rolled through her mind, the scene of rock and ocean became a blurred kaleidoscope as tears coursed down her face, her brain slowly becoming as cold as her body.

Paddy lay there watching her, his tortured body was in crucifying pain from a smashed cheekbone and deep lacerations across the chest; his shoulder hung down by his side, dislocated. If he dared open his mouth, a scream would escape. He craved for black oblivion, but the pain was not allowing exhaustion to claim him, so he lay there, the waves of intense pain mirroring the waves washing up onto the beach. He recognised the look of hopelessness in her eyes, as she sat there staring out to sea and knew he should move, but he could not, all he could do was croak a muffled, "Help!" He also knew without the basics of survival, water, shelter and warmth, death was not too far away. His first attempt to sit up was unsuccessful, the world tipped over onto its side, his vision somersaulted, his bowels emptying as he retched again. Paddy's body flopped back onto the rocks, the overpowering stench of his faeces now adding to his physical misery, once again his voice rasped, "Help."

Rose crawled over to him and weakly crumpled beside him. An 'ugh' of disgust escaped as the smell reached her. "You need to have that covered." Her nails began to flick out dirt and shell from the mash of skin and blood, her face showing disgust as her nails scraped on the protruding bone. "You really should wash off that dirt and that stuff," she said, her eyes pointing towards his vomit-stained shirt and then the puddle of brown liquid that now seeped into the beach. Rose staggered to her feet, offering him her hand.

"Can you get up?" Paddy slowly mouthed 'no', trying not to shake his head, the pain was too great to be of any practical use to himself or his condition.

Rose kneeled behind him, trying to push him into a sitting position; again Paddy's world tipped over. Bile and sea water erupted from his nose and mouth, his stomach cramping with the loss of much-needed fluid. "I think I've really hurt my head," he whimpered.

Rose grimaced as the stench of bowel waste and vomit teased her nostrils. "You've more than bloody banged your head," she replied. "Well we can't stay here, are you sure you can't get up?" Paddy's white bloodless face gave her the answer. Her pale, cold hand found his work-calloused one, and holding it gently she said, "I'm Rose, and you are?"

He managed to whisper, "Paddy."

"Well, Paddy, I need to find some shelter and some fresh water, I'm going to walk along the beach, to see what I can find, maybe someone else has survived. Will you be okay for a while?" He slowly gave a single nod. Rose stood up, her young slim body bruised and sore, her clothes torn, determination written on her face. Brushing off small stones and sand from her jeans, she walked away, her destination a rocky point that jutted out into the ocean.

Paddy watched her walk away, calling out as she went.

"Hello, anyone out there!" It seemed like just minutes had passed before he heard her footsteps again as she ran back to where he lay. He watched as she slipped over seaweed, stumbling in her haste, the shrill fear in her voice palpable.

"There's nothing or no-one for miles, we are on one bloody great rock in the middle of the ocean." Her deep blue eyes were still searching the horizon as she spoke; her tears shimmered, ready to fall once again. "Nothing but black and grey rocks that go nowhere but upwards." Rose hunched over, her arms wrapped around knees as she rocked back and forth. "Paddy, what the hell are we going to do?"

Paddy had managed to push a small sandy stone into his mouth; thankfully, saliva now wet his tongue. "What about up there, Rose?" His voice calm, but his mind screaming, *Jesus, help us,* his broken body tearing apart with pain.

Rose turned her face upwards; tears dripped off her chin, "It's just a huge rock, Paddy." He knew he needed to encourage her, if they were to find a way out, it would be Rose had who needed to find it.

Her eyes searched his face, now a mottled grey-blue, the cheek gash had formed two puffed purple lips around itself. The bleeding had almost stopped, but a wink of cream bone still stuck out through his skin, making her stomach churn. She looked at the cuts on his chest, the ripped cotton T-shirt he wore was meshed onto his skin, his dislocated arm lay like a dead fish beside him. Rose was evaluating whether or not she could move him, Paddy knew it was more important to find shelter and fresh water as soon as possible.

"Rose – more – rain – climb – find – help." Each word was punctuated by needles of sheer agony. Rose stood again; her face pinched with exhaustion. Without an answer, she marched off. He could hear her scrabbling uphill; small rocks began bouncing onto the beach as she climbed higher. He could hear her muttering to herself as she grunted and heaved her body up over boulders that formed part of the rocky island they were stranded on.

It seemed such a short time before she was kneeling beside him once again, Paddy's injured cheek was now very swollen, his eye shut, the colours of yellow, grey and green had taken the place of pale skin. The urgency in her voice woke him.

"Paddy, come on, move, now." His brain was fog, and he was feeling numb, almost warm. "You have to move, Paddy, there's another storm brewing, it's already raining out there." Her hand flicked out towards the sea. "Come on, mate, can you move?" Together they inched closer to the base of the rock, Rose grunting and half dragging, half carrying Paddy, while she babbled about a small ledge she had found, halfway up. Paddy's feet scrabbled for a hold, his dead weight proving too much for her, she stopped, pushing him onto his knees. He retched; his vision now spotted with red dots. His silent mantra was, *I have to do this.*

Rose sobbed at Paddy's inability to do anything except mutter. Finally, he gave up, sprawling facedown on the beach, his strangled gasps for breath telling Rose he could go no further. She knew all the pleading and begging was not worth the effort, Paddy could not move one more inch, let alone climb up to a small ledge.

"Leave me here, Rose, find shelter."

"Don't be such a bloody hero," Rose snarled at him, "I can't get us both up there, so I'll have to find something down here." Paddy attempted interrupting her, but her anger and frustration at being in this situation had taken over. "Paddy, you can't do squat, so shut the hell up, and let me sort it."

Rose walked away, hands on hips, a damp cold wind seeping through her thin clothes. The storm was almost on top of them, the sodden clouds above laced with lighting, the oily waves building once again. Suddenly she saw them. A little way down the beach; big dark rocks that could form some sort of shelter. She walked back to where he lay. "Come on, we can do this." Rose put his good arm around her waist, his shoulder tucked into her armpit. After a slow process of slipping, sliding, and pushing till there was nothing more to give, Paddy collapsed into a heap, the rocks not one metre away. She dragged his unconscious body up to the rocks and pushed Paddy into the slight alcove.

Rose looked up at the sky, the black curtain of rain was already hitting the shore. she rolled two large rocks around to form the base of a shelter, forming a miniature, semi-roofless igloo. It would have to do, Rose crawled inside with Paddy. She knew it would not keep them dry but would hopefully shelter them from the wind.

With the arrival of a grey drizzling morning, the worst of the storm had gone. Her body screaming for water, Rose wriggled out of the rocky cocoon and lay face up on the beach with her mouth open for the rain to splash into it and quench her thirst. She noticed small rivulets of fresh water splattering off the rocks onto the beach. Filling her mouth with the gritty mix, swallowing gagging, she then carefully wriggled back into the rocky hole to deliver water from her mouth into Paddy's. He stirred as she pressed her lips to his to trickle the slimy gritty mix into his mouth. He groaned and swallowed.

Rose patted his arm. "As long as it keeps raining, we have water." She repeated her journey twice more, drinking in the muddy water until mud and grit coated her face and teeth, and a taste of slimy earth sat on her tongue.

As the weather cleared and the sky turned a greyish blue, it was time for Rose to explore the rock a little more. She knew, but could not admit it to herself, their survival depended solely on her.

·

"Paddy," she said, giving him a small shake, "I'm going to climb up and see what I can find, won't be long." Rose climbed till she stood on the small ledge she had previously discovered. Above it jutted out another small ledge, once more she climbed up till she scrambled over the edge, feeling like she had won a war – her small fist punched the air as she let out a triumphant, "Yes!" Two seagulls screamed their fear and hate at her; in response she screamed, "Piss off!" her arms windmilling. The larger of the two dived at her. "Go on, bugger off," she yelled.

Two blue-grey eggs sat inside a nest of sticks, feathers and mud. Rose grabbed a few small rocks from the ground and heaved them at the two birds that still swirled and screamed at her, she was determined to win this prize. "Finders keepers!" she yelled at them. *At least Paddy and I will have something to eat,* she thought. As she sat down on the ledge, the sun warming her face, Rose cracked the first egg open and poured the contents into her mouth. Her gag reflexes kicked in as the taste of rotten fish poured down her throat; her mind pleaded, her stomach roiled, but begrudgingly the oily muck stayed down. It took a while to settle. She tucked the other egg into her t-shirt pocket. With great care she lowered herself back down the rock, with each step she fought the urge to vomit the rotten mess back up, her anger erupting into loud verbal abuse, "Stupid friggin rock, stupid bloody eggs and shitty water."

With one last soft thump, she landed on the beach. The rock igloo was not too far away. She wanted to run, to fling herself at the one point of safety that housed Paddy.

"Wake up, lazy, guess what I've got for you?" Rose shook him gently; "Come on, Paddy, wake up." She thought his colour was a lot better, although the gash and bone still looked disgusting. Taking the prized egg out from her t-shirt, she held it between her thumb and forefingers and displayed it above him, like a king's prized treasure. Paddy stayed mute and still, Rose's heart gave a quick flip as she noticed his chest was not rising or falling. Pinching his arm hard and twisting the skin, she screamed, "Paddy, you bastard, answer me!" laying her head on his chest expecting a soft thump. It remained still. "God no, please, no," Rose whimpered. She began to wriggle outside, the fear of death overtaking the fear of being shipwrecked. The prized treasure now lay broken on the ground beside Paddy, the stinking yellow fluid vanishing into the wet sand.

"Don't leave me here!" erupted like a volcano from Rose's throat as she sat on her haunches. The wind snatched the words from her mouth, whirling them up into the crannies and niches of the rock. The ocean was creeping closer, high tide was on its way in. Rose knew her only salvation was the ledge; the sea was already lapping around Paddy's pale feet. She walked away, the half-moon shone on her face as she nudged herself close into the ledge where the eggs had been, her sobbing wail of, "I want to go home!" bounced off hard surfaces that gave no quarter. Fear sat beside her: fear of falling, fear of dying, fear of never being found.

Her gut was still roiling, her bowel wanting to rid itself of the liquid poison. Her hands were ripped and torn; the sharpness of small rocks was unrelenting as she scrabbled to keep her balance on the ledge. Her eyelids fluttered with exhaustion. A terrifying night began as she wandered between sleep and hallucination, a fever raged through her body. She knew that if she was not rescued soon, she too would be dead. *Would that be so bad?* whispered inside her head.

Dawn, the most beautiful time of the day arrived, glowing warm pink and orange on the rock, it lightly brushed her skin in gold. Rose could barely see, her eyes were gummed together with pus, her lips split with dehydration, trickling a line of pink blood down her chin. The two seagulls flew around her, their screams sounding like maniacal laughter in her ears. She sat. not daring to move as dark shadows danced inside her gummed eyelids. Dusk arrived, and with it a cool breeze. Night bought silence, except for the sound of waves searching for the shore – she knew they were searching for her; they had already claimed Paddy. The rock creaked and groaned in agreement, Rose pressed her ear closely to it, hearing its deep voice. Once again, the dawn touched her face; this time she did not turn her face up to it, the rock told her to hide from the bright yellow eye. She heard one lone seagull land close by, its white head cocked to the side, staring at her. It asked to come fly with us. Rose's laughter matched the screech of the seagull as it flew off; both voices filled the still dawn air.

Rose leaned forward. Her slight body somersaulted over boulders and rocks, finally landing with a sickening crunch. A small patch of beach changed from pink to red as her blood seeped into the sea water, the white ooze of brain squelching out of the split skull. Rose stood, looking down at her body. The sea was now claiming what it had wanted, since the time Rose and Jack were shipwrecked. With greed it rushed in, whirlpooling around her broken limbs, sucking her body back into greener deeper depths. Rose now wandered the beach with the many other shades, their moans, and wails of grief mingling, echoing in and around the rock, bouncing off the barren rock walls. The sound was one of despair, a warning to others who would one day join them.

CHAPTER 1

My name flashed up on the big screen; this was another first. A story I had written had been made into film. As the director and producer of my script gently pulled me to my feet, soft lights blossoming around us, applause scattered around the theatre. As we moved towards the exit, members of the movie industry elite surrounded me, some stopping to say, "Well done, Tara," and, "Congratulations." I looked over at Gordi, with his unruly hair slicked down, the black tuxedo, the crisp white shirt that illuminated each time a flash bulb went off. Excitement was written on his face. It felt like a dream, my gown with black sequins scattered over metallic silver material glistened like oil under the flashlights. My dream had come true. I found it hard to beleive this was happening. It felt surreal; everything was happening in fast mode, I wanted it to slow down, to savour every minute of our success.

Riding to the afterparty in a stretch limo, I thought about the bright white smiles and flashing cameras that had greeted us, me tucking my arm into Gordi's as he whispered, "Big breath, Tara, we can do this." I had felt a niggle of annoyance at the time, as only an hour earlier Gordi had been in such a foul mood; I thought I would be attending this event on my own.

It had been two years since Gordi had encouraged me to write a short story for a local writing competition. He had edited it and proofread it, making suggestions for improvements along the way. I appreciated his honesty and polished it up until we were both happy, and posted it off.

I had never written a ghost story prior to this, so I was surprised and delighted when I found out it had it won. My prize was fifteen hundred dollars and an escorted trip through the Fremantle movie studios – of course I asked if Gordi could escort me, as it was his prompting and encouragement that had led me to participate. I thought it was wonderful that it had been read by a film producer, but I was completely gobsmacked when they offered to purchase the script. The surprises had kept coming, and now we were on the other side of Australia at the Cairns short film festival, having just watched a thirty-minute film based on my story. A picture flipped through my mind of the two of us, not so long ago sitting outside our motorhome, slurping billy tea out of tin mugs, dressed in beanies, jackets, woolly scarves, jeans and boots.

I had to admit, my success was no accident, but due to hard work and my willingness to embrace every opportunity offered. After writing my stories, I had to put them out there, which involved diligent marketing on social media. It was not a smooth pathway, in the early days I was screwed over by some less than ethical publishing companies; I had been on the receiving end of disgusting insulting emails that, in hindsight, should have been handed to a lawyer. I tried to keep smiling through it all.

My biggest break came to me in the oddest way. Some of my work was being exhibited with two other local artists; we had organised a well-marketed exhibition opening to get noticed and to sell. I was experienced in publicity, so I was given the job of inviting the editor of the arts page in the Perth weekend newspaper to open the exhibition, and to our delight he agreed. It all went well, and sell we did; it was exciting to see red dots appearing beside paintings as the night progressed. After the excitement was over, and the busy flurry of exhibiting finished, I received a phone call from the same editor, asking if I would consider being interviewed for a half-page editorial in the weekend newspaper. He was interested in writing an article focusing on me, my art and writing, and Dwan, the young videographer I had hired for the exhibition. Dwan was currently working on a video for my website. I was delighted and accepted the offer for us both immediately; this meant an even bigger exposure for me and my novels and for Dwan as well.

The interview went well, I requested that the interview be held in my backyard, which looked like a magical green oasis after the warmer than usual weather. The birds and butterflies flew around the garden, adding to the ambiance. We, the editor and I, connected immediately, he asked me if I had ever thought about writing a script for film or stage as another way of honing my writer's skills. I told him that I had in fact written one already, it was a prologue to an unpublished book, but had done nothing with it. He offered to read it and to 'see where it goes from there'. Embarrassed, I handed over the single copy, dog-eared and all. He did not seem fazed; he accepted it and deposited it in his satchel.

I forgot all about it, until some months later he called to say he had enjoyed it immensely; saying I had a gift for the paranormal genre. In fact, he had passed it on to a mate who made films, and who was looking for something 'different'. The weird thing about it was that, when I was writing it, I had a gut feeling it could be the book that put me in the bestselling author category. I knew it was good and had entered it as a short story in several local writing competitions; so, when it was emailed back with rejection messages, disappointment had settled around my shoulders.

For the previous year or so, anything I entered into any Rockingham art or writing competitions had failed. However, for some reason, my intuition told me to try again. Fast forward and here I was, signing contracts and all kinds of papers, meeting the actors, shaking hands with the famous as well as the folk who would turn my script into a thirty-minute film.

The local papers were informed and wanted interviews. These led to invitations to speak at writing festivals and libraries in regional areas in my home state of Western Australia. On my bucket list was to be a speaker at Margaret River writer's festival. So far, I had been unable to achieve this one elusive spot. You would think that after many years of self-marketing, I would be an author they would want on their panels, that they would all want an opportunity to meet and greet. But in real life it is not so.

I called my ever-patient publisher for advice. He said, "Go for it, Tara, my advice is to hire yourself an agent. I can connect you to someone who may help. Her name is Elsa, she is very good." This all felt very strange, a little bit too professional for me – a big step up from my life as a writer, artist and writing mentor. This was one of the main reasons I travelled, to encourage others to write, wherever and whenever I could. But then again, a part of me had always yearned for the spotlight. I agreed to have a conversation with Elsa, but my tummy did a little blip at the thought of where this step would take me. *One step at a time, Tara*, kept running through my head.

Gordi mapped out a route that would allow us to meet all requests. First things first; I had already accepted invitations to speak to a number of local writing groups. Planning a road trip was where Gordi excelled. I wanted to involve him, so I had agreed to let him plan the route which would take us from our home in Rockingham to Margaret River writer's festival, travelling through the wheat belt of Western Australia and home again. We would be away for a month; well, that was the plan.

I had forgotten all about the ghost story I had written until we were packing up to drive back towards Perth. With the itinerary almost completed – just three more small townships to visit – Gordi decided to stop along the way and make us a pot of coffee. I took the chance to open my laptop for a quick catch-up on news. I read the most exciting email: my script had been accepted for a short film festival in Cairns in northern Queensland!

Success tasted like fizzy wine in my throat.

Neither of us could believe it at first, then Gordi let out a huge 'woo hoo' that sent the black cockatoos screaming from their treetop perches. He grabbed hold of me and did the weird jigging dance thing he did when he was excited. As we were tucked up inside our home on wheels, I had no option but to bounce around with him.

"Mate, you've cracked it!" he yelled. I was too stunned to do anything but sit down and let it sink in. I had had a feeling that my life was about to change. I thought about the life I loved, involving travel, billy tea around the campfire, meeting new and old friends along the way, writing about my experiences and painting. It was perfect, did I want it to change? I re-read the email: *your story has been accepted by Bluefin Films.* My presence was requested for a meeting with the producers and investors in Sydney in two weeks' time. They would organise the plane tickets and a reservation at the Sydney Hilton Hotel for four days. Everything was taken care of, I just had to be there.

Gordi re-read the email with me. He was so close I could feel his whiskery stubble lightly scratching my cheek, his strong arms now around me. "God, Tara, I am so proud of you!" I knew that without Gordi pushing me none of this would have happened. From the first day we met, he had been there for me, even though I fought our relationship for a while. Our life was not perfect, we were still finding our way to be together, but I felt that I was the lucky one. I put my hands around his face, kissing him with all my heart, wanting to convey what I felt for him, while Gordi pulled me so close we became one breath, one heartbeat. My body and spirit joined in the joy of our love, it felt like there were no secrets, no lies, just two hearts beating in unison as our bodies joined in the age-old ritual of passion. His whispered "Tara," causing me to catch my breath as he buried his head between my now bare breasts. What had started off as a soft kiss had ignited into a fierce desire for one another; soon our clothes lay in a tangled heap around our feet. As my body arched in answer to his searching hands, the pot of hot coffee was forgotten.

CHAPTER 2

My body was still reeling with the explosion of emotions as I sat up on the bed. Gordi lay beside me with a look of smugness. I dug him in the ribs. "Come on, lover boy, time to finish this tour and get home, we have a meeting in Sydney to attend." The trip had been planned in a way that we could stop along the route and take in some local scenery. I had three more speaking commitments, but we both realised we would need to adjust our program a bit in order to leave for Sydney.

Our next stop was York, a farming town little bit out of the way, but I felt it was well worth keeping on the itinerary. I was scheduled to attend a *Meet the Author* session at the local library. There were six ladies present, all from a small writing group. Gordi whispered that 'the senior parade' was out in force. I could pinch him at times, his Kiwi humour could be very sarcastic; thank God we were in the motorhome when he said it. They were a bright bunch, eager to learn, and I was happy to spend two hours with them. A tasty lunch of hot pumpkin and watercress soup with cheese scones was served afterwards – I went out to invite Gordi inside to eat with us but by the looks of the breadcrumbs and eggshells on the bench, he had already eaten. I had no idea where he had wandered off to, so I rejoined the ladies for lunch. I must admit I was very happy he was not around, as Gordi more than often had no filter where 'seniors' were concerned, I do not think he thought or saw himself as getting older. Maybe we needed a new mirror in the motorhome.

I was feeling positive when I got back to our home on wheels, commenting that the session and the lunch had been excellent. Gordi seemed annoyed; he did not reply. We pulled out of the car park, our new destination was Corrigin, a bit of a detour, but again I felt it was worthwhile. The scenery along the way was beautiful, we stopped briefly so I could snap some photos. Corrigin is another small farming township containing a pub, post office and second-hand shop. After my meeting there, we drove on for another couple of hours to Wagin, pulling over to make hot drinks beside the huge white statue of a ram.

Whoever sculptured this beast left nothing to the imagination, underneath it hung two ginormous testicles. I watched Gordi from the window of our motorhome as he walked around to stretch his legs; he had not seen the ram's appendages, but when he did, his eyebrows shot up. His only comment was, "Lucky bugger." I offered Gordi a coffee plus one of the two scones I had smuggled into my handbag. We were both grinning insanely, me because I had smuggled two scones and no-one saw me (I hoped), and Gordi because of his appreciation for the ram with the spectacular testicles. He took lots of photos from all angles.

"My mum and family will love these." I had once met his family and had not been impressed with their behaviour.

When I replied, "I bet!" Gordi immediately took offence; I could see it in his eyes and the puce colour of his face.

"What's that supposed to mean?" he asked as I got in the driver's seat. I felt an argument was brewing. I eased the handbrake off.

"Come on, sourpuss, I'm expected in Hyden."

Gordi could not let go of my comment, so he tried another way to get me to react. "That's right, it's all about you, Tara the famous." There were times I was so tempted to just open the passenger door, unclip his belt and push him out, life would be so much simpler. Deep breathing helped me stay calm. The scenery in midwinter here is amazing; the paddocks and trees are so alive with green. After one of our long scorching summers, it amazes me to this day that they survive in temperatures that can reach forty-plus degrees; with over a five-month summer period or more, we were in a drought now.

The road to Lake Grace is one of my favourites, it has a roadside art gallery, nicknamed Tin Horse Highway, with tin horses in all kinds of wacky, comical poses. At the end of this road someone has added two tin scarecrows and a piebald cow. Once again, I got out my trusty camera, knowing my grandson Jess would love these photos.

We needed a spot to camp for the night. There are plenty of lay-bys to choose from, and at this time of year, few travellers. We chose a site close enough to a heavily wooded area so we could enjoy the dusk and dawn choir of birdsong, and hopefully spot some wildlife. With our deckchairs placed on each side of the camp table, Gordi erected our portable BBQ; soon the smell of grilled pork chops filled the air. I put together a green salad and a potato salad, unpacked a small loaf of sourdough bread which I thinly sliced and buttered, then opened tin of apple sauce to go with the pork chops. Once the meal was on our plates, it smelt and tasted lovely

Dusk had settled over us and the birdsong softened from its raucous chorus as the woodland prepared for the oncoming night. Gordi opened a bottle of red wine for himself; I made my favourite, cranberry juice with ice and mint. After the dishes were washed and put away it was time to catch up on my blog, social media and emails. It was the biting sandflies that drove us inside. I packed my laptop away and snuggled under the quilt, while Gordi had another glass of wine. Recently I had noticed that Gordi was drinking more than usual, never just the one glass as we used to, now it was often two large glasses with dinner, and perhaps one when he cooked for us. It was hard for us to have a conversation when his words came out more and more slurred, and even worse, he would fall asleep. I gave myself a mental note to have a chat with him about it – or was I simply being alarmist? I fell asleep to the sound of the night-time hush in the bush.

A fabulous dawn erupted quietly in the sky, first a faint blush turning dark blue to mauve, then a pink stain in the sky grew as I made myself a hot cup of tea and made sure my camera was charged. Quietly sitting outside with a rug around my knees, I felt like I was the only one on earth to witness the awakening of life in the woods. A faint mist was lifting from the plants around the motorhome, a soft kaleidoscope of colours began turning and twisting across the sky, from deep mauve to pale orange, a splash of turquoise – then the sun suddenly popped up on the horizon. To me, this was a message from nature, to remind us to stop, to enjoy and breathe deeply. Looking at my photos, I saw I had captured the sunrise beautifully, a golden glowing ball sat perfectly for one moment, right between two pink salmon gums; I had to admit it was stunning. The bird life had now switched from mellow tweeting to megaphone loud.

I went inside to wake Gordi, but he grumbled a 'not yet', pulling the blankets over his head. I had noted the empty wine bottle on the outdoor table, leaving painkillers with a glass of water beside the bed. I began cooking. I was ravenous. The smell of morning coffee with hot toast and fried eggs woke him. In our little motorhome the table was part of the double bed, it was too much trouble to pack up the bed and raise the table, so we often had breakfast sitting on the bed. Today I balanced plates, egg and toast on my lap; Gordi sat up with pillows behind him, his breakfast sat on a tray. He looked grey and haggard; sadly, a miasma of drink and body odour filled my little home, I felt disappointed as I been so very proud to make our motorhome feel so fresh and clean before we had left.

There was no rush; our last stop not too far away, we had figured with good timing we would be there by lunchtime. The Hyden tourism had kindly booked us both into the hotel overnight, with dinner and breakfast included. I was to give two two-hour talks, six ladies were booked for the noon session, and six again at night.

Hyden is a small town with a huge hotel-motel in the middle; it also is a very popular stop on the tourist trail as they have a massive rock rising up from the ground called Wave Rock, which is formed just like a wave. As you look up it feels like it is going to crash down onto you. People of all ages climb over it. On a path not far from this rock is Hippo's Yawn, and true to the description, it looks like a hippopotamus yawning. It even has rock-like teeth! But my favourite place in Hyden is The Lace Place, a time capsule with beautiful lace from all over the world. There is also a wedding gown collection, I am proud to say mine was one of them. I was keen to see if it was still there, although I knew it would lead to old memories flooding back. I also knew Gordi did not believe in rehashing the past.

CHAPTER 3

A few years after, Rus, my husband's death, I had finally gotten around to cleaning out the loft. I had become used to shoving all in sundry up the stairs and into this dark place of memories, but amongst the junk were a few treasures. As I sorted through a few boxes looking for photos Rae had asked for, I came across a large blanket-bound cardboard box. My wedding gown was inside, my fingers suddenly feeling fat and clumsy as I untied the old string Russ had used to bind the parcel tight. Blowing off many years of dust and removing the protecting woolly blanket I saw it had kept the box in almost mint condition (apart from a smattering of yellowing patches), I slid the lid off. The tissue paper around my gown had also yellowed; I held my breath, expecting to see a fair amount of damage to this gown that I had treasured. Thankfully, it was still untouched by insects or mould, and I could still smell the faintest of the perfume I had worn on that day – French Roses by Lancôme. Or was it my imagination? As I unfolded the tissue paper, the wedding dress I had designed myself fell softly into my lap. I held my breath as I turned it over in my hands, it was still perfect. The emotions were so deep, as can only happen when you love another with your being, not just your heart, when you remain in love no matter the highs and lows as we had had. Russ' death had proved that none of us are immortal. I felt that we were soulmates. I had to remind myself to breathe.

I spied the photographs I was looking for tucked underneath my gown, that one day of yesteryear suddenly swam before me like I was reliving it. Memories I had tucked away for many years in my mind now flooded back: a short courtship, engagement – being young and impatient, I began to experiment with my body, and thankfully Russ taught me the art of making love, not sex. His engagement ring I still wore. Then there was my wedding day, it had begun with my folks waking me in the early morning after I spent my last night as a single woman in the twin bed beside my matron of honour Valerie who slept soundly. Of Irish Māori heritage, her raven black hair spilt over the pillow, her olive complexion was smooth, her mouth always upturned in a smile, even in her sleep. Val was my best friend, she was a beautiful women inside and out in every way, when she loved she did so with open arms that completely enfolded you.

Dad put his finger to his lips stopping me from waking her, they waited for me to put on my dressing gown and to join them in the kitchen. As I sat and listened to their plans for all the things that still had to be done, the excitement hit me; I was getting married today. Mum was plaiting a blue and white ribbon to attach the silver horseshoe I was to carry; inside the last knot that attached it to my bouquet was a lucky four-leaf clover charm of pewter that she had been given on her own wedding day. I was to carry the horseshoe with my bouquet of flowers that had been delivered the night before.

The two bridal bouquets, along with Dad's buttonhole and Mum's wrist corsage lay on the bench. They were stunning, made from white baby's breath and pink carnations, with the smallest of day lilies tucked around them. The simplicity made them beautiful.

Dad was busy making toast and a pot of tea; they had both aged considerably by now, Dad was slightly stooped, a hardworking man all his life. At the age of eleven, my grandpa had taken him out of school to work with a cart and horse, his job was to deliver anything and everything to anyone. He was one of four brothers and two sisters in a family that had migrated to Australia from Ireland when my father was five years old. When I asked how they could afford it – as we were always told they were poor, his answer was to tap the side of his nose. Dad was always ready with a story to tell, whereas my mum claimed an indirect line of aristocrat blood line that she truly believed, as her great-great-aunty was a serving maid to Queen Mary. She and her family had been born in Sydney, Australia, her education was exceptional for that day and age, reaching her college years, before being hired out was almost unheard of in early 1900s she was not a young apprentice, and because of her maturity she became dressmaker to a large well-known home in Melbourne, then met my dad at a dance hall. Apparently one dance and Dad was hooked, whenever Dad talked about that night, Mum would smile and blush. Of course, ever the storyteller, Dad would change the story each and every time, and occasionally Mum would say, "Richard, enough of your nonsense."

The only taboo subject in our home was World War II when Dad had been an ambulance driver. No matter how much they tried, to the day he passed away, they could not hide his nightmares. His advice to me was, "Tara, war is an awful mess, thank God we went to war, so you could live your life in peace." Mum, who had only recently retired as the dressmaker to the lord mayor's wife and their two daughters, her once beautiful long fingers and hands now lumpy with large blue veins and arthritis, but her stories were just as full of glamour and decorum or juicy village gossip when the lights went out, as Dad's were of his days as a lad in the old country, full of adventure. Being the youngest had its advantages, being a postwar baby of the family, my sisters had married and left home many years ago, I was an aunty to many nephews, and I loved it. I became the shoulder my sisters sometimes cried on. Tiredness their main complaint.

My folks had never wanted to be empty-nesters, yet that day was here, I was to leave my childhood home, and I knew between them was a sadness I would never understand until I was a parent myself. Once we had settled at the breakfast table, Mum and Dad sat there looking at me, at their baby girl, both of them filled with love and pride, yet fearful for me in a way only parents could understand. Mum reached under a cushion beside her; "Your dad and I would like to give you these." Dad took over opening the velvet box, his hands shook a little, tears slipped into my mum's eyes. Inside the small box, nestled into dark blue velvet, sat one small teardrop pearl on a gold chain. On each side of the chain sat a set of tiny teardrop pearl earrings, I had never seen them before. Mum explained they were family heirlooms from both sides of the family; the pearl drop from my maternal side, and the earrings were from my paternal grandmother, to be passed to the last daughter.

Dad stood, placing his hands lightly on my head, "To wear on your wedding day and to give to your daughter to give to her daughter, may the line continue with you." A blessing I will never forget. I had done as they wished, blessing my daughter the same way when she had married. I picked up another photo, so many wonderful memories bringing sharp stinging tears to my eyes, my Russ so young and handsome in his tuxedo. I found a photo of our wedding cake, then a photo of our first waltz as a married couple, marvelling at the love and desire that shone from my young husband's eyes. Suddenly I did not know what to do with the gown or the photos, it made my heart hurt too much.

So many memories whirled and churned through my mind. My daughter Rae was not interested in wearing the gown; I also felt that keeping the gown was not fair to Gordi, my new partner; he should not feel he was being compared to a memory. I rang the local wedding shops and was given information about The Lace Place, a museum that collected antique lace and wedding gowns. The curator Beverly arrived two weeks after we had spoken on the phone. She accepted my dress with joy calling it a 1960s triumph of champagne oyster silk, she delighted in the bodice of hand-crotchet lace, and asked if she could also display the photograph of Russ and I hand in hand beneath the elm tree we had been married under. Later that day, as I carefully passed it to her, I felt my hands tightened around the box with dress and photo sealed inside. Beverly understood, reassuring me they would be treasured. After she put the box of my memories into her boot, she gave me a hug and said, "Make yourself a sweet tea, Tara, you are quite pale," and drove away. I had to admit I did feel sick, my stomach lurched and I rushed off to the bathroom, throwing up what I felt was guilt, feeling I had given a part of me away.

CHAPTER 4

Now I was here at The Lace Place. Excitement gripped me as Gordi and I entered the foyer, and there, displayed behind a red corded-off area, was my wedding gown, and alongside the display was a description of where we were married, and the photo of Russ and I in front of the one-hundred-year-old elm tree, its lime green leafy branches bending down towards us as we were pledged our love for each other. I could feel my heart thud; my eyes pricked with tears, one drop escaping down my cheek. Gordi's large hand found mine, "You looked beautiful, Tara."

"I still do," I replied, as a watery wobbly smile tried to emerge. The photo was more than twenty years old. If the truth be told, right at this moment I felt terrible, wrapped in many layers of warm clothing, plus scarf, beanie, and bright red nose – it was obvious, I hoped, that I was travelling. Then it hit me, my gown was part of a museum collection of lace and wedding gowns where more people passed through than were at my wedding. We – Russ and I – were now part of history. I knew had done the right thing. I left the museum without seeing the curator, passing on my gratitude to the receptionist.

Thankfully, the rooms in the Hyden Hotel were heated the water was super hot. I enjoyed a long shower, quickly dressing in my clean clothes, but adding, once again, a scarf, coat and beanie, as the air outdoors was really cold. Then off to the first of the two-hour meetings arranged by the tourist department. I enjoyed introducing myself as an author, urging the aspiring writers to relax and enjoy what they wrote. To flex the brain muscles, I included a game for them, asking them to describe what they would wear if invited to the Mad Hatter's tea party. This helped them to relax; their descriptions brought laughter into the room. It was creative writing at its best, and I loved it. The time flew and the participants all seemed to get the information they were after. I was asked for my autograph and three people purchased my books, so not a bad outcome.

A small bouquet of wildflowers was given to me as a thank you gift. The afternoon tea was enormous, more than enough to go around the folk present, there were plates of food going home with everyone, including us. Plates of food were pressed into my hands as the organiser insisted, "We won't eat all of this." Walking back to our accommodation, it was a wonder the bouquet of flowers did not freeze on their stalks. It had become so cold, once again the heated room wrapped its warmth around us. I made two hot cups of Milo, offering Gordi some pumpkin quiche or the beef rissoles we had been given. I was not hungry, so I left him to it, it was time for a nanna nap for me or some reading while I stretched out on the comfy bed. Soon 5pm rolled around and it was time to repeat my authors talk to another group.

This time there was one male in the group, I appreciated the effort they had taken to brave the extreme cold that night. It went well, almost a repeat of the morning. As I packed up the pamphlets and spare books, my phone rang.

"Hi, Mum, how's it all going?" my daughter asked. I could hear my grandchildren in the background, the telly was also blaring away, Rae's words were shouted at me. Gordi mouthed *say hi for me* as he disappeared through the door into the hall foyer. He looked quite happy talking to the one man who had attended with the group. Rae and I chatted about my author's tour, where I had been and where it would end up – she had been rung by the local papers for an interview on having a well-known author/screenwriter for a mum. I could hear the question in her voice asking *is this okay?*

"Go for it, honey, if that's what you want to do."

I knew my daughter well; there was something she was not telling me. I could also see Gordi signalling that he wanted to go back to our room; the heating in the hall had been turned off and only one last flickering light remained on. It was time to go, this phone conversation would have to wait.

"Rae, I will call you back." Both Gordi and I were feeling the deep icy-cold weather settling into our bodies as we walked back to the hotel, our footsteps crunching on the settling frost. It was close to eight o'clock at night. We could smell the roast meal that was waiting for us at the hotel, it wafted past our nostrils in the cold air, tantalising us as it drifted past.

Gordi pushed open the heavy wooden doors, holding them open for me, a large fire crackled in the fireplace. The room was alive with warmth, the roast meat smelt divine. We were shown to a small corner table, it had been made from one large circular piece of wood. I had heard once that you can tell the age of a tree by the rings on the inside, it soon became a competition between Gordi and myself as to who was right about the number of rings. Gordi is highly competitive and if he were proven wrong, he would go to any lengths to be correct, he asked the waiter for a pen the begun to add up the numbers of rings on the serviette claiming it was 150 rings, so I shrugged and agreed, choose your arguments, right? Plus, I was really hungry, soon we were both tucking into a large plate of roast vegies, roast lamb and rich brown gravy.

As we discussed our day, my phone call with Rae, and the next stop on our itinerary, Gordi ordered a carafe of red house wine, I was about to ask, *Gordi, why not just one glass tonight?* He had already anticipated what I was going to say. He became sullen, I saw his jaw tighten. The question for me was, should I stand up for what I feel was right, or simply shrug and say it was okay? When do you say to another you want to love, *I think your favouring the wine a little too much?* In the end I said nothing, my attention being drawn to the faint piano music which was coming from an adjoining room. It was superb.

CHAPTER 5

The piano music being played was so beautiful, it lifted the atmosphere as well as my spirits. I had to find out exactly where it was coming from and who was playing. Excusing myself from the dinner table, as Gordi finished off his first glass of wine, I found my way through the main bar, where a few regulars sipped their brews while watching sport on the telly, and on into the snug, which was empty. Still the music drew me on, it was entrancing. Chopin ended, then Strauss took over. Walking into a small lounge, I was immediately surrounded by the sound of music. A fire crackling away in the stone fireplace around which were placed four red leather, button-studded armchairs. In the corner, next to a huge potted palm, was a baby grand piano; but on the seat was the real surprise – two young black men were playing a duet. I was mesmerised. Their long fingers caressed the keys, their combined playing was pure poetry. I sat and listened to their repertoire; it was delightful see these two men playing the baby grand piano with such passion. They stopped and greeted me; two huge white smiles lit up their handsome black faces. I stood up and shook their hands, knowing that this experience would definitely be added into my next novel.

Jabari and Omar were such polite young men, they had travelled around Australia before settling into Perth. Jabari was a medical doctor working in a Perth hospital, while Omar was an accountant with a well-known legal firm. Both were excited to meet a local author and artist, the two young men asked if I would care to join them in a song. Now, I am known for my dulcet tone within my family, as my grandson Jess will happily confirm – his polite way of saying I was tone-deaf was, "You sound like a frog in a tin bucket."

Tonight, I thought, *Why not?* I asked them to play one of my favourites, *You Are My Sunshine*, a song everyone knows. I sucked in a lungful of air, their voices joining mine, and what voices they had! I shut my mouth with a snap and listened to them play and sing; my heart soared to the rafters as they finished that song, then another rippled out. Neil Diamond would have been proud of their rendition of *Song Sung Blue*, this time I did join in, loving every minute of it, that is until Gordi made his appearance.

I heard him before he saw me; it was obvious that he had finished the carafe off by himself. Imagining he was amusing, no doubt, he began bellowing out the same song, but the fun stopped as Gordi slurred loudly, "Encore," and tried to clap, but his hands missed each other. He stood there swaying and giggling, The top of the piano was closed down, the two young men walking away. I sat there completely horrified, then I also left the room with Gordi yelling, "Jesus wept, Tara, what have I done now?" as he slumped down into one of the red leather chairs.

I walked through the lounge area on our way to our room. Jabari and Omar were there. They both smiled and waved to me, I don't think they realised that Gordi was with me. Jabari asked if I would like a coffee, I opted for herbal tea. After the waitress took my order the three of us discussed places to visit in Perth. They explained they were a couple but had only recently admitted this to their folks. They had fallen in love over ten years ago, while both living in Uganda which was considered taboo within their family culture, so they decided to live in Australia where they would be able to live openly with each other, not be made to feel ashamed of their feelings. Again, I felt embarrassed, I had always associated Africa with drums, loincloths, lions, and native villages full of African arts and crafts, I knew from the news it was becoming a nation to be reckoned with, even though unrest was still prevalent. These two men were nothing like the poverty or unrest we see on the news, they were tall, healthy, obviously talented, both professionals. So what if they loved each other? I liked them because of their enthusiasm for life. I stood to leave, they both stood as well, gathering me up in a group hug. "Goodnight my friends, sleep well," I said as I left. The door to our room was wide-open, the room freezing. Gordi was fully dressed lying across the bed, softly snoring. Locking the door, I pushed him over to one side and fell into bed, I was exhausted, too tired to even consider why Gordi was acting up again.

Tomorrow we were moving on to Balingup. I woke to a misty frosty morning, I felt so alive. For Gordi it was a different story. A hangover is never nice; he grumped and moaned his way through a shower and room service breakfast. After I had packed my small bag I made more tea, then sat opposite him, the painkillers I had given him earlier on were working, his face and shoulders not so tense. It was time to have that chat about his attitude towards drinking. But it came out all wrong, the words I had practised that morning, *Gordi, please watch the amount you drink*, came out like a slap: "Stop your boozing, Gordi, you're ruining everything!" It was like a red rag to a bull. Suddenly we were having the nastiest fight we had ever had; his insults hurting deeply. I was accused of being a bludger, a nagger and I was up myself. I was shocked, if this is what he called a loving relationship, he could have it. Picking up my overnight bag, my wallet, and keys I walked out of the room.

I had no idea what I would do. I was a ball of emotion as I walked into the breakfast bar and ordered a hot chocolate from the waitress; with fat teardrops rolling down my face as I stared out the window into a winter-bare courtyard. No-one spoke to me like that, I was not going to lower myself by answering him. I had made a promise to attend the Balingup writer's festival, and that is what I decided to do, on my own. Gordi would have to learn I was not his teacher. His hangover had slowed him down; by the time his hand had reached for the passenger door, I was backing out of the parking space, my anger at his insulting behaviour sat like a bubble in my throat, there was nothing I could say or want to say to this man who, I had thought, loved me. I was obviously wrong, I had blamed myself continuously as nearly every day since we had arrived back from out last adventure, he had found something to criticise, most of the time subtly, and I had made the mistake of saying 'don't stress I'll make it better'. I was not his mother, nor did I want to be, time for some lessons for us both.

Today it hit home what the problem was: if I stayed with him, I would be critiqued continuously in one way or another. Together forever? Not for me. I drove all morning till I reached Katanning where I stopped for fuel, it was nearly midday and my stomach demanded food, so I purchased an egg and bacon roll with sweet coffee.

In another two hours I would be in Balingup. As I sat in the cab, the tears fell, the food tasted like mud, however the coffee was a lifesaver. I sobbed till I could sob no more. I checked my phone for messages. There were many from Gordi and one from Rae, her message insisted I ring as soon as possible. "Please, Mum!" I did as she asked, thinking there must be an emergency at home, to find out Gordi had rung her and told her we had argued and I had run off, leaving him alone. He had no idea what to do. I repeated the words that he had yelled at me; Rae was shocked. "He said what? You're joking aren't you, Gordi said that?" Now she was angry, my little firecracker daughter was on the warpath on my behalf. "Right, that little sucker needs a lesson in manners, I'm going to ring him, I will ring you back, Mum." I have no idea what she said, I presume it was not pleasant, but within ten minutes my phone rang.

I could not resist, I no sooner said, "Tara speaking," when Gordi began apologising profusely, asking me to return to Hyden to pick him up, so we could finish the journey.

My reply was curt and to the point, disappointment and mistrust had now entered our relationship. "I would rather not, Gordi, however I will see you back in Perth; we can then discuss if we have a future together." I informed him about Sydney: "I will be going on my own, Gordi; I really don't want you to be involved."

Ringing Rae, I told her my decision, she asked, "Are you sure, Mum, you're not cutting off your nose just because of a silly spat are you?"

"Yes, I'm sure, honey, I want to do this on my own, maybe Gordi and I need this time apart." I had one more night to find a place to rest up before Balingup. Boyup Brooke was just ahead, it is the cutest little township. They proudly display signs all over the buildings advertising the local blue breasted robin; blue breasted it is, a bright deep blue, and so pretty. This tiny bird calls with such a high, sweet trilling song. I have driven this way before and spent an afternoon taking photo after photo of this bird. Being here also raised memories of Russ, as it was to this little township we would often drive to and book into the one and only caravan park with its tiny little cottages that were set on the bank of the Blackwood River.

Rae had learnt to kayak on this river; I could still see Russ holding his little girl by the hand, laughing together, flicking water at each other while he patiently taught her the technique of rowing smoothly. I drove in and booked a space for the motorhome, attached the water hose to the tap and the power cord to the outlet. The tiredness I felt was draining. In fact, I felt too old to be having such a tumultuous relationship like a teenager. Gordi and I had not argued for a long while, but recently, as my skills as an author and artist had become more in demand, there had been tension between us. His jealousy was demanding, he had opinions aplenty about 'other people's stupid choices in their lives', as he called them, but not once did he heed his own advice. Lying down on the bed, I ran through this morning's argument in my head, recalling what had happened, and trying to work out what I could have done that was so offensive to cause him to erupt like that. I knew that the journey we were on was not easy for Gordi. There were many fond happy memories of Russ no matter where I travelled. Here in Boyup Brook again had so many memories for me, this was where we had often holidayed as a family when Russ was on one of his week-long breaks. Gordi didn't like me reminiscing, he would often snarl, "Stop chewing over the past, it's time to let it go!"

CHAPTER 6

Memories chased each other that afternoon, one after another, the tension from my stiff shoulders leaving as I thought about one particular day. A stifling hot day, we had been swimming and picnicking. Not too far from where I was sitting now, in the middle of this river, were shallow rapids. Rae was bursting with energy, not wanting to leave the coolness of the water, so Russ made up a game for us. I walked her out to the middle of the stream, lowering her into the flow, Russ was down the other end ready to catch her. As I lowered her into the flow, it gently caught her, and with her water belt holding her up, she bobbed quickly along the shallow river towards Russ. I could still hear Rae's shrieks of delight as her daddy caught her, raising her high in the air, sunlight catching in the drops of water as he quickly carried her to shore, Rae begging for more, running back to me for a repeat swim to her adored daddy.

When Rae was, finally, deeply asleep, and we were exhausted from repeatedly sending her down the river, we quietly cleaned up our dinner dishes and sat outside in the cooling air. It was a nice kind of tired feeling that required no communication between us, but Russ, always full of surprises, had quietly checked on our daughter, tucked her in to her little cot, locked the cabin door, then led me back to the cool waters of the Blackwood River to make love as the water rippled over our bodies. What wonderful memories of our youth. If I had mentioned any of this to Gordi he would have sulked for a day, but loving, beautiful memories of times filled with love are never forgotten.

Sleep claimed me, however at 2am I was wide awake. The argument between Gordi and I would not go away, it clambered around in my head wanting me to take notice, to come to a decision: What was I going to do? Did I want to have a relationship with this man? I hated this internal questioning, surely by now I was settled, yet was I prepared to be the ever-compliant housewife of his dreams? Would he encourage me to grow as an author, in the same way I encouraged him in his holistic work? Yes, he had been a godsend in Coober Pedy when I hurt my back, and in many ways had continued to be loving and kind. It was this whiplash temper he had that bothered me. I had seen him rile Jess once, both of them red in the face, yelling at each other, Gordi had been determined not to back down. I had wondered who the adult was.

Jess was now fifteen, his world was an open door, his oyster. Gordi, however, saw the need to father him, giving advice which, to be honest, none of us thought was good advice at times. Sometimes it would erupt in a yelling match between them; Gordi had a way of annoying people with his unwanted critique with a bite of sarcasm. Then when he realised he had hurt someone, he would apologise with a joke, or blame the other for not listening. I put it down to him being a bought up differently to us. He had only stopped when Rae took him aside to warn him Jess had a stepdad, and it was Kane's, not his, opinion that mattered to them.

There were times I could see Gordi and his over-sarcastic opinion did not fit in. When we went out to an evening with friends, I could see Gordi's discomfort; he became easily bored, which turned to accusations. According to him, my friends and I, who were all a little older than him, had too fixed an outlook on life, we treated him like his opinions did not matter. He sought understanding in the wine, and his drinking was becoming a problem. Recently my friends had commented on his high colour, his deeply bloodshot eyes and shortness of breath, not just after a drink or two, but whenever he exerted himself. I had insisted on a medical before we had done this recent trip, only to be told I was an idiot. Apart from slightly elevated cholesterol, he was told to lose five kilograms and exercise more. When medication was offered, it was refused. I was in the foyer as the doctor and Gordi walked out, Gordi's face was puce, he had obviously not seen it the Doctors way, who said, "Well, Gordi, these are the facts, do with as them as you will."

Maybe that was the way to shut this man up, simply walk away, maybe this trip to Sydney was what we needed; it would give us a good break from each other. I snuggled back down in my bed, waking again when the pearled frosty morning arrived, and with it a choir of birdsong to welcome it in. I was to be in Balingup by the afternoon, it was maybe a half-hour drive away. Taking my time to shower and primp myself up a bit, tidy up and wash the dishes, by eight in the morning, I was ready to go. I felt fantastic; a worrying start to my night had worked its way free. Clear-headed, I knew exactly what I wanted to do: finish my author's tour in Balingup, head home, clean up, pack a case, then fly out to Sydney in four days' time, without having to check twice with anyone, to make sure they were happy and sober.

Balingup is a small township in the countryside that relies on tourists to keep it open. The children's book festival was a key event, along with a medieval festival held at the same time of year, which Gordi, Jess and I had attended a year ago. I loved the atmosphere, lords, ladies, knights, dragons all dressed in period costume. Innkeepers, cutthroats, robbers, princess, and kings all mingled together in one happy crowd. Food trucks sold hot chips, candy apples and candy floss, stall holders touted their wares, all manner of farm produce was for sale, as well as homemade wares, fancy dress costumes and gorgeous silver jewellery. It was a busy, dusty day, made even better when it got dark; Gordi and Jess had found two hay bales, dragging them over to a circle that had been prepared earlier. In the middle of the large circle stood a twenty-foot-high wooden dragon, ready to mark the end of this festival. We had no idea of what was to come next as dusk settled into a crisp cold night. In the middle of the circle appeared fire-eaters and flamethrowers, making the crowd gasp with delight at their skills.

Fire-dancers danced into the middle of the circle, their dancing and swaying with the fireballs they held they seemed to float through the dark night. As if no-one had any control over them, they bobbed and weaved in the darkness, leaving trails of light behind them. I heard them before I saw them, the beat of a drum, I felt goosebumps grow up and down my arms, as panpipes were added, next came the ringing rattle of a tambourine and from the woods surrounding the circle stepped a family of fairies, tiny children dressed in multicoloured tutus, silvered wings fluttered on their small backs. Ribbons of rainbow colours flooded the field as they began to dance around the dragon, then this magical band of musicians appeared from behind trees.

I had never seen anything like it in my life, the musicians glowed with tiny lights as the fairy band struck up a tune that was slightly off-key – it made me feel slightly uncomfortable, the music made my skin prickle, I would call it haunting, as to this day when I remember, it still brings me out in chills.

Among the tiny dancers that circled the dragon were beautiful witches, gorgeous fairies, strutting elves, a princess or two, each with a handsome prince holding her arm. The costumes were amazing, each one of them lit softly with fairy lights. Drums, panpipes and a violin all kept a steady beat. They swayed in time to this slight off-beat music, then they would move forward, stop once again, sway, then move forward – it was as hypnotic as the music, the blurred twinkling of lights mesmerising. I savoured every minute. A tall wizard in black robes strode into the circle, the squeals of the fairy folk and their children reached fever pitch, as they ran into the woods for cover. The wizard cast a spell over the dragon, his hunchbacked servant sidling up to him, with a torch of fire. The wizard asked if anyone amongst us had anything to add to his curse, to rid the land of the fire-breathing scaled serpent. There was deep silence, all the lights had been extinguished, no sound from any one or thing, then the wizard threw the torch up and onto the dragon's wooden body. The torch looked like it was about to extinguish, then *whoosh*, up it went.

The fairy folk came back out dancing amongst the crowd; it was a real medieval night to be remembered. Jess was lost for words, but when we arrived home the next day he finally did have something to say. As he spoke, he would stop mid-sentence, I could see in his eyes, he was remembering the night before, every fairytale moment. Balingup was full of memories for me, old ones from the past, and new ones made with Gordi and Jess.

My heart softened towards this opinionated angry man who had entered my life, who would never take no for an answer. I had agreed to sow our seeds for a future together; it was time to ring him and tell him how I felt. After I informed the event manager for the children's book festival that I was here and found out where I was staying, I planned on settling in and then having this much-needed honest conversation with Gordi, before we went any further. The events organiser for Balingup gave me the directions and informed me that I was billeted in the log cabin with five other artists for two nights. It took me a good half hour to find the right road and follow it through a forest of paperbark trees, the road ending in a large clearing. Four cars were parked around two log cabins, smoke from both cabins' chimneys billowed up to the clear sky above. The magpies greeting my arrival with their warbling song, the front door opened wide to greet me. I checked the time, exactly midday.

"Where have you been, it's time we got this party started!" There was no time to make that phone call to Gordi I had promised myself; a glass of mulled wine was pushed into my hand as I was still locking up my motorhome. My night case was taken from my hands and put in my room, then I was literally sat down on a chair at the table and served a meal of hot corn soup with warm cheese and onion bread. The main meal was meatballs and spaghetti with a very strong garlic flavour. Hot chocolate, tea or coffee was offered. The large room rang with knives and forks busily scraping plates empty, and laughter from old and new storytellers.

The time came to introduce myself properly. Some of the folk I knew from last year, while others were new to me. I loved being amongst the other authors, playwrights, drama coaches and scriptwriters who surrounded the table. Soon any awkwardness had passed, and we were chatting freely. The event team arrived with our itineraries for the next two days; I was booked by one café to read stories to the children, five kiddies to a group that afternoon, starting in two hours. Then for the next two days they had booked me to appear at the library for a poetry reading, as a guest speaker that night at a dinner at the local hotel for the adults, as a storyteller for another group reading for children, at the small local church another poetry reading for another hour, and then, with my mission completed, it was time to drive home. All meals were paid for, any money on gas was recompensed, and all I had to do was entertain. I had an hour to call Gordi and start a conversation about our future, I dialled his number but only got his message bank. I decided I would try again after I had finished entertaining on my first day.

CHAPTER 7

The children at the café seemed to enjoy my reading; I had written many stories for children and published two of them. I had been delighted with the outcome, two of them had been accepted by the royal families of London and Denmark and I had the letters from the royals to show anyone that queried this. This afternoon I would read these two books I published to to see what the local children thought of them. When I had finished the first one, to my delight, I was asked for the next book, the mothers in the room echoing their children's pleas. I enjoyed myself immensely, as did my young audience, asking me to come back and read to them again the next day.

By five in the afternoon I was on my way back to the log cabin. It was that time of day in the winter when it becomes so quiet, I knew now was the best time to pull over and make that phone call. Gordi answered it on first ring, his apologies tumbling out before I had a chance to say, *Gordi, it's me*, I listened, knowing full well that, like always, he would have found a way to blame something or someone. As I expected, he had excuses, he claimed he had found the trip exhausting; he thought a tipple or two would relax him. He did not realise I was offended by his having a few sips of wine, when he had finished, it was my turn to be brutally honest; our future depended on his understanding.

"Gordi, I have to speak honestly, it's not a few sips, Gordi, and you know it. If the drinking continues, I don't want to be with you, to be your whipping boy when you're drunk or hungover, I find your behaviour embarrassing, I don't trust you around alcohol. Your drinking stops now, plus your constant critiquing and opinion of what I do or say has to stop, or we don't have a future together." It felt like he was holding his breath, then a soft exhaling of air as he at last admitted his drinking was out of control.

"Sweetheart, I can't seem to stop, one is never enough, you walk into a room so comfortable with who you are, you have an air about you that says *I'm here,* you are greeted by many people who know who you are, and what you do. I often feel like I don't matter, I'm your chauffer, or if I join in a conversation when asked for my opinion, I feel I'm being judged by your acquaintances. Drinking takes all that away, I feel like I belong."

"Then we have a problem, Gordi. If you feel like that, you need professional help, I will let you think on it tonight, and we can talk tomorrow, but I cannot continue like this. There's love, Gordi, and then there's ownership, you have to decide." I felt awful, Gordi was obviously honest enough to tell me how he felt and there was nothing I could do but support him to overcome his emotional insecurities and his crutch of alcohol.

When I arrived at the cabin, the fires had been lit, a meal was being prepared for us, and all I had to do was unpack, shower, change into a track suit and comfy slippers, and discuss my day with my fellow artists. All through the meal, I could hear Gordi's voice, by bedtime the fire was low, I could still hear the misery in Gordi's voice.

I quietly let myself out the back door, the frost had settled, mist had strung itself between the trees, the coldness seeped inside my clothes, I was shivering by the time got into to my motorhome and tucked myself under a quilt. My tears were rippling in a salty cold streak down both cheeks as I rang Rae, her sleepy voice telling me I had woken her, but her instincts alerting her that I was having a problem and would appreciate some time to talk. I needed to say out loud what I was thinking instead of it rattling around in my head while I tried to sleep.

When had the role of mother and daughter turned around? Rae was now my confidante, I sat and let it all spill out of me: the confusion, the anger, but most of all, the role I felt Gordi wanted me to play, of the helpless housewife. Rae's gurgle of amusement when I said this, made me giggle as well.

"Rae, what am I going to do?"

"Mum, come home, once you have finished all you are doing with your authors workshops, come back here till you fly out to Sydney, Gordi is here safe and sound, and full of moans and groans about your driving off and leaving him to catch a bus to Perth."

I was shocked. "He's with you? Why?"

"That's just it, Mum, he also needed to offload his anger, so Kane and I picked him up from the bus depot, we invited him to stay with us till you arrive home. He literally has nowhere else to go, what else could we do? So finish what you're doing and once you're here, then you can sort it out between you." Her voice changed, it took on a happy vibe "Mum, I also have news," she informed me that she had taken a huge leap of faith and had entered the Mandurah Wearable Arts competition.

Rae enjoyed creating like I did; I had entered the same competition last year, getting so much pleasure out of doing something so radically different. Rae's talents had always been knitting, crochet, quilting, and recently designing baby clothes for christenings, whereas my artistic outlets had always been floral art, dress design, abstract art, and of course, writing. When I had my website designed, we also had a one created for her; we were so pleased with both of them. Rae's little home boutique business had grown, proving a steady growth in popularity. She had the perfect model, my eighteen-month-old granddaughter Shauna.

I was very proud of the turnaround Rae had made in her life; and now she was advising me on my relationship with Gordi. When did she grow up and become so wise? And why did I need so much help trying to discover what made Gordi tick? Was it my age? Was it the fact I had become too busy to be bothered with this sort of emotional claptrap? Or was it simply that I was trying to wear two hats, where the one as Gordi's partner was a tad too tight for me, and the other hat which was *me, Tara*, the person I had grown into and treasured. The road of becoming an adult is fraught with stress in some way or form, but I felt like I had proved myself so many times and I was now highly capable of wearing the mantle called wisdom. But I had to admit Rae was right, I needed to finish what I was here for, and then drive home to sort it out with Gordi, once and for all.

The festival lasted two more days. Two more days of reading to children, one appearance as a guest speaker, one more night with the craziest funny bunch of people I had met in a long while, much sharing of great food, and feeling like I belonged to the funniest and most adventurous group I had met in a long time. Of course, while I was not running a workshop, I did a little touring, finding a gallery just outside Balingup called the Stone Dragons. Dragons of all sorts and sizes hung from the gables inside the studio, some with weird-looking googly eyes, feather and beads adorning each one, some had incense smoke spiralling out of the nostrils, some had a coy flirtatious look, while others seemed to be challenging me with one raised eyebrow set just so, daring me to have an opinion. All the dragons were made from the local clay pit which happened to be on their property. I rummaged around for an hour or two, I loved it so much, taking many photographs.

I finally decided on a small green stone dragon with long blue feathered wings and a mane of white spotted pheasant feathers. I knew Rae and Kane would love it for the new herb garden they had recently built; well, Rae, like me, had a zany sense of the ridiculous, I knew she would love it. Then it was home time, we had all been invited back for the next year of the Balingup children's book festival, and I was asked to consider the opportunity of once again being the resident writer for ghost stories. I had no idea how they cottoned on to that but was only too happy to agree to returning next year for the TellingTales book festival. I left with half an egg and bacon pie wrapped up for my lunch, a thermos of hot tea to keep me fuelled up until my next stop, and a bottle of champagne we were each given as a thank you gift. Plus, a healthy amount had been deposited into my bank account.

My road map had been marked with large rings of purple around places I wanted to stop and see. Nannup was to be my first stop, then Donnybrook overnight as I had a workshop to attend there, it had not been widely advertised, so it was not a big turnout. However, we had a great time; it was more like a personal conversation between writers. Then on to Harvey for a cup of tea at one of the wackiest cafés I have ever been to, Waroona was another pit stop and refuelling station, not that I was hungry, but needed to keep awake till I reached home. Waroona has amazing hand-carved totem poles depicting the area. I fully intended to stop off at all these places and take as many photos as I could to add to my growing blog site. I planned to take photos of the rose gardens and swinging bridge at Pinjarra before moving onto Mandurah to catch up with my favourite arts festival people, a team of creatives that did an amazing job for the arts in the area, always coming up with exciting ideas to showcase artists' work, then back on the road to home.

CHAPTER 8

Well, that was what I thought would happen, but there were too many stops and too many people to chat with, and the three days it would take would leave me just one day to get back and catch that all-important flight to Sydney. I had made it to the creative writer's group in Donnybrook, here I found the communication with their social circle was really advanced, their president stating, "We may be in our dotage, but we are not that old we can't use what we have left," she said, tapping her head. It was a small mix of men and women, all very switched-on about writing, the memoirs of what their life is all about, their mental energy put me to shame. Our lunch turned into dinner with this group of amazing storytellers, I was talked into staying on, camping in the communal fairgrounds for the night, to refresh for the next day's trip. It was a safe option for me.

I left the grounds the next morning feeling refreshed and happy with my decision, life was simpler without the complications of a grumpy passenger.

At Harvey I always stop off at the same café, the manager is a race bike fanatic, bike wheels hang off the rafters and walls. He remembered me from a visit some time ago, when I had introduced myself to the local arts group. He saw me pop my head around the door, "I remember you; you're the writer lady, aren't you?"

"Yes, I'm that same lady," was my reply. Just then Geoff, the event manager of this group who had invited me to speak, introduced himself, then ushered me through to a small group of artists. It was lovely as poets, artists and writers of all genres were in attendance. After I had chatted to them for an hour telling them about my experience with wearable arts, they asked me to describe my creative processes. I showed them the website over a slice of cream and jam sponge with a cup of mint and chamomile tea, convincing them it was an international competition of some importance to the area, not a little sideshow to a festival that they could pop anything into, which is what they thought. By the time I left to drive off, it was late in the afternoon, I was exhausted, and I knew by now stress, not so much tiredness, was the cause. I had certainly had enough of that recently, that familiar throb behind the left eye had begun. I intended to take two painkillers as soon as possible, then find a space to park. I knew that here, also was a free campsite in the municipal park grounds. It was one overnight stop-off, sleep was necessary for me to operate properly. Finding a bottle of water in the fridge, I swallowed the medication, followed with cup of sweet black tea and a shortbread biscuit, switched off all the electrics, locked up and curled up under my doona and slept the night away.

The next morning was Pinjarra; I rang Pearl, the president of the creative writing club, asking about where the art festival was being held, explained this was only a quick stop. This small community put on a fabulous art exhibition every year. As I walked around a corner of the exhibition, I noticed two things: firstly, the lighting was perfect, and secondly, one of my pieces had a red sticker on it. I felt my face light up, I had a sale. But what took my breath away was an incredible floral art exhibit. A large wooden handcart was filled with bush flowers, gumnuts, leaves, flax and branches of golden and red leaves. I examined the contents of the wagon and introduced myself to the artist, such a humble lady who would take no praise, only that she loved to garden and show off her beautiful plants to the public. My camera got busy, I was looking forward to adding the photos to my blog site – to present an attractive and interesting page was my aim, and it was working; my blog was growing in leaps and bounds with all the places and photos I had added.

It was late afternoon by the time I had finished at the festival and put my laptop away. Mandurah Council would be closed; Pearl invited me to stay for a hot home-cooked dinner and to set up in her driveway overnight. The meal smelt divine, curried sausages with mash spuds and mushy peas. By the time we had finished dinner and chatted over coffee about being a writer, it was past ten at night, I fell asleep with the thought, *Tomorrow I'm home, back to family, including Gordi.*

The dawn was magnificent, I felt like I was being enfolded in arms of peach and gold, in the one place I love, the coast of Perth. I made myself a quick breakfast of muesli and yoghurt. I had dreamt of Gordi; I knew deep down I had a strong connection with him. All I wanted was to sort out was what used to be mood swings were now part of his every day communication with me? Anger, resentment and dislike flicked off his tongue whenever possible. I had hoped that our love for each other would override our personality differences, but the mood swings and the alcohol had to go. I phoned Rae. It rang out, so I left her a message, "Nearly home, honey, I'll be there for dinner, put an extra spud in the pot for me."

As I drove through Mandurah, I saw the posters up on billboards advertising the next wearable arts competition, I felt a little niggle of remorse. But Sydney was calling me, but there was nothing to say I could not have beautiful memories, I also knew if Gordi had been with me, he would have been annoyed, his memories were not happy ones. And that was the part I did not understand, surely he had some nice memories? I had never heard him reminisce, he always said best to get on with it, why bring up the past? I was very different. I loved my memories, and I loved my albums of old family photos. Gordi had maybe one or two of his family, I had loved that time in my life when my art really took a huge leap in creativity.

When I entered my first wearable arts competition it had been called 'Flight'. I asked Jess to be my workshop model. He was perfect, I cut and sewed hundreds of silk scales; I just knew Jess was the model to wear it for the competition. I also spent many nights designing and making a headdress of feathers, I worked on the ensemble for months. It looked amazing when the costume finally came together. Rae and I stood back and what we saw was a proud avatar, a young man tall and strong, the costume of multicoloured silk scales softly shimmering across his body. On one of our walks, Jess had found a long tree branch. "My staff!" he cried. I could see the possibilities, and after we got it home Gordi offered to work on it, turning it into work of art. He had smoothed it right down then burnt a design into it, decorated it with all sorts of bibs and bobs that I had collected during our travels. I added a string of plaited leather, weaving any remaining feathers into it. The ensemble looked amazing; I was speechless as Jess displayed it for us. However, to my disappointment, on judging day, my costume was not deemed a winner. One of the judges asking what my costume had to do with flight? It seemed obvious to me, feathers and dragon scales spelt flight, correct? The answer was, "It's not what we are looking for." The papers I signed specified that *the judge's decision was final, any contact with judges would disqualify the artist.*

Whether it was to compensate the artists who did not get onstage or not, I accepted the opportunity when invited to display my costume front and centre in the foyer on the showcase night, when all the winning categories displayed their creations onstage in a wonderful musical. It was no use being precious about not being included in the stage show, being shown in the foyer seemed a nice gesture, so I agreed to it. Gordi was angry I was not one of the chosen few, I was only too happy to be part of it, so when I replied "Gordi, it's not about winning, it's about being part of a creative community," I might well have spoken to the wall, he was adamant I deserved to win. Which I guess is nice, to a point, but then common sense should prevail. Shouldn't it? Well, those were my thoughts on it. On the day I was asked to place my costume in the foyer, Gordi spied a judge from the competition having a coffee in the café opposite the foyer. He strode over, hands on hips, then in a very loud voice he demanded to know why my magnificent costume was shown in the foyer, not onstage. I knew by local gossip the competition was so popular plans were being made for a repeat next year, and I now understood why I was not invited back. No-one likes confrontation, well except Gordi, even if his theory was proved wrong, he would argue the point till his target or opponent would walk away. I was happy he thought I was the best, but Gordi had to learn his opinion did not matter in this art world. A lot of apologising and soothing of egos took place from me that year. But today I had one thing on my mind, it was time for me to go home to Rockingham, pack my case and leave for Sydney. My tum whirled with excitement.

CHAPTER 9

Jess was the first to greet me. The front door was flung open, his arms open, waiting to give me a bear hug. With this one action of his, I knew I was home. He was nearly sixteen and taller than me. He was physically maturing fast, his once chubby baby face now all sharp angles of the adult he would become, "Glad you're home safe, Nana," his voice seemed deeper. The next out the door was Rae, with a bundle of joy in her arms, my granddaughter Shauna, she too had grown from a helpless babe to a wriggling, smiling, happy child. Rae looked tired but happy and content. Kane stood beside her; he had a settled mature look about him now he was a dad and husband.

I spied Gordi standing inside the doorway, his face a mask of uncertainty. After hugging everyone in front of me, I walked towards him, opened my arms and held him close to me; now I felt I was home, part of a loving close family. Dinner was on the table; Shauna sat in her highchair beside Gordi who obviously doted on her, Jess was beside me, and Kane and Rae at each end of the table where Russ and I once sat. It felt weird, but looked as it should be, Kane offered a blessing for the food on the table, then and only then, could we help ourselves to the food. I was not a religious person, did not pray all that often, I preferred to meditate and feel the energy, but this felt right, soon all that you could hear was cutlery scraping plates, as the chicken & corn soup with crusty cheese bread was devoured, I complimented Rae on her culinary skills.

"Not me, Mum, it was all Gordi's hard work." I was then told what a blessing he was around the house; he had either cooked or cleaned and had offered to babysit, while Rae and Kane had a date night. Nothing was too much trouble for him. I was not surprised at all; I knew how caring Gordi could be. I knew when he put his mind to it, the meals he produced were lovely, in fact, when I considered what he could do in the home, he was amazing, what we had to sort out, though, was his anger and drinking. Still, there would be time for that later, for now we discussed my plans for Sydney, and what I was expecting from any contract offered to me, which was financial security. Now Gordi in this mode was the one I liked. He saw the opportunity for me.

My days of wandering wherever I wanted, to take an overseas trip or two and buy a granny flat somewhere nice, safe and secure could now come true. I had learnt that helping others and allowing them to become dependent on me financially had not done me any favours. As the saying goes, money does not grow on trees. To say I had bent the money tree and given it a good shake was closer to home. It was time to build up my savings or become a government-paid pensioner. I do not have any objection to the latter, they have earnt their money, worked hard for it, I simply hated what they went through, I had seen for myself the ton of paperwork involved when applying for an age pension, the less you had the better it seemed, I had witnessed what an extra dollar to make ends meet, could mean.

Volunteering for the local soup kitchen rounds one year had opened my eyes, not only the homeless arrived for hot soup and a buttered bun or two, older people and families on low incomes were among the recipients of community kindness. There is only so much a soup kitchen can do; I always left them thinking of what else could be done for those people in need. When Rae was a solo parent, the number of papers she had to fill out was incredible; the continuous battle she had to get what the government said she had a right to was enough to show me the value of financial independence – and the big money, if it was offered, would help me to achieve this. But I had not seen the paperwork yet.

My lawyer had already rung and informed me he was Skyping into my meeting with the production company, he had made all the prearrangements, my job was just to be there, if we both agreed, then I would sign the papers, so I really had no qualms about what was to happen.

As we were tidying up the table after our dinner, stacking dishes into the dishwasher, Gordi took me by the hand, leading me into the study; it was his room while he lived here. His apology was from the heart, he asked for me to trust him with his decision of going to AA for help. I did not have a problem with any of it, if he admitted he had a drinking problem and was seeking help. When we embraced, it was with love and forgiveness on both sides, there was no mistaking that Gordi and I could really love each other. He asked that I stop comparing him to Russ, to which I answered, "They are my memories, Gordi, I can't agree to that." I asked him to stop his drinking and curb his sarcasm. It sounded easy enough, hopefully with this new honesty between us we could grow as a couple. Gordi asked to fly to Sydney with me, I shook my head, this was something I wanted to accomplish on my own.

Gordi had one thousand reasons why he should accompany me; Trust was the one reason why he should not, Gordi then produced the silver turquoise ring he had given me a year ago. It was the engagement ring he gave me. I had taken it off as we had stacked tonight's dinner dishes. My hand shook as I held it out to accept it. "I love you," was all he said as he slipped it back to where it had left an indent. Our foreheads now pressed against one another; Gordi feathered small kisses over my face. I was relaxed in his arms, returning his embrace, but when he whispered, "Marry me, Tara," I froze.

Marriage? Where did that come from? My first instinct was to say no. Taking a big breath I asked, "Why, Gordi? Why not stay as we are?" I began to search for the right words, but they would not come.

Gordi's face turned puce he exploded. "Why not? Why do you have to take everything apart and write or verbalise everything we do? Why do you take pleasure in being on your own so much? I'm here as your partner, either I'm an active partner or not? Tell me, Tara, how you see my role in your life if we stay as we are?"

I did not want to argue on my first night home with my family around me. I felt bullied into giving him an answer; I left the room saying, "I'll stay in the motorhome tonight, Gordi." Just being one room away was not enough. The flame of embarrassment touching my cheeks as I walked past my family as they watched television; I knew they had heard Gordi's outburst. Outdoors, the night air cooled my face, his proposal had rocked me to my core, I questioned myself: *Did I want more from our relationship?* I slept badly, Gordi's proposal echoing around inside my head all night. The banging on the door woke me with a start, my head aching, my eyes felt gritty. The alarm clock told me it was 5am, the voice calling me was urgent.

"Mum, wake up, you have to be on the plane in four hours." I shot out of bed in panic, I had not even started to pack my case, or sort what I wanted to wear, I had three days in Sydney, two of them in meetings, one of them to explore.

Then the excitement hit my gut, this was really happening, and if I kept my head screwed on right it would be well worth the effort. Rae stood there as I opened the door, a mug of tea in her hand and little Shauna attached to a baby pack in front of her. "Better get up, Mum, you have to be there two hours before your flight." From that moment on, apart from a quick hug from my sweet-smelling granddaughter, who thought grabbing her nana's glasses off her face and trying to chew them was an extremely funny game, time flew. I hugged Gordi with a promise I would give him an answer when I returned to Perth. My open suitcase lay on my bed, my bathroom bag had been packed, clean underwear placed in a cotton bag and packed, all I had to do was throw in some clothes and shoes.

As I showered, Gordi's hand crept inside the shower curtain, his hand began to caress my breast. All I could gurgle was, "Gordi, not now," his chuckle at my discomfort made it worse. Slapping his hand away, shooing him out of the bathroom then locking the door, I dried and dressed in a hurry.

Gordi's face was at the door when I opened it, he was softly chanting, "You wanna hold me, you wanna love me." It was a line from a Sandra Bullock movie we had both watched, it had become a saying Gordi had cottoned onto, especially if I was grumpy with him.

"Not now, buddy," I said as I packed my clothing, each item I put in was taken out and refolded by him, which was annoying the hell out of me, I felt like he was approving of what I wore, not too short, not too see-through, just like my father. Finally, make-up on, hair dried, shoes on, and I was ready to go, Rae offered me a ride to the airport, asking Gordi to babysit Shauna for an hour or two, I knew this was going to be question time from Rae, I also knew by Gordi's face that he was really put-out at her request.

His plan was to drive me to the airport and usher me onto the plane, all with an ulterior motive, to put pressure on me to say those two words 'I do'. So, it was, "Yes please," to her offer, "let's go." Kane had to go to work, and Jess who I hugged onto for a wee while longer, was going back to his boarding school. They had said their goodbyes and congratulations the previous night.

As we drove, the sun was just creeping up, and what I had thought about would happen, happened, it was not so much question time, but an interrogation time.

"So, what's happening with you and Gordi, does he stay or go?" I was not surprised by her candid honesty, I expected nothing less from my daughter, but what came next was unexpected. "Mum, you really should make a decision about Gordi, it's not good to leave him hanging, he feels like a third wheel around us, he is trying to be part of our family, but you keep him at arm's length all the time. It's about time you decided what it is you want, and act on it. The poor guy is trying so hard." Before I could say anything, Rae continued with her tirade. "He has no-one here but us, Mum, if you don't want him in your life, then say so, send him away for good, and don't look back, let him grow with another, you seem to be just standing back and when he mucks up, which he does, and often, then you look uncomfortable. He's a friend of the family at the moment, not part of our family. How would you like to be in his shoes?"

Wow: all this from my daughter, I felt like I was ten and being reprimanded by an adult. At first, I was frustrated as some of her words were true, I did hold him at arm's length. And yes, in a way it was unfair to keep him here if I was not serious about our relationship. So, my answer was short and quick, "In my defence, Rae, I'm not used to the abuse Gordi seems to take pleasure in. He flip-flops from kind and loving to mean and sarcastic. I was married to your dad for a long time, we grew together in love and friendship, it did not happen overnight and that's what I'm trying to show Gordi. Let's be friends, lets grow with each other. And his family, Rae? They are not nice at all. We no sooner take one step forward as a couple, he chats to them, then it's two steps back."

Her hand reached over and held mine. "It's okay, Mum, really enjoy

Sydney. Once you're home try to sort it out for all of us. I know it's your life, but there is nothing like famiy which you taught us, so do we encourage Shauna to call him Gordi or Grandad?" And somehow that question unsettled me. Both of us laughing when she said, "At the moment she sort of burbles 'Grunch' which may stick."

To which I added, "And at the moment, appropriate."

CHAPTER 10

The airport turn-off came up, our conversation stopped with the need to concentrate on what entry to take for the drop-off section. Rae grabbed my suitcase out of the car boot; she knew I was hurt that she had literally taken his side. As I hugged her goodbye, she said, "Knock their socks off, Mum, ring us tonight to let us know you arrived, okay?" I loved this daughter of mine, yes, I was a trifle offended, but, in other ways she was right. I really should sort my feelings for Gordi, for good, for now I was off to Sydney. Once I was through the check-in and the metal detectors, I sat inside the Dome café with coffee and a ham sandwich, and the papers my lawyer had emailed through. I had printed them off once I had arrived home, and they were well and truly thumb-marked from reading and re-reading them many times. Whether I signed either option, I was going to be financially stable. My flight was called, I boarded, and the next step was to arrive, find my hotel and settle in for the night.

At three o'clock on a Friday afternoon the city of Sydney is frantic. Everybody wants to go home, and taxis are few and far between, I was maybe twentieth in line at the airport terminal when the women behind me asked if I was heading towards central city, I informed her of my hotel, she said it was not too far away from where she wanted to be dropped off, so we shared a taxi. I choose to be dropped off with her simply because I wanted to experience Sydney from a tourist's point of view.

Walking down the busy street filled with traffic fumes and noise, people crowding together, it was exciting to think I knew no-one and no-one knew me. I was a total stranger in this huge metropolitan city. My hotel soon came into view. The glass doors whooshed elegantly open at my approach, the desk staff beaming as I walked towards them. Within ten minutes I was in my room three floors up, the noise of the city muffled by the double glass windows. In front of me the Sydney harbour bridge rose, a black metal majestic monolith. Built in the 1950s, a tribute to engineering and the flood of immigrants who were encouraged from Greece, Croatia, New Zealand, Italy and Britain to work on this bridge.

They had long gone; it was their descendants who now walked these streets. The forefathers of a yesteryear from varied nationalities, a global family that worked, lived, loved, and died, making Sydney what it is today, an international city of merit on the world stage. Today I was a small part of this heritage, just another face that looked up at the bridge in wonder from the windows of my room, while below me a mass of humans swarmed with their heads down. But that's a city for you; it's no different worldwide.

The white gauze curtains that should have billowed with fresh air, remained slack and motionless; the windows were shut tight, aircon softly blowing cold air into the room. It felt lifeless. I was about to go downstairs to the café when my phone rang, my lawyer was on the line making sure I had all the correct information, and that the camera on my laptop was working. I'm not that computer-savvy, so he walked me through the steps of logging in and pressing the right buttons, if all failed then we could communicate via Facebook Messenger, that way he would be included in the conversation.

"This is important, Tara, from all sides, so just make sure you get it right." Was it me, or the men in my life that insisted on treating me like an idiot?

By the time we had finished our conversation it was dinnertime. I dressed in a short red cross-cut dress that I loved. It flared slightly from hip to knee, otherwise it hugged my body. I added a gauzy black wrap for my shoulders and strappy black high heels. I enjoyed this part of dressing up. Dinners around a campfire do not provide much opportunity to be glamorous. I made the most of it, gel spiking my silver hair, adding puffs of my rose perfume, diamanté earrings and bracelet, and applying fresh make-up, I felt great. Making my way down the corridor, stepping into the lift, I pressed the down button. What is it about elevator music? I find it unnerving, almost suffocating, while others find it calming. As I entered the restaurant the sounds of tinkling plates and glassware and stilted conversation filled the air, a three-piece band softly played lounge room jazz in a corner. The tables were filled with couples; I was the only one who seemed to be on my own.

The waiter showed me to my seat, I ordered a cold white wine with a serving of pan-fried parmesan bread for my entree, and for my main meal, a fillet of white fish and lemon herb butter sauce with a fresh side salad of apple, carrot and cucumber. Everything was perfect, the food and wine delicious. I was about to leave when a waiter appeared with another glass of white wine, I informed him I had not ordered it, he replied, "No, Ma'am, that gentleman over there has sent this over to you."

I looked up into the deepest brown eyes, before I could refuse, the gentleman the waiter referred to was now standing next to me. "Mind if I join you?" His voice washed over me like warm honey, it had a slight European accent, and with a start, I realised I was being flirted with, it had been a long time since this had happened.

He held out his hand, I noticed his nails were manicured, his white shirt-cuff spotless, a silver cufflink winked at the edge, mesmerising me. He introduced himself as, "Ramón. And yours is?"

"Tara," I blurted. I went to shake his hand and he held onto mine, lifting it to his lips. My legs turned to rubber. "Ramón, I think you have mistaken me for someone else."

His hand still held onto mine. "No mistake, Tara, you're the beautiful women in red. You will dance with me?"

"Yes."

Ramón led me to the dance floor, then his arm went around my waist as we danced to a very slow twostep. His hand on my back was placed just above the hips, his thumb lightly rubbed my lower spine. I wanted to purr. Ramón was a tall, slim, good-looking man, his silver hair tied back into a small ponytail, a tiny stud diamond glittered on his right earlobe. It was if I had no control over myself or my body, I was enjoying every minute of it, my mind crying out *Tara, stop,* my body betraying me, becoming relaxed within his embrace. His peppermint laced breath sighed into my hair, as my name rolled of his lips, "Tara." No conversation was needed.

Ramón was an expert at seduction. He glided with such ease across the dance floor, his body so tantalising close, close enough for me to feel his muscled body through my dress. My body was responding, it had been such a long time since I had danced a slow dance with a man who knew how to make a women's legs go weak at the knees. Ramón and I walked out into the beautiful night, the harbour bridge was lit up, tiny soft glowing lights surrounded us as we stood in small courtyard. Ramón's lips brushed my ear, his hand cradled the back of my head, our lips met in the lightest of kisses.

Our drinks had been delivered to a small table beside us; Ramón passed me my glass of cold white wine, "To tonight, Tara," his glass only just touched mine, his hand slipped around my waist, "Tara, shall we take our wine to your room?" Again, my mind said, *Whoa, Tara*, but my body agreed, I felt like someone had offered me the gold ring off the carousel. It was when he slipped his business card into my hand, I glanced down to read *Ramón, Male Escort* written in gold script across a black card. The shock of what I knew was being offered, which, I realised, had been encouraged by me, bought me to sudden halt. I was being invited to pay for this night. Ramón was a male prostitute, high class, oh so sexy and handsome, he sold sex and had targeted me, a woman on my own, as a client for his services. I could not believe how I had thought this man would be in interested in me. I left the restaurant and Ramón's embrace, almost tripping up in my haste to the lift, quickly tapping the up button a dozen times in my haste to retreat. The doors slowly responded, they were in no hurry, finally they opened again with a quiet *whoosh*. I was soon outside my room, the key card slipping out of my hand twice before I managed to swipe it. Once safely inside, I closed the door on the dimly lit hallway.

I sat on my bed in the dark, stunned by what I had just done, and was very tempted to do. How easily I had been deceived and how I had responded. Sleep took a long time to come to me that night, my mind retracing over and over my encounter with this handsome gigolo, it was my very first and it was going to be my very last. Yet the naughtiness of it all made me smile. I woke early feeling confused, a little ashamed of my lack of control. Although my relationship with Gordi was not the most stable; he did not deserve this, if the boot were on the other foot, I would have been disappointed in him. Yet my face broke out in a smile when I looked in the mirror.

Breakfast was served in my room; this day was D-day, the day I was to sign over my script. I decided to dress smart casual, so I put on my dress jeans, long loose top, the sandals I had borrowed from Rae with a little bling on them and a dainty gold heel. Adding sunglasses, a spritz of hair spray and minimal make-up, I was ready. I was making sure I had all legal papers, my laptop, and my bag, when the phone rang. "Madam, your car is waiting," said the concierge. I did not expect what was outside waiting for me, a mauve-coloured stretch Jeep. I loved it. The driver opened the door for me, and as I got in the back, I realised there were three other people inside the dim interior, all eyes settling on me.

CHAPTER 11

It seemed my preparation the night before was not necessary. In the moving mauve Aladdin's cave, soft lights twinkled, and the soft music that played as I had entered the vehicle was now turned off. The other three travellers were holding iPads or mobile phones. A misty, ice-filled glass appeared, I sipped slowly expecting champagne, but instead, one of my favourite drinks, an ice-cold mint and ginger tea, they had done their homework. How refreshing. Helena introduced herself to me and then introduced Keiko and Serani. They were all dressed all in black, Helena and Serani in black trouser suits and wore gold and diamonds at their throats, wrists and ears, Keiko, the male of the threesome was dressed in black suit and white shirt, his wide smile was welcoming, while the eyes were serious. We all shook hands, and Keiko asked for my laptop. I popped in my password, he then popped in a code and within two minutes my lawyer's face zoomed in, I felt like I was in a spy movie, a member of a secret service working out the world's problems, keeping it safe from evil, it would not have surprised me to hear one of them say, *For your next mission ...*

It was time to get down to business. Their main concern was whether I would sign over total copyright of the manuscript, now a filmscript, to the movie company? Or did I want a say in the making of the movie, and was I to be involved in the casting of the lead characters? The options were simple; if I decided to sell everything, including copyright of the book I was writing (which included a new scene written into it as they requested), I would be offered more money. If I wanted to be part of the production team, it would be a lesser amount. Both figures shown were healthy enough to live well for many years, if invested wisely. My lawyer left the Zoom session saying he had heard all he needed to, he would listen to the recording once more and would be in contact. Keiko said the two contracts would be emailed to him.

These film people knew what they were doing; although the smiles were genuine, it was business all the way. I had left the hotel in the early morning; it was nearly midday when we cruised to a stop at a small restaurant. The outside veranda was covered in deep green vine leaves, the building itself a nondescript ochre. Lunch was amazing, fresh calamari in a spicy tomato sauce. There were tall jugs of water filled with ice and slices of bright yellow lemon, and a bold red wine was offered, which I refused. I was not here to drink, I was here to make deal, to keep clear-headed was imperative. It was at this lunch when I met the director and two sponsors, who immediately put me at ease. As we discussed the script, I couldn't help wondering at all this fuss over sixty sheets of paper, it all seemed surreal; so much wealth casually tossed about like leaves in the wind. All I had to do was decide what I wanted, to sell completely or to have a say in what and how they made the film, which would mean regular flights back and forth to Sydney, but it was made clear that this option would be at my own expense – I immediately saw the dollars flying away. By 3pm I was back in my hotel room, numbers buzzing around my head as I mulled over my options. I felt it was time I rang Gordi to get his input. Simply out of respect as it was his idea in the first place.

I knew deep down I wanted to get on with the life I had created, writing stories and poetry, being published and running art and/or creative writing workshops around the countryside. If I accepted the second offer, there would be no time for anything else but working with and on the movie. No doubt meeting and greeting many more influential people.

Gordi's voice was full of concern for me. "Is everything alright, honey? What's the news?" I almost choked up. If I ever needed a wise word or two it was now. There were times that Gordi's opinion mattered, and I needed to make sense out of all of this. Not a lawyer's point of view, just a friend's opinion. He suggested that I email him the two written options, he would read them and get back to me, then it was time for a chat to Rae and Jess. Rae wanting to know had I thought about our conversation on the way to the airport and Jess wanting a part in the movie.

Some things never change. I informed Rae, "Yes I was seriously thinking about it," and to Jess it was, "Not this time, Jess."

His argument was simple, to the point, "I'm in drama class at school, I've done three major shows, I am enrolled with a modelling agency, what more could you want?" I did not want to spend the night explaining my actions to my grandson; maybe Gordi was wearing off on him, the 'what about me?' syndrome was too familiar. I cut the conversation short, sending my love to all.

A change of scene was needed, the reception desk was not busy when I approached to enquire if I were booked in for dinner or was I to make my own arrangements, I was informed a menu was in my room I could order in if I preferred. As I walked away, I spied Ramón, his beautiful brown hypnotic eyes never left mine, although he had another attractive older woman by the arm. Her eyes were glazed over with lust. I wanted to rush up and warn her; then again this was her choice, instead I turned my back and walked into the lift to go back to my room. It was none of my business who or what he did, he made a living by hunting the vulnerable. I knew if I let it get to me, I would end up confronting Ramón and embarrassing myself. I decided that a hot shower and a hot cuppa were better options. I ordered a light supper in my room and flicked through the movie offerings. *Life of Pi* came up. I had taken Jess to see it and we had both loved it, but this time I could sit back and watch it uninterrupted, without the demands of a bottomless-pit grandson who inhaled popcorn, ice cream and coke throughout the movie, I smiled when I thought of Jess when an exciting part came on screen, Jess got such a fright, he had yelled out, "Shit!!" and guess who wore the popcorn?

Wrapped up in the hotel's massive fluffy bathrobe, I munched on my room service supper, a very small pizza with a pot of tea and relaxed. I realised I had drifted off when I was woken by my mobile phone trilling. It showed 11:30pm.

"What's wrong?" Gordi was surprised by my abruptness.

"Well hello to you too, I just rang to chat to you, Tara, I received your emails I thought we could talk while the house is quiet."

Gordi had forgotten about the time difference; it was only 9:30pm Perth. He was right though; it was a nice time to sit and chat with no disturbances.

"So, what do you think, Gordi, which contract would you go for?"

He hesitated. "Okay, Tara, I would go for the contract that says you sell outright to them, sign away the copyright, not the money. Sell outright as long as your name is on the screen as the author, the second option would be very time-consuming for you. You would have to be wherever they are filming, and to be honest, I feel it would make a huge difference to our lives together." I was seeing the sense of it, by now I was yawning, my body demanding sleep.

"Gordi, let me sleep on it, I know what you're saying, and I am thinking it over, really I am." We both said, "Bye, love you," at the same time, my words sounding empty. It was ages before I could settle, my mind was so full wondering about the right thing to do. The movie contract I was almost decided on. However, if I declined Gordi's proposal of marriage, I knew I would face an outburst of angry emotions.

I knew that I did not want to spend the rest of my life alone, however did I want to spend it as Gordi's wife? Living with his expectations reminded me of the days when a wife was seen and not heard; this was not who I was. I had the uneasy feeling that there would be more unexpected emotional upheavals to come.

I was the one who claimed I was so good at writing lists, I thought maybe I should write one for myself. What did I expect from my partner? As I finally dozed off, I spied through the curtains the Southern Cross in the sky, my dreams were filled with our travels together, the people we had met, the fun and laughter, and the many campfires Gordi and I had built together, it had once been fun.

I woke with clarity; I had a plan. My first call after breakfast was to Gordi, I had decided to take his advice on selling the whole thing, kit and caboodle, to the film company and as he suggested my name stay on credits as the author. My life as a writer and traveller was too important to ignore, and our life as a couple was also important. I was in my mid-sixties, I knew this man, I knew he loved me, our relationship was fiery, I was the first to admit, but it was real-life, not like the one-night stand offered to me by Ramón. Maybe it was time to knuckle down and accept Gordi's proposal.

Next, I rang my lawyer, my decision had been made, I was selling the manuscript, lock, stock and barrel, my name would be on-screen as the author; that was what I had asked for and that was exactly what I was getting.

Scrambled eggs on toast at this hotel were the best and lightest I had ever tasted in my life, they seemed to float over the golden buttery toast. Set out on a pure white tablecloth with polished silver cutlery, and accompanied by two hot cups of steaming black coffee, I was in heaven. The silver service topped it off, none of the serve-yourself breakfast buffet scenario. The light through the windows was soft, lemon sunlight was diffused through the long white net curtains. With only five or so other diners dotted around the room, it felt like a private occasion, put on just for me. Thinking about what was going to happen with the contracts must have put a smile on my face.

"Thinking about me, Tara?" The honeyed voice sluiced through my thoughts like cold water. Ramón stood at my side, as handsome and immaculate as ever, his dark eyes smouldered with an unspoken invitation. It was then I noticed how pale he looked, smudges of grey under his beautiful eyes, his Bay Leaf aftershave surrounded me, it was stronger than ever, and this morning it annoyed me.

The look of shock on his handsome face when I said aloud, "Young man, why don't you go out and get some fresh air, get some sun on your face, and for heaven's sake stop bothering me!" It had the effect I was after. Ramón made a hurried exit.

My time in Sydney was coming to an end; I had one day left to hit the tourist spots before flying home that night. The car and chauffer, courtesy of the film company was available at any time – all I had to do was call. I booked them for an hour later, which would allow me time to pack, make phone calls, and put my life in order.

"Woo hoo, luv ya, babe!" Gordi's shout nearly deafened me when I said 'yes' to his marriage proposal, and also told him that I had accepted the contract that offered no involvement in the movie, meaning his opinion counted.

Rae's comment was just as warm and welcome. There was laughter in her voice as she said, "Can't wait till you're home safe, Mum, from what I hear we have a wedding to plan."

I called my lawyer and advised him of my decision, I did not want to be shackled to what may be a year or two of hard work, and repeated travelling.

He agreed that what I had decided was for the best. As I was dressing, he rang back and gave me the good news that the film company was delighted to accept my decision, and a cheque would be deposited within the next twenty-four hours, meaning I was going to be financially secure.

It was time to pack my case, and head home to family and friends, and the life I loved of travel and adventure.

CHAPTER 12

After I checked out and walked through the doors of the hotel for the last time, there was no stretch limo waiting for me; a white Peugeot stood in its place. My case, which I had packed and left in the room, was already stowed in the boot, a dapper older gentleman dressed in a navy suit, white shirt and navy tie with a gold tiepin introduced himself as Daniel, held the door open for me, taking care to ensure my clothing was not caught up as he closed it.

"I believe you would like to do some touring?" Daniel suggested first we go to the Blue Mountains, I admitted I had already been there, perhaps two years ago, so he suggested a drive that would lead me out to Palm Beach, stopping off at Chatswood and Mona Vale along the way, where a Sculptures by the Sea, an outdoor exhibition, was on now on display. All he had to say was 'art' and I was hooked. We drove into the Sydney traffic, it was mid-morning and the harbour looked beautiful, the Sydney Opera House a stark white against the light blue sky, deep blue water and golden sun. While we drove, Daniel informed me that Mona Vale was his hometown, it was not a tourist mecca, which to me made it all the more interesting, as that meant there would be artisans of all sorts in sheds or workshops; we just had to find them. With my driver being a local, I knew he would know where to go.

Daniel pulled over at the Armchair Collective, and immediately my art instincts were aroused as I noticed the eclectic muddle of art displayed, from huge bouquets of fresh flowers and locally dried flowers, to delicate handmade pincushions, the old fashioned over-stuffed armchairs that were scattered around small marble inlaid wooden tables. The counter was an old piece of sea flotsam that had been water-damaged and weathered; the owner had salvaged it and polished it so it was now a beautiful piece of art in itself. We were offered iced teas, and while Daniel stood and chatted to the owner, I wandered around the shop. I stopped still in front of a piece; I knew as soon as I set my eyes on it that Rae would love it. It was made by a local artist called Suzanne; in my hand sat a fragile glassblown hatpin, handpainted with blossoming pink roses on black lacquer, on the tip was a diamanté, perfect to go with the costume she was making for the wearable arts competitions. Jess was next, a metallic skull mobile phone cover, then for Kane a magazine on wood-turning, Shauna's gift was a cute hand-sewn baby bib with 'best granddaughter' printed on it. I searched for a curio for Gordi, there was nothing that said, 'pick me'. Gordi loved knick-knacks, like weird keyrings, but there was nothing that took my eye. I decided to wait till I was at the airport; perhaps the tourist shop would have something of interest for him.

Apart from that one shop Daniel had suggested, everything else was spread too far afield; he suggested we drive to the sculpture exhibition have our lunch then head back towards the airport. It sounded good to me. It didn't take long to get there; there was not a lot of traffic, which surprised me, as I had heard it was a very popular exhibition. Once out of the car, my camera went to work, I loved it, everything about this exhibition was superb, the number of talented artists that exhibited here was amazing. My favourite was a silver stag situated on a grassy mound and looking out to sea; its antlers fascinated me, they appeared to be made of pure silver but were, in fact, long branches of sticks and twigs painted silver. It was the sort of sculpture you wanted to pop in your case and take home to show off in the garden, but logically it was far too big to consider. Daniel had unpacked a picnic hamper and after I finished wandering around the artwork, he invited me to join him. While we ate, I encouraged him to tell me his story. He was a little shy about speaking about his life, so I chatted about the purpose of my trip.

Daniel finally began his story. He was a Vietnam War veteran; he described his job in the army as 'just another grunt'. His opinion was that war was senseless, I sat and listened, my opinion was of no value on this subject, Daniel was one of the many veterans with mental scars. "They call it post-traumatic stress disorder," he said, "I call it getting the shits every two hours." I nearly choked on my egg sandwich, I did not know whether to laugh or cry, he had obviously been through hell and back, and black humour was the way he dealt with it, that was my guess anyway. It seemed silly that here we were, two adults sitting in the sunshine, with the blue sea in front, golden sand around us, the waves gently lapping up on shore, gulls calling overhead – a beautiful peaceful calm day, secure and safe in this beautiful country, and Daniel was talking about the horrors of war. I sent up a whisper of thanks to the universe that we lived in this country, not in a place where ducking bullets before breakfast was considered normal.

His biggest sorrow was watching the small village children collecting a day's water for the household, not knowing if they would return home in one piece, or at all, "It's a god-awful friggin' mess, nothing in the whole world can make up for what we saw." His grey eyes were troubled with his memories. I suggested it was time to pack up and go, there was nothing I could do to help; this man was one of the many casualties that brings war home, and it hurt to know that sitting next to me was the foregone conclusion of bravery, one who had done his duty for our country, and there was nothing I could do to help him forget what he witnessed. Soon enough it was time for me to go back to my home and take up the life waiting for me. And yet, once again, I had this gut feeling what was waiting for me was not for me. Daniel drove me to the drop-off point at the airport; we had not spoken further during the time that it took to get us there. Both of us were immersed in our own thoughts, once I was out on the pavement, with my suitcase beside me, we shook hands. I wished him well, he wished me a safe journey home and drove off. It was while I was sitting in the plane ready for take-off that it struck me, Daniel and I most likely would never meet again. He had made a deep impression on me, and I might write about it one day. My thoughts were about Daniel, isn't it weird who and how we meet people, and we never know when that one small piece of conversation may change another's life? Listening to Daniel's story had certainly given me food for thought, one of these being very grateful for what I had, and also for the information that I might use in the next book I was writing.

The flight from Sydney takes about six hours, depending on the wind, or so they say. I had an aisle seat, I snuggled into my seat and studied the film menu in search of a good movie and ordered a hot black tea. I'd have a snooze, and soon enough I would be back home with my family. One of my mothers' sayings kept rattling around in my head: "One drop of rain can make such a mark; its rippling effects can change a whole community." With that thought, as we climbed higher into a cloudless sky, reclining my seat, I drifted off. Maybe that's what Daniel was for his community, a mark of change, of the need to care more for each other. It was a ripple effect that one day may affect us all.

I was woken by the flight attendant announcing dinner was served. No foil-wrapped package for me this time, I was flying first class thanks to the film company. A chilled champagne was offered with my dinner, I asked for a spritzer, half orange juice and half white wine; nothing was too much trouble. I felt very spoilt when I was offered warm lemon-scented handtowels, a fresh water or orange juice with a dinner menu. I chose the roast duck with a white rice salad. There was a choice of magazines or today's newspaper, I just wanted to relax, so I chose the movie *The Red Tent*, I had loved the book, so why not watch the movie?

Well, that was my intention. In the window seat was an older woman who had tucked into her dinner with gusto, then ordered a brandy. She introduced herself: "Billy's my name, and you are?" I introduced myself and we chatted as the plane flew through heavy clouds. Billy gave a big sigh. "I wish it was that easy to go to heaven!" My eyebrows went up, "You know," Billy continued, "just book a seat when you have had enough of living and fly away." I thought it was a little weird, but everyone has the right to an opinion. I knew if I asked why, it would be seen as an invitation to chat, and right now all I wanted was some space in my head to work out what was going on with my own thoughts. The closer I got to Perth the more I felt like I was being given a jail sentence. But Billy had other ideas, her voice trembling with age, she warmed up to her audience of one – me.

She had been visiting her husband's grave site in a small suburb of Sydney, he had been a World War II veteran who had been hospitalised for trauma after he came home in 1944. They had married when she was just a child of fifteen, lying about her age and running away to marry him. I did a quick calculation, Billy was in her nineties if she was a day; she talked about her soldier husband like he was here with us. A small smile played around the deeply lined mouth; her eyes soft with love. They remained a childless couple, no sooner had they married than he was taken away from her to fight a war they had no idea about. Once he was shipped back to Australia from Gallipoli, he was too ill to go back home so they led a married life from his hospital bed. As I listened to her story, it was not of hardship, but of love for her husband who fought as an ANZAC, a kind caring man whom she adored. It did not matter to her how many medals he was given for bravery and courage.

All Billy had wanted was for her man to wrap his arms around her and be her partner in life. "I loved him then and I still do, he will always be in my heart." When I asked if she had ever remarried, her rheumy eyes looked into mine. "To be honest, I thought about it, life as a widow was really hard back then, I was not short of offers, I even lived with one man, as his housekeeper. His family and the community pressured me to marry him for decency's sake, it became extreme. My heart said no, but as a young woman, out of respect for the church I agreed. On the day I was to marry him, I left him at the altar, running away to the very back waters of Northern Queensland. You see I still loved my soldier boy, and I always will."

It struck me, then, that was how I felt about Russ. Was this a sign to end things before it was too late to turn back? I helped Billy to pick her hot cup of tea, her arthritic fingers were unable to curl around the cup properly. These bent fingers told of hardship; her nails were ridged and yellowed with age. Her next comment sealed what my heart had told me for the past five years: "Once you meet your true love, or as they say today, your life's partner, then no-one else can hold a candle to them. I guess I could have settled for second best, but I was not prepared to settle. I did alright for myself though, we both know it's not too long before we are together again." With that she put her small head back and closed her eyes with a sigh, no doubt dreaming of her soldier boy.

I did not watch my chosen movie; my head was busy with the what-ifs of arriving and announcing that I did now want to be married, that I was happy to stay as we were. Would marriage settle Gordi down? Would it make Gordi or either of us happier? Or, should we call it quits and stay friends, as we had done in the past? I watched the Perth city lights growing larger, my mind still a whirl of what-ifs. Soon the captain made his announcement: "Ladies and gentlemen, we are approaching Perth city, thank you for flying Qantas." The flight attendants were making sure our tray tables were stowed, our seats upright and seatbelts pulled tight, our bags under the seats; soon we glided onto the tarmac.

CHAPTER 13

I love the lights of Perth, I have done so since my first flight into Perth city, and this time proved no different. At the airport it was a short walk to the bag carousel. I helped Billy with hers, making sure she knew where the cab rank was. I was surprised there was no-one to greet me, thinking maybe they are waiting downstairs. Again, no-one greeted me, no-one called out my name, no-one smiled at me. I felt slightly abandoned, to be honest. My phone rang; it was Rae saying Shauna my granddaughter was teething and not at all happy, Gordi was caught in traffic but would be there soon. "Just wait for him, Mum, he will be there to pick you up."

Somehow it was relaxing not having to smile and greet everyone; I envied Billy in a way. Walking over to a café with thoughts of buying myself a coffee whilst I waited, I heard my name being called out, looking up, there was Gordi, his arms full of flowers, his voice full of love, his eyes tender as he saw my face brighten up.

"Welcome home, my sweetheart." The ride home was full of questions: "What did you do? Who did you meet? What did you eat? Did you do any sightseeing? What was Sydney like? Was the weather good?"

I talked as much as I could about the hotel, the travelling, sightseeing and the contract meeting. I omitted talking about meeting Ramón, I was still embarrassed about how I reacted to this gigolo, maybe one day I would tell Gordi, but for now I was going to enjoy being home and spending time with family. The Rockingham lights were, as always, welcoming, the café strip busier than ever before. Over the past two years it had really blossomed with so many folk moving over here to find employment in the mines up north. The turn-off to our road appeared and then our home came into view;

it was lit up like a Christmas tree, with cars parked all over the place. Inside were the many faces I loved, Jess just about sending me sprawling with his enthusiastic greeting, Rae hugging me and Kane placing one gorgeous, growing granddaughter in my arms. Gordi stood to one side as my friends and family greeted me.

A surprise party was in full swing to welcome me home, I felt mean and petty, bitching about there being no-one at the airport to greet me, when all the time they were planning this welcome for me, it really hit me how much all these faces meant to me. Gordi knew I was exhausted; as the last of the friends left he announced, "Bed for you!" His tone brooked no arguments, and to be honest I was looking forward to a good night's sleep in my own bed, which meant, of course, the motorhome.

With Gordi tucked in beside me I went to sleep instantly feeling safe. The trip had been fun, I was glad I had done it on my own, I was glad I had that time to consider what was being offered to me, I also knew there was a lot of catching up to do, as while I was away in Sydney, Elsa my agent had finally agreed with the organisers for me to go to Margaret River as a paid participating author at a writer's festival, Geraldton had also put out feelers for me to attend the Big Sky Writer's Festival, obviously there was our wedding to plan, and a week at Cairns at the short film festival, in which my script was featured. With all these activities ahead, I knew that what I had wished for was coming true, so why did I feel there was something seriously wrong? I had tried to shake this feeling since Gordi had proposed. What was wrong with me? I should be so full of joy and happiness. So why wasn't I?

It was autumn in Perth, although we don't get the gorgeous rusty red leaves the eastern states display – the leaves here in West Australia have a yellow tinge. In three months, we would be well into winter, a time for fires, hot meals, snuggles under the bedcovers. My two grandchildren were growing up fast. Jess was a firebrand, his temper was always simmering close to the surface; he seemed to take great pleasure in being overly opinionated on every topic, and he had begun to use sarcasm and accusations to get his point across. It was agreed between all of us, a little empathy his way would not go amiss, so we listened to the tirades about how boring school was, and how stupid the teachers were, the only time he stopped was when his mouth was full or when he was asleep. However, his little sister was the apple of his eye, when they were together Jess treated her like spun gold; she adored him and vice versa.

There were times I would have preferred not to have been in the room when his sarcasm overtook his good sense, mostly aimed at his mum or his friends at school. He was still at boarding school, home only on weekends and holidays. At times he was so disrespectful, but it was really up to Kane now as his stepfather, they had formed a bond of friendship with respect. I left it up to them as I had more important things to consider, this was a normal modern family with the world at their feet, it did not need myself or Gordi to step in and say what we thought should or should not be adhered to.

Gordi began to push for a wedding date. I definitely did not want a big wedding, but he requested we give some thought as to the timing, so that all his family in New Zealand could attend. I suggested February or early March in the new year but Gordi was impatient, suggesting I was delaying things. I showed him my itinerary for travelling, expecting an argument, to my surprise his response was, "I agree, we are too busy this year to take that time away to be married." At first I thought he was being sarcastic, but he was genuine. I guessed this meant he was travelling with me. We set the wedding date for 27 February; I suggested the wedding be held at sunset at Shark Point in Mandurah. Gordi had made no comment and did not seem to wish to commit. However, true to form, Gordi loves the shock factor so surprised us all one night when we were having dinner, suggesting we all, as a family, go back to New Zealand for us to be married as it might make his family happier.

"I rang Mum today to tell her we were getting married, she was not that keen on the idea nor was the family, I of course asked why. You, Tara, are an older woman with a family." In their opinion he had a life to live before he settled down. "In fact," he added, "Mum said you are not what she would have chosen for me – she thinks you're a cougar."

There was a sudden silence at the table, I looked over at Rae; her mouth was open. Kane had a bemused look on his face. I was gobsmacked – cougar, me? Before Gordi could say another word, Rae pushed her chair back; it toppled over with a crash, Shauna burst into a frightened cry, all of us were surprised at Rae's reaction; "I agree with everything you mother has said, except I feel the opposite. My mother is too good for your family, how does your Mummy feel about her little boy being a kept man, or does that not come into it? Did you tell her you have bludged off this family for over a year? We asked for nothing as we supported you, and that's what we got in return, insults." Rae spluttered, pausing for breath before adding, "What a rude bloody cow your mother is; I won't be attending your wedding if your mob are going to be there, and they certainly won't be welcome in this family."

CHAPTER 14

Where had my sensible daughter gone, the one who had railed at me when driving me to the airport about giving Gordi a fair go? Rae stomped out of the kitchen, followed by Kane. I took little Shauna out of her highchair, wiped her face and popped her into her playpen. Gordi was nearly in tears. I moved outdoors and sat inside our mobile home, muttering to myself, "I loathe weddings, they are just too hard." I felt hurt by Gordi's family and their criticism of me, but to be honest I had expected it. I did not like them, and they did not like me. When Gordi had his accident in Bali, I had witnessed their true colours; trustworthy or likeable were not words I associated with his family. Gordi poked his head around the door, I could sense he was winding up for an argument, "Gordi, let's wait for a while, please. You have informed your family what we intend to do, we are not children, now let's get on with our plans for this year and see how it all pans out." My instincts were yelling, *Tara – run for the hills!*

He knew he had spoken out of turn; he knew there are some things that are better left unsaid. I did ask him to explain to his family, and particularly his mother, that a cougar I was not, that I was a respected women amongst my peers in the arts world and my community. Gordi was four years younger than me but treated as an equal partner. As for being a kept man, it was true he had not worked for over eighteen months, but this was only because we had travelled overseas and around Australia, we had agreed it would be a fifty-fifty share basis all the way, if and when possible, when it came to hard work, I had no complaints. Obviously, Rae had not taken that into account and had had a knee jerk reaction, and once again I was trying to mop it all up. Maybe my suggestion that we stick to a quiet wedding, only inviting close friends and family, would sink into Gordi's brain.

While these thoughts were running around my head, I was reminded of an article I had read about handfasting, a Celtic ceremony popular among those that loved each other but did not want to take the legal road of marriage. This was a thought I had tucked away as a possibility; the anxiety over the idea of marriage to Gordi would not budge. When the words *marriage* and *Gordi* were put together, what is that saying, 'It is best to wait, then to hurry and fail'.

Our first stop in two weeks' time was Margaret River. Gordi had not been there; soon we were both caught up in the excitement of another road trip. His family and their opinions were put on the backburner. I told him about all the things we could do down that way as he pulled out our well-worn Hema Australia road map. It's the best way to go to sleep, wrapped up together in a warm quilt, with strange names of places to see tripping off your tongue, a hint of adventure in the air.

I still had two important meetings before we drove away. One of these was my own prearranged Skype interview with the MS station in the USA, this was my chosen charity. Elsa, my agent, had also arranged for me to speak on BBS RadioToni in the USA. The interviewer for MS had a hard time understanding my accent, her gurgling laughter in-between bursts of, "Oh I love your accent," soon had us both in stiches. She asked the questions and I answered, quickly forgetting that this was a live broadcast interview. It was the easiest interview I had ever done. When they played it back to me it sounded like I had a peg on my nose, however I was pleased with the outcome. An hour later, after a much-needed cup of tea it was time for an interview with Radio Toni. To my surprise Toni lived and broadcasted from North Queensland in Australia. Again, Toni's laughter put me at ease with the interview; hopefully this would help raise my author profile in the USA and Australia.

I had a goal for this year; I intended to be a bestselling author with global recognition, Gordi said it was too big a dream, I disagreed; it bought out the female warrior in me, I knew it was within reach – I just had to persevere, to press the right button, meet the right person – that was all I needed. And maybe that was it, I wanted to reach for the golden ring, to be on that merry-go-round, to shout out loud, *I am a woman, hear me roar!* It was the sticking point as I felt Gordi wanted me to be subservient, to be a writer by all means, but we both knew by now he was not ever going to enjoy my being in the spotlight.

When I was offered the position of co-host for RadioToni, his jaw clenched with anger; his advice was, "Decline, you are far too busy with festivals all over the place, then it's the wedding."

To be fair, I took this into consideration for an hour or two as we packed the motorhome, when I phoned Toni, "I would love to do a co-host show with you," popped out, Toni was so warm and welcoming, a kindred spirit if I ever met one. A true professional with a big heart. An appointment was made for a date after I had finished my tour, so we could discuss what to do and how to bring a broadcast about.

The packing and repacking of a mobile home may seem easy, but when you're sharing it with another, it can become a chore; Gordi still had no idea how cold it was going to become. Although we lived in Perth, which is considered to have a four-season weather pattern with cold winters, hot summers, warm gorgeous spring and chilly autumns, we were heading south, a four-hour trip from here to a place by the sea; we would catch those cold onshore winds. As he packed his side of the wardrobe with summer gear, I packed mine with winter woollies, jackets, scarves and leggings. I had explained it all to him, but his response to my warnings was, "Stop fussing, Tara, I'll be fine." Okay, I had raised my concerns, but I was not one for mothering a grown man, so I let it be.

The weather stayed fine in Perth, till four nights before we were to leave, it got cold; I pretended not to see Gordi repacking his shelves with his winter clothing. We gave Rae and Kane a weekend to themselves, while we had our own memorable weekend with the kids. Gordi and Jess wanted to go fishing but we caught nothing, so it was fish and chips on the beach for dinner, the food reviving us sufficiently to splash cold water all over each other. I don't know where the most noise was coming from, us, or the screeching seagulls. It was exhausting, but fun. Gordi and I cooked a family meal on our last night and they played cricket on the front lawn. Little Shauna was an absolute dream, playing quietly in her playpen with her toys.

As Gordi made the gravy for the roast lamb, a lovely wash of contentment enfolded me. *This is how it feels, as a family,* went through my heart and head, Shauna was now resting happily on my hip, then Gordi and I swapped chores so I could put the potatoes into the roasting dish. Gordi looked every bit the contented family man as Shauna poked her fingers in his ear, before deciding his glasses were much more fun if she chucked them out the window.

This felt right, I was happy, my noisy family were all healthy and well; what more could I ask for? As I looked outside it was picture perfect, a camera could not have adequately captured that single moment in time: the pink and orange sunset, a sinking golden sun, green grass, the veggie patch in full bloom thanks to Gordi's recent care. I had planted sweet potatoes, but instead of giving us vegetables, it had covered the patio in a beautiful green vine. The many pots of herbs had blossomed to overflowing, the green stone dragon I had given Rae sat proudly on display, a stray pumpkin plant had wound its way through the garden then decided to climb up a fence post, boasting large bright yellow flowers against dark variegated leaves. It all worked together. A golden peace rose blossomed beside the mint and parsley, the gnarly old climbing pink rose, a treasured gift from my Russ now spilled out of its pot, just kissing the ground with a delicate display of budding roses. I loved this house, and I loved my family living here; this house needed this family, not one woman living on her own.

I acknowledged in my heart that life had being good to me, now I was being offered a different road – another opportunity; it was up to me if I took it with both hands. I knew from past experience that life is full of opportunities, you just have to recognise them when they come along as often they are not offered again.

My lawyer had rung me the day Rae and Kane had left, his words, "The film company has paid you, Tara," gave me goosebumps. He was waiting for the cheque to be cleared. Hopefully by the time I was back from Margaret River it would all be done; I had arranged a meeting with him once home to spread the money across stocks and shares. This time I would involve Gordi, if he was going to be my husband he needed to know where and what it was all about. The doubts rushed in, so many what-ifs, but as I felt them rise up

I did some deep breathing to quiet the anxiety. I had given my word and accepted Gordi as my partner, to be petty now was wrong of me.

The time to leave for Margaret River arrived. We were dropping Jess off at his boarding school on our way, I knew he wanted to come with us; this young man was like me, travel was in his blood, he yearned to be on the road. As we drove, Jess started his new favourite teenage game called badgering Nana and Gordi, but this time it was a little different as his question took us both by surprise, one I had not thought of.

"If you guys are getting married, what do I call Gordi?" It was food for thought. Jess was not into the hugs and kisses of yesteryear when I dropped him off at primary school, this time it was a high five for Gordi, a hit and miss hug for me. Jess whispered, "Love you guys, see ya soon." My little man was all grown up, almost. I felt melancholy sweep over me as memories of a sweet blond baby boy being born flooded in, of being asked to cut his cord, then holding him while his new mummy was made more comfortable. Russ, the new granddad, held him like he would break, the joy we felt being part of his little life.

CHAPTER 15

Jess was now in a different team, he had a new dad, a new set of grandparents – Kane's folks who lived in Tasmania, as well as a new sibling, and Gordi his new grandfather. We all loved him, but I wondered how Jess felt, how he was coping with such a new colourful family in his life. I guessed only time would tell. Our next stop was Bunbury for lunch and a hot drink, Gordi was quite happy to drive, and I was happy to relax, reading through my notes and making a few phone calls. As we pulled into the Bunbury township at around 1pm, the sky was a little overcast and the sea breeze chilly. While we found a decent park out of the wind, I rummaged around in my notebook for places I wanted to visit in Bunbury: the Silk Teapot Shop, and an aboriginal art gallery I had been told about. We couldn't see both, so the teapot shop won. We ate the lunch I had made that morning – pulled beef and homemade beetroot relish sandwiches, followed by a hot cup of tea and fresh muesli bites I had made a few days before, with a little bit of white chocolate baked inside as a nice surprise.

After lunch we took a slow walk around the pretty park which led to the public toilets; the first rule of camping is to keep your own toilet as clean as possible, which means using public toilets whenever we come across them. Once back in the motorhome we headed off to Koombana Bay to find the teapot shop; I wanted to see what the fuss was about, as this place had made such a name for itself.

Once inside I could see why. Aladdin's cave opened before me, from delicate tiny, beaded key rings made in India, to huge bolts of cloth enriched with gold and silver thread, delicate designs of budding flowers on vines, or golden peacocks and silver palm trees. Some were plain, others so richly decorated in seed pearls and what I assumed were semiprecious jewels. My mind was a tad confused as I had been to Bunbury many times before, but here before me was Baghdad or Persia. One bolt of cloth took my eye, it was the colour of rich jade green with a design of lotus flowers in red sequins and gold thread. To actually view this cloth, I had to ask the shop assistant, who, with a dramatic flourish put on a pair of white cotton gloves, removing the tissue around the bolt of cloth and displayed it. I was not allowed to touch it; this was understandable as these were jewelled works of art.

Gordi could see I was in awe; I wandered around the shop before going back and looking at the photo of the beaded art that was attached to each bolt. I saw him talking with one of the sales assistants but didn't take much notice as my watch said I was running out of time to get to where we should be next. It was while I was driving out of Bunbury that Gordi told me the cost of the one bolt I had admired, adding that they were actual gemstones, not glass. My reaction was instant.

"How much? No! We could buy a house for that."

Gordi's chuckle filled the cabin. "That's my girl."

Margaret River was a two-hour drive, not including a couple of stops to take photos; I had stopped apologising a long time ago for my hobby, and Gordi did not seem to mind. In all it took us three hours to reach Margaret River; our first stop was the campground we had booked into, I offered to put together some dinner for us both. I had pre-booked a campsite with all ammneities with an private ensuite on site, which meant we could hook into the campground's electricity for the duration of our stay, instead of using up our batteries. It worked better for us this way; it was much roomier if we used the camp's facilities, instead of squeezing past each other to use the motorhome's tiny bathroom.

In the caravans, campervans and mobile homes around the campground, the blue light of televisions flickered on as night set in. Gordi opted for a poached egg on a toasted muffin, which was fine with me. I made a hot drink for us both, then after washing the small number of dishes, I settled down to read my book about the tourism spots in Margaret River. Gordi stepped outside for some fresh air; I soon heard him in conversation with another man, I fell asleep as their voices were rumbling close by. When Gordi came inside I was woken by the strong smell of alcohol. My eyes flicked open as he got into bed beside me. I kept still, knowing from experience that Gordi liked to pick an argument or else complain about some imagined attack on him after a few drinks. Thankfully, he fell asleep immediately, while I was the one left awake with an argument brewing. He knew my stance on his consumption of alcohol; he was the one who had made the commitment to stop drinking. It felt like a huge stone lay on my chest, knowing what the next day would bring.

I woke with the smell of fresh coffee filling my nostrils. Gordi was outside, the barbie was fired up outside and he was cooking breakfast. He looked happy and healthy; maybe I had been wrong, this time. This was to be my first day at the Margaret River Writer's Festival and I was quite excited; soon Gordi had breakfast on the table waiting for me – baked beans with a golden egg yolk on top, a plate of toast, and a teapot full of my favourite hot drink, green tea with mint and ginger. It was time to wash and get dressed, I had one large yummy, buttered crust to finish. As I walked into the motorhome, Gordi wrapped his arms around me, his face snuggling into my neck.

"Mmm, you smell great, do you want to leave immediately, or shall we go for gold?"

I took a huge bite out of the crust pushing what was left in my hand between us like some sort of buttered mini defence system; "Not now, Gordi."

He rolled his eyes, "Yes, ma'am, anything you say, your royal ruddy highness."

I sent up a silent prayer, *Dear Lord why me? Why today? God give me strength.*

I felt incredibly nervous, I had spoken to perhaps fifty people in a seminar before today. Today among the audience would be experts on the field of writing; *You're an imposter,* rose up in my mind, *what do you know? Breathe and just be yourself,* I kept saying to myself over and over. I had written down a few facts and figures; but decided that speaking from my heart might be the best idea. It was time for me to go; we quickly stacked the dishes in the sink, deciding it was a nice enough day that we could walk into town, and hopefully it would help calm the nerves.

CHAPTER 16

The township was packed with cars and people everywhere, owed partly to the fact that this was a long weekend, not only tourism but the writer's festival was just as busy, with attendees standing shoulder to shoulder. My stomach did a huge flip when I saw the marquee was already so full, it heaved at the seams. People were seated with notepads, iPads, laptops, all ready to extract the wisdom of the speakers. There were six talks over the morning; I was the second. I introduced myself to the organiser and she walked me to the table that was set up for guest speakers; each of us had a microphone and a half-hour chat with the audience, with time for questions afterwards. I was informed that the audience consisted of more writers than journalists. I listened to the first speaker, trying to find calmness in the way she rolled her R's when she spoke, a New Zealand lass from the very tip of the South Island, her new book a romance set in the high country called *A Sheep Farmer's Daughter*. The book had achieved great success.

When it was my turn, I stood and looked into a sea of eyes. What came out of my mouth was not what I had prepared; I sounded like a two-year-old with a cold, saying 'umm' and then rabbiting on till the bell rang. I sat down wanting to cry, I felt I had made a complete idiot of myself. "Any questions?" the organiser asked, not one hand went up, obviously I had not made an impression. She shook my hand, congratulated me on my success with my movie script and ushered me outdoors. I was then asked for an interview by the local newspaper. In a small annex off the main tent stood four journalists and two cameramen – as soon as I sat down for the interview an explosion of flashlights went off. The interview felt more like an interrogation, the questions I had expected from the audience were fired at me from all corners. In all it was a half-hour stint that I did not enjoy; the relief when Gordi's arm went around my waist to walk me home was immense. I felt like I had been on trial for a crime I did not commit. My dreamed-of spot as a speaker at Margaret River was over. This experience had been awful, not because of them, they had been welcoming and professional, but for some reason my own confidence was rattled.

There was a beautiful sunset, the autumn sun was kissing the tops of each wave as it swept onto the shore. Gordi poured us both a cold dry white wine; as I sipped and ponderd, I watched the seagulls sweeping past on the sea breeze, and silhouettes of the last surfers raced over the darkening water. I summarised my day, telling Gordi the writer's festival was all I had expected so the problem must lay with me. His answer made me realise I was right, this was what I had wanted for a long time, it was what I had prayed for, as he put it.

"If this is your reaction to the public now, imagine how you're going to feel in Cairns?" He was right, the fact I had accepted the money, signed the contract, and the flights and hotel bookings had been made meant it was too late to back out, to say, *Sorry, I've changed my mind.* I was going to have to grin and grow up and get on with improving my speaking skills. Maybe speaker training virtual sessions would help. I was passionate about delivering a powerful speech on being a success in my field, I also wanted to bring to the conversation never be afraid of your age, which it seemed some writers were, they treated aging as a taboo subject, not to be discussed. I wanted to change that. In my years on this earth, I was very proud of being me, it had taken a while to understand with age comes wisdom, I would often say to my older friends don't insult this gift by pretending to be anything else but yourself, warts and all. Our flight to Cairns was our next step on this advenutre called life.

Cairns has always reminded me of an old lady showing off her handmade lace petticoats. The old nineteenth century buildings with all their immaculately maintained fine fretwork stood in stark contrast with the modern concrete and steel architecture. The tall stately palm trees and bright bougainvillea clung to the older buildings and climbed into the crevices. We were booked to stay at the Cairns Casino for three nights; on arrival, I was greeted in the foyer by a well-polished, smiling, super white, toothy young man, who kept assuring me he was there to assist. Gordi was ignored. The young man made sure our bags were taken care of; at the reception desk I was given a small gold-embossed wallet, with the emblem of the film studio emblazoned across it. Inside, there a Casino Visa card, a room key card plus documents for a self-drive hire car.

The toothy young man made sure I understood exactly what 'no expense' meant, waving the Visa card in the air like conductor with a baton he stated, "No expense spared, madam."

Gordi snatched the card off him, stuffing it back in the black wallet. "Our room, please!" he growled. I could tell by his tone; he had had enough of this young prima donna. We were both itching to explore Cairns; the car was ordered and would be ready in one hour. I should have said two hours; what is it about a gorgeous hotel room that makes men think of sex? I was busy admiring the range of toiletries in the bathroom and zhooshing myself with a face freshening spray when Gordi suggested we try out the bed. I'm not naïve, nor did I feel the slightest bit inclined, so I declined.

To Gordi, a refusal is a challenge to his ego. He put his arms around me, pinning my arms to my sides, then lifted me up and literally dragged me out of the bathroom, throwing me onto the bed. It was like a red rag to a bull, no-one handles my body, unless I give them permission. I had thought he would know by now, I had boundaries, and you don't cross them. I enjoyed sex when it was fun and loving, but rough sex was a definite no. He saw my face, and resorted to sarcasm, his last line of defence.

"Who's not a happy camper then? Has fame gone to your head? Come on, girl, relax, it's time to do the horizontal tango."

I looked at him in disbelief; who was this person? Pushing him aside, I stood, reminding him we had a car arriving in twenty minutes and I for one was going to explore Cairns, if he chose to stay in the room, so be it. Gordi grumped and grumbled, lay curled up on the bed and sulked, calling me old-fashioned and starchy. From where I stood right now, Ramón from Sydney looked rather good, I wondered if he would like to take Gordi's place, I had to smile to myself as a memory slid back; I had enjoyed being seduced, who doesn't like being flirted with? A slow seduction that simmers, feeling your pulse react, looking into their eyes as desire slides into the pit of your stomach. It was still my secret, I hugged it close.

We headed out of Cairns towards the famous Skyrail Rainforest Cableway. This attraction takes guests on a slow ride in a glass bubble gondola up into the Daintree Forest, it gave me goose bumps to look thousands of feet down, and know with certainty that no man had ever set foot in some of the places below us. I settled in with my camera, it was just us, two people in a plastic bubble. No doubt through boredom, or maybe he wanted to give me a scare, Gordi rediscovered his childhood; he began rocking the cable car from side to side and then he hung out of the window – which had a very clear sign on it: *Do not put your head out the window.* Thank heavens the doors were locked, or he would have tried to swing from the car itself. He had me rattled; I pointed at the camera, trying to take photos while fear was pumping through me, was impossible.

"Gordi, stop and calm down!" It was an order – I was not playing. To my surprise he did, until we arrived at a stopping point. We were both keen to discover the story of this amazing wonder of the modern world. It was eerie. Huge, weird vines and ferns covered the treetops, birds called out from within the dense foliage, but we could not see them. This is where the prehistoric cassowary bird lives. There are forest breaks along the way where you can hop off the skyrail and an Aboriginal ranger will take you for a walk into the forest and explain native herbal remedies. As we were shown around, it seemed Gordi was enjoying himself, he asked a million questions and took photos with the iPad. When the ranger asked why we were visiting Cairns I saw a shadow cross Gordi's face. Disappointingly for me, he answered, "Just visiting the area."

We caught another large plastic bubble which rumbled us up to the top station, we had spent a good two hours walking the Daintree with the ranger, this was our next and final stop at the Kuranda railway station, where a steam train would take us back down into Cairns. The train guard said we had a three-hour wait. There was some lush vegetation to look at, but in forty-plus degree heat with high humidity I was after some shade. Along the station were massive – and I mean massive – potted plants, reminding me a little bit of the movie *Little Shop of Horrors*. All I could say was "Oh my God, everything is huge!" Gordi was as fascinated as I was as we looked up at a peace lily; we were completely dwarfed by this twenty-foot giant with creamy blooms as big as a serving dish; the bougainvillea vines were as thick as my wrists, its flowers so bright they looked like disco lights. We wandered down the main street of Kuranda, a tourist village; in the middle of the street stood massive ancient fig trees that had wound into and around each other; the girth on one of them was forty feet. There were souvenir shops everywhere, but we were not here to buy, we were here for an adventure. I noticed a small handwritten sign: *Day Tours Ferry*. I made enquiries at the railway station, and sure enough, if we scooted down the steps immediately, we would just catch it before it took off.

CHAPTER 17

The river boat owner-operater who was now providing tours greeting us with enthusiasm, his words, "Welcome folks, I'm still tightening up the nuts and bolts," as he put it. Plastic chairs were screwed into the wooden deck, an awning of striped canvas flapped lazily in a soft breeze. We paid our ten dollars each and the skipper cast off, also onboard was a family of four. This little ferry putted down the deep green glassy river very slowly, the skipper pointing out the egrets, storks, birds, foliage, fresh water crocodiles, and a large python slithered down a tree into the tepid water, just like a scene from a *Tarzan* movie. It was the white eyebrow turtles that fascinated me the most. The freshwater crocodiles gave me the creeps; they sat on logs and rocks sunning themselves, their mouths open, making them look like they were smiling at us.

    I adored watching the antics of a red-breasted swallow. This little mother had made a nest amongst the life jackets above us; she raced around the boat, comfortable with the idea of having large clumsy human guests in her home. Chirruping happily, she flew so low that she brushed my hair with her wings. The skipper told me it meant good fortune was on its way. On the way back to the jetty the skipper stopped the boat so we could feed the turtles. I was in awe of these small amphibious creatures that so gently took food from our hands; I was also very aware not ten metres away sat a very large crocodile.

    We came to a soft bump as we docked, I heard kids yelling and saw them running towards us, pointing up into the bush. I saw something about five-foot-tall standing in the deep shade where the forest met the riverbank, silently watching us. A cassowary: my spine tingled, the Aboriginal children had shimmied up the trees – these birds are exotic to look at, but very dangerous, they can disembowel a person with one stroke of the middle toe on their feet. Gordi wanted a closer look, but the skipper warned him to stay put. It slowly moved off and we were encouraged to disembark; the kids scuttled down the trees, mischief was written all over their faces. The skipper picked up a handful of large bright purple berries: "This is what that bird and those bloody kids are after," he said; "It tastes sour, almost like a plum, the cassowaries love 'em, and so do we. Every year it's a fight about who's going to get them, us, or them." He offered us one each to taste; he was right, they were sour but nice, it made the saliva run in my mouth as I bit into it. The skipper then proceeded to tell us of the health benefits of the purple berry, its amazing antioxidant properties, and high vitamin C content, I made a mental note to look into this potent fruit, for my own use.

The train whistled; there was just time to race back and grab a seat. I managed to buy some water and some sandwiches for afternoon tea. We settled in for our ride back to Cairns, both of us ready to snooze, well that was the thought. In fact, we spent the most interesting two hours as the train made some gut-wrenching twists and turns around the tightest of corners, the distraction for me was the narration of interesting history about how the railroad was built and by whom; once again the government bought in Italian, Swiss and New Zealand immigrants to help build this amazing railway that literally hung off the side of this mountain. And although I never said a word as Gordi would have made a derogatory remark, my own father and uncles had worked in this particular railroad before he married my mum. I was never more proud of my ancestors. To look out the window was to look out onto a sheer drop many hundreds of feet into the forest below. I also had an audience which greatly amused me, a young Asian girl decided I was more interesting than her folks. She spoke very clear English, I could see her parents were struggling, so I helped her understand the bigger words written on the brochure, she was soon translating what I had said to her folks.

Once back in the car Gordi pulled out the road maps. "Where to next?" he asked.

I for one wanted a hot bath and some nourishing food. "Let's sort it out over dinner, I'm starving." Travel weary and dusty, we arrived back at the casino, where I was still a little overwhelmed by the huge room we had been given; it was a penthouse, or the closest thing to it.

Gordi sank onto the bed with a groan, "My Lord, this is heaven" he sighed. I went for my longed-for hot bath with all the beautiful-smelling lotions and salts provided. Just before I put my foot in the bath I heard a distinct snore from the bedroom. Ahh! Time for a peaceful soak, with no interruptions.

Gordi slept for a good hour while I soaked in deep hot water, washed and dried my hair, nibbled on some fruit from the fruit basket, and ate two or three chocolates. I was feeling tired and intended having a nanna nap. The next thing I knew, I was woken from a deep slumber by Gordi's hand inside my dressing gown, stroking my breast, circling down to my stomach to my groin, igniting a reaction. This was more like it. "You smell great, sweetheart," he whispered as his tongue circled my nipple, and my body responded. Gordi always whistled in the shower after we had made love, while I felt like a bag of foam rubber, relaxed but a bit wobbly till the senses had settled down. Gordi strode out of the shower, full of purpose. "Guess where I'm driving you tomorrow!" then it was, "No, don't guess, it can be a surprise." I was happy with that. There was time for me to have quick shower and dress in some casual gear. Rae rang to say hello and ask how it was all going. Was I excited? We had a ten-minute conversation as I applied some lipstick and brushed my hair, then I was off to have a meal with Gordi, who was now standing by the open door stepping from one foot to the other. "Hurry up, Tara, I'm a man on a mission!" Well, nothing had changed there.

CHAPTER 18

Dinner was going to be a relaxed affair; there was a choice of restaurants within the casino, it looked like the pizza bar was the place for us tonight. I love my pizza, as long as it is a real pizza, not pastry and melted cheese with some sort of flavouring or tomato sauce smothered on top of it. We ordered a glass of red wine each to sip as we watched the pizza chef make our meal from go to whoa; he spun that pizza base like there was no tomorrow, then added the filling – mozzarella cheese with a tomato and garlic sauce, topped with sprigs of fresh basil, then the whole pizza was dotted with big chunks of pineapple and big dots of white goat's cheese. It was just enough for two, so delicious and filling. We took a wander through the casino after our dinner; we were not gambling people, my only vice was buying a weekly lotto ticket. Gordi didn't care one way or the other, so we agreed that an early night was what we both needed, wandering back to our room, quite happy in each other's company. By ten o'clock we were tucked up in bed, I went to sleep happy with my thoughts that tomorrow was another warm day, and I had been promised a surprise road trip.

I was woken by Gordi at around two in the morning. He was sitting up in bed, talking quietly to his brother Ryan in New Zealand. I overheard the words "Mum," and, "let me know how she is." I sat up, Gordi's face was sad and pale in the moonlight. I knew his family disapproved of me and our relationship but felt I should enquire what was wrong; maybe I could help in some way.

Gordi's reply was terse; "Nothing we can do, Mum's had a bad fall, she's in hospital, they think there may be internal injuries." I was about to offer my sympathy when he continued, "We are a very long way from New Zealand; even if we were back in Perth, it would still be an eight-hour flight." It sounded like he was trying to convince himself that staying here was the right thing to do; I left him alone to sort it out and snuggled back into the doona and soon fell into a deep sleep.

The warm sun shining on my face woke me; Gordi was already up, sitting out on the veranda, talking on his phone, he was not happy; his body language and weird face pulling made that obvious. I was over this game of 'guess how I feel', just bloody tell me, don't do a pantomime about it.

I empathised that his mother was ill, but it seemed to me from being on the sidelines in the past, Gordi was not able to live a full life without his family asking for money to help out, or without his sister going on about how Gordi should share the responsibility, which I felt he certainly did – he had often flown back to his homeland to give them a reprieve from caring for their mother, often paying for that reprieve himself, so they could all have a decent break. I had commented on his generosity to them more than once, he would always challenge me by asking, "If this was your parent, wouldn't you do the same?" He was right, I had no argument with him there. Again, I left him alone to sort out what he wanted to do, ordering a room service full breakfast for us both. When it arrived, I ate mine; while Gordi's went cold, he talked to each of his family members, who were around his mum's bedside.

I had the impression that if she died it would mean the glue, the matriarch, of his family was gone. I knew how my little family in Perth would feel once I had taken that step myself, they'd be lost for a while, but hopefully I had passed on enough strength for them to pull together and remain close. Gordi's secret daytrip for us was falling apart, so it was up to me to order the hire car for the day, and it was me who planned the trip. Gordi had no life in him, his head was full of his family in New Zealand. He insisted on escorting me, even though I suggested he stay back and get some sleep, and if his family rang, at least he would have some privacy.

Port Douglas was our first port of call; I did not want to do the tourist thing, so I drove into the hills, stopping at a magnificent lookout that encompassed a huge stretch of beach. The sea sending its waves crashing onto shore was the Coral Sea. I had been here many years ago, this place was unknown then, now I had to find a park, put money in a parking meter, then put more money into a public telescope to see how this once small community had flourished with the advent of tourism. I nudged my way through the crowd while Gordi stayed in the car, his face drawn, his hand moulded around his mobile phone.

I made the decision to drive back to Cairns via the inland road. A place called Mareeba was advertising a coffee plantation with a tour and light lunch. After a two-hour drive we arrived; I was looking forward to the tour, but Gordi's emotional pain was again obvious. The luncheon was great, a coffee infused pastry with fresh mango sauce, then a massive slice of coffee banana cake and cream. Gordi picked at his share, it was too much for me to eat on my own. Excusing myself, I went to the ladies' room to freshen up, inside the bathroom was a backlit window that covered half the wall, and inside this window was a bricked-in courtyard with a large pool with huge rocks and a stump of a tree inside it, dotted on the rocks, tree and walls were live frilled-neck lizards of all sizes, some small, some not so small. These lizards are real characters, the frill is around their necks, some have frills of yellow, others a deep pink, they flare them if they see or feel danger. Today the danger came from one of them, two males were fighting it out, the display of hissing and 'frilling', as they call it, was fascinating, I could have watched them for ages.

When I went out to see what Gordi was up to, full of my news about what I had just witnessed, he had left the café. I found him in the car on the phone to his family, his face alight with smiles as he announced 'Mum' had come through the operation she was going to be fine. From that moment on Gordi was a different man; he had his mojo back in full throttle, wanting to drive and continue our touring. It was alright with me, as I said, I enjoy being a passenger, it means I am free to take photos to add to my blog site. Our next stop was a blip really; Walkamin has one small shop attached to a peanut farm, selling all things peanutty, as you can imagine. I love peanuts; Gordi does not, so I purchased a small bag, for my pleasure only.

Off we drove to view the Tinaroo Falls, sadly with no rain over last three months. it was just a trickle, I had read there was sunken 1900s village here, sadly I could not see it. The next stop was not meant to happen, but I just had to yell, "Stop!" so I could take photos of the cutest little township I had ever seen. Atherton was built as a circle of approximately six small homes and two shops, each home is circular, with a shingle outside of each house announcing the name of the people who lived there and what they did. The shops were delightful, there was a very snug café-come-art-gallery-come-post-office, both owned by the same person – or maybe it was a family business. It was then that I noticed all the surnames on the shingles were the same. My camera came alive, I could not believe I was looking at what I would term as a hobbit township. Gordi thought of it as quirky, his effort of getting out the car ended up with him shouting, "Bloody flies." He got back in, slamming the door behind him. I ran around trying to get the best shots before we drove off to Millaa Millaa.

I happened to agree with Gordi the flies were bad, but this was outback Australia, what did he expect, a royal tour with flag bearers? The tourist trail map advertised that close to here was the biggest wild fig tree in the southern hemisphere, called the Cathedral Tree. It was another two-hour drive. As we pulled into the car park Gordi muttered about flies and drain smells. We were in the middle of a huge rainforest system, humid and wet and completely on our own, just the two of us amongst this forest of great age and beauty; Gordi's nonstop moaning about flies, mosquitoes and smells was beginning to get to me. Why couldn't he just stop and breathe, take in the scenery? Then I saw it, the Cathedral Tree, it was so huge they had built a boardwalk through it and around it; it rose two thousand feet in the air, its girth was almost the same. Its age, as far as the scientists could tell, was four thousand years. It was majestic! Standing inside this tree was magical, feeling it enfolding me, breathing its energy. Gordi had the camera, I stood still for him to capture me inside the tree, it was so huge you could place twenty people inside it. "Okay, my friend. It's your turn now," I said.

Gordi's comment was, "That must be what a coffin feels like." I had had enough; this man was intent on squashing joy like one of the flies he kept slapping at. This adventure was proving too hard for me, I walked away, so close to tears.

CHAPTER 19

We were back in Cairns city at around four in the afternoon. I still wanted to see more, but Gordi wanted to have a sleep. I dropped him off at the casino and drove off towards Palm Cove which is a thirty-minute drive north of Cairns. This time I was happy to leave him behind, as Russ and I had visited there many years before, we had docked there for supplies, when we were crew on a leaky old tub named the Ibis, we were so young and so in love with each other, we did not care what the world thought, we had one another.

I parked beside the small café and walked over to the beach. The ramshackle beach store that held all the supplies you could wish for had long gone, a modern café had taken it place. Memories of how we had seen the advert for two deckhands and decided that would be our honeymoon, it was like stepping from one world to another. I had never been on a boat let alone a boat like this, Russ had had experience in the past as a decky on a crab boat, telling me it would be fun. My first day on this rolling tub was awful, it stunk of old fish and wine, I was so seasick all I could do was lie down and cry. Very soon I found my sea feet, I loved the freedom, 1 lived in a bikini, Russ in cut-off jeans the whole time we were at sea, our bodies becoming bronzed, lean and healthy We had our whole life together ahead of us, the world was ours.

The captain was a wine-sodden old man, who seemed not so much to steer but aim the boat with a 'she'll do' as his finger would stab at the maps. I was cook and cleaner, Russ the decky, we fished for our food, calling into small harbours for fresh water and fuel for the boat. It was here I soon learnt to look for fresh foods, barter for eggs and fresh veggies, I soon learnt how to handle the two-burner stove on a Gimbal, I was not a great cook but soon mastered sticky fried rice and pancakes. Our captain, however, drank his ruby red wine from a jam jar from sunup to sundown, very often passing out while the Ibis chugged her way to the next port. Our open-air bed, a blow-up mattress on deck, as the stars glinted softly down on the night ocean we would lie in each other's arms, watching for shooting stars, often listening to the sound of whales as they passed by. Or watching the dawn arrive tinging us and the ocean in pinks and golds as it rose above us. Youth has so much going for it; we loved every minute of our adventure. I had not told Gordi; it was not worth the argument of 'not memories again' that it would encourage.

As the sun slipped onto the horizon it coated the sand and sea with an golden glow. As the waves gently lapped onto the shore, I allowed tears to fall; sometimes I missed the love Russ and I shared so much that it made my heart ache. With us, there had never been a need to explain, no need to be the best we could be all the time, no petty jealousies. Russ and I were together nearly twenty years, we had grown up together; now, somehow, life would go on without him. I packed away my memories, washed my face in the warm ocean water, and drove back to the casino. My heart was a little lighter after my one-sided chat with the person I had trusted above all others.

It may sound crazy to some, but I always felt better after having a chat to Russ. I guess that was why I had so much trouble understanding Gordi, his troubled personality, his love-hate relationship with his family, the you-belong-to-me attitude, the mood swings. He was always ready to explode or disagree, yet on the other hand he was a kind, gregarious man who claimed he loved me. The one question that had constantly plagued me settled in my heart again: Why was I trying to fit in with him and not be who I was?

On my return, Gordi was full of life after his sleep; he wanted to know where I had been, and what I did. I told him I had found a beautiful beach and sat on the sand, collecting my thoughts about tomorrow night. I felt if I told him the truth he would feel I was unfaithful in some way; to be honest, though, I did not want to change. I enjoyed my brutally honest chats with Russ. I felt it was time, however, to tell Gordi about Ramón. As we sat on the veranda with the lights of Cairns twinkling all around us, I told Gordi the whole story, even admitting I was a little attracted to Ramón. I knew he was angry, the long silence was awful, but I did not know how angry, till he threw his glass against the wall. Red wine ran down the wall and puddled at its base, the shattered glass stuck up inside the dark puddle looking like shark fins in a ruby red pool.

Gordi was shouting at me, "Christ almighty, Tara, how could you be so easy? One night on your own, and you're ready to part your legs for another man!"

The insult took a minute to sink in. I stepped inside and shut the door behind me, locking it. No-one spoke to me like that, ever. I lay on the bed listening to Gordi knocking on the glass patio door, his voice muffled by the heavy glass partition. If I had opened it, I would have pushed him over the balcony, how dare he.

Amazingly, I slept, waking to a gorgeous sunny morning, the temperature in the mid-twenties. I had no desire to see or talk to Gordi; I had made the decision; if there was no apology for the insult he hurled last night, he could return home, I did not want to be with him. I decided to have a swim in the casino pool, it felt good to feel my body stretching through the water. Breakfast this morning was at the buffet, I chose fresh-squeezed orange juice and spelt flour toast with fresh cottage cheese; it was delicious. It was around 8am when I got back to my room, Gordi had obviously slept on a sun chair, he looked a mess standing by the patio door, waiting for me to open it, which I reluctantly did.

He made a run to the bathroom; I went to the bedroom locking the door behind me, I had no intention of associating with Gordi until he apologised; in fact, I was trying not to let my emotions guide me into confronting him and demanding he leave Cairns. Should I ring a friend or family? No, this was my problem, not theirs. Maybe it would have been better if I had been honest with him immediately on my return to Perth. I could hear Rae's voice in my head, *You're going to have to sort out this relationship Mum or it's going to end up seriously hurting you, and Gordi,* I had to agree.

Taking a big breath, I went out to confront him, Gordi was laying on the couch watching a TV show. His body language spoke volumes.

"Gordi, can we talk? I'm sorry if my honesty caused you any pain, it was not done to hurt you, but to be honest with you, I don't want to start a new life with secrets." His arms went around me as I sat beside him.

"Tara, you scare me sometimes, I have to accept that I will be sharing you with Russ for the rest of my life. I do not want to share you with anyone else." His kiss was light, testing the waters, to see my reaction; I was surprised he had said the very same words I had been thinking last night when I drove back from the beach. It was time to heal the hurt I had inflicted, time to admit that Russ would always be there in a big corner of my heart. To me it was natural, Russ and I had built a rich life together over many years. But it was the difference between Gordi and myself that worried me, we seemed to struggle along, then fall off the *together forever wagon*, then after a bit of soul-searching, struggle back on. Was it worth it? All I was after was peace and quiet within our relationship, a moderately happy life, one that stretched me in all kinds of creative ways. I told him how I felt, waiting for him to reply. He slumped on the couch.

"Whatever, Tara, I can't compete with the wonderful Russ." I was itching to leave the room, this was not a competition; it was simply a matter of trying to be the best we could be for, and with each other. Gordi's apathy and anger had invaded every corner, it was time for me to go for a walk around the park-like grounds that surrounded the casino, hoping to give him a chance to mull my words over.

Outside was fabulous. The sun was bright, its hot rays sinking into my body. I stood under a magnificent old frangipani tree, the sweet smell from its cream-coloured flowers was heavenly, the air fresh as the ocean breeze rippled through the grounds. I felt my body relax, my emotions almost together. Finally, the truth had been spoken out loud; I knew in my heart there would be no wedding. Gordi had some real personal problems, and me, a ghost called Russ, who had once treated me as an intelectual equal. If I allowed Gordi to shout abuse at me, it was me who was at fault. I also knew he had his family calling him home, in his heart of hearts that's where he wanted to be; I knew it and he knew it. As I walked, I took in the sight and scent of the bush around me, the lake filled with koi carp, the quaint Japanese-style bridge over the lake, and as the path continued, a Japanese-style building. There was a flyer advertising a recent seminar on *feng shui* flapped lazily in the wind, its dried edges curling. The words written on the flyer saying: 'Only you *can* change your thoughts, do that and you can change your world.' It took maybe a minute to sink in, my heart agreeing, my mind arguing with my decision to have one more go at this gasping sagging relationship with Gordi.

CHAPTER 20

I rang Gordi to ask him out for the day. His phone rang out, so I left a message to say I was going for a drive in ten minutes, and would he care to join me. One miserable, sad Gordi almost limped like an injured dog to the passenger side with his head hung down. He looked dejected – or should that be rejected?

"Come on, my friend, buck up, we are on an adventure, let's go for a drive." I knew this was going to be a painful afternoon with Gordi oozing rejection, but I was buzzing, those few words I had read had energised me into action. Life was too short to be sad 24/7. I grabbed his hand. "Gordi, look, an open road; where shall we go?"

He pulled his hand away. "Just drive, Tara, anywhere will do."

It was not what I wanted to hear, but at least he was talking to me. Gordonville looked good to me, it was a two-hour drive, and we would be back on time for my debut into the world of short film festivals. I was getting those familiar butterflies in my tummy. Gordonville is a sugar cane county, not a tourist mecca, just a small thriving shopping centre, but I was here to see the royal poinciana trees. I had overheard two women at my morning swim raving about their spectacular colour and abundance; they weren't wrong, gorgeous bright red flowers and lime green leaves, and stately height as they overgrew the local palm trees – they were magnificent. In northern Queensland, this tree is considered a noxious pest, it certainly grows wild in some areas.

I pulled over into a café park and went in to buy two ice creams, a strawberry one for Gordi which was his favourite, and chocolate for me. Parked under a shady palm tree, we sat munching on our fast-melting ice creams. I leaned over to wipe some ice cream that had dripped onto his shirt, giving him a quick kiss on the cheek. "Am I forgiven yet?"

Gordi's hand squeezed mine. "It's not you, Tara, it's me. I can't seem to move away from the fact that you almost slept with a stranger. I'm disappointed that I'm not man enough to keep you interested." While he was revelling in self-pity, I decided this was not the time to go into a full explanation; I suggested we discuss it when we flew home to Perth. I drove back to the casino, the ice cream doing a huge sour flip-flop inside me, those wise words I had read on the flyer repeating themselves time and time again, I did not know if I was strong enough to carry Gordi's problems as well as my own insecurities about this relationship.

I was not surprised to find our room cleaned and neat, with everything folded, tucked, creased and hung up. I wondered if the room service team had hidden out of my sight, ready to come out and do their thing as soon as I left the room, then secreting themselves once again in a cupboard somewhere. On my bedside table someone had placed an envelope full of vouchers. I had only a minute to read that a massage had been booked before there was a discreet knock on the door. Gordi answered it, in stepped two beautiful young Aboriginal girls, the casino badge proudly displayed on their white uniforms. The massage had come to me; this was a first. The ladies erected a massage table in the palatial bathroom; inside the many cupboards was an assortment of phials and bottles; they selected a few and invited me to lie down and relax. A quilt-like blanket was wrapped around me while they massaged my feet. This, and the murmur of their voices, put me to sleep. They woke me when it was time for me to turn over, then once more a gentle waking to say they were about to finish. I felt rested and so very calm. They had buffed, polished and kneaded every single muscle in my body, I felt like I was floating. The ladies quietly cleaned up the room, I was then asked to sit on the pink plush two-seater couch. This amused me, who had ever heard of a couch in the bathroom? An array of beautiful bottles was fanned out in a bright rainbow of colours across the small table in front of me for a manicure/pedicure. Heaven. When it was time for me to stand, they warned me that I may feel lightheaded after such a long time on the massage table. Wrapped in a large fluffy bath robe, I literally floated out of the bathroom. Gordi's face was filled with envy.

"Well, where's my massage?" he demanded. I had no sooner sat down in front of the telly when one of the ladies asked me to put my feet up as the nail polish was still damp. One reached for the large pouffe, the other placed pillows around me. I could not keep the smirk off my face; this was very different to life in the mobile home, I felt royal in every way.

Gordi was not happy. He ushered the ladies out with a sour look on his face. As they left the room, the phone was ringing, Gordi answered it, then muttered a sentence I did not understand. Once again there was a discreet knock on the door. Gordi literally stomped over to open it. A small team of ladies carrying small work boxes entered. And I was asked to 'please sit in the dressing room'. All the lights were blazing as the team of beauticians went to work while the hair stylist slipped a cape around me and set about curling, primping and spraying. After they had left the room, I did not know who was looking in the mirror back at me, I looked totally amazing, tanned glowing, gorgeous. Tara looked ten years younger, the stress of Margaret River and the last twenty-four hours had completely left my face and body, Gordi took one look at me, and said, "Bloody hell, what's all that muck over your face? Your hair looks like you have had an electric shock, and I don't like the red nail polish."

I felt the tears gathering, stinging my eyes. How come other men found me attractive? Why did I put up with this silly little man when I had a choice? Gordi was the epitome of sarcastic rudeness when he was not the main attraction and whenever I was being made a fuss of. When he saw the look on my face, his arms went around me – I knew where it was heading so I broke off the embrace.

"We only have an hour before we have to be at the casino theatre, I do not want to arrive smelling of sex!" Gordi once again did his foot-stomping, door-banging thing that he does well, this time with added yelling and swearing. "That's right, it's all about you, the bloody princess!"

I surprised myself, this time yelling back, "Yes, it is, grow up for one bloody night, try to behave like a man." This was becoming a nightmare; I had wanted this night to be so very special, a badge I wore with honour and hard work was being recognised. Now I just wanted this night to disappear fast, so I could say, *Gordi, it's over, just go back to your family.*

Once again there was a knock on the door, by now Gordi was almost beside himself. "What the hell!" he mumbled. If it had not been so serious, I would have been laughing at his actions, even so a chuckle escaped. Gordi reminded me of Jess with his temper tantrums, on and off like a frantic light bulb.

My dresser had arrived. "My what?" I asked.

A young man had bought up my costumes for the night. He introduced himself as, "Lassiter, ma'am, and ma'am has a choice of three gowns." Once again, I was ushered away from Gordi into the small dressing room off the bathroom, where the choice of gowns was displayed. One was a pale blue powder puff design that would have looked wonderful on a slim thirty-year-old, the next was a vastly beaded and tassel creation – a black evening dress with a short train attached, high neck and long tight sleeves in gold and silver. Against my skin it made me look pale and ethereal, a little like Elvira the black widow.

CHAPTER 21

We were down to Lassiter's final choice. He unwrapped a long ribbon of glittering black sequins on silver material. I lifted my arms and it slithered down my body, moulding itself around me. One shoulder was bare, on the other was a small cap sleeve. This dress was made for me. Lassiter's eyes lit up as he stood back, rocking on his heels, his thumb and forefinger of his right hand massaging his chin. Tattooed on his wrist was *Carpe Diem*, Latin for *seize the day.*

Lassiter studied me. "Ma'am, I think we have it." The shoes that went with the gown were black patent leather with dainty silver and diamante buckles on top. They fit perfectly: the spiked heel would have proved lethal if used as a weapon. I had to ask how they knew my size; he smiled.

"The company rang your daughter, Ma'am." Ahh, the mystery was solved. By the time I was primped, prodded and pleated, Gordi was preparing to shave. To our surprise, Lassiter flicked open a black cape, saying, "Sir, may I?" Gordi smirked with satisfaction, at last he was being noticed, he allowed himself to be guided to the chair I had just vacated. I did not stay to watch the shaving procedure; in fact, I was politely ushered into the lounge by Lassiter, a chilled glass of pink Champagne was placed in my hand. Once Gordi was shaved and a mix of citrus aftershave applied, Lassiter produced a white cotton suit hanger: "Courtesy of the company, sir," unwrapping a black tuxedo, white shirt and tie. Gordi was all smiles.

As Lassiter was brushing down the jacket, I realised I had no idea how to tie a bow tie, but Lassiter stood behind Gordi, and with a couple of flips and twists of his hands, the tie finally rested as it should, perfectly. It was time to take the lift downstairs.

The Cairns Short Film Festival was everything I hoped it would be. I loved everything about it, I felt beautiful and Gordi looked very handsome. The lights were dimmed, conversation was muted and the movie began. A huge storm filled the screen, and soon the script I wrote was being played out before me. I sat breathless throughout the movie; the two actors were so talented. I was stunned at how realistic it was.

There was light applause as my name flashed up on the silver screen as author/scriptwriter. Dylan, the director and producer of my script, gently pulled me to my feet and the applause once again filled the theatre. Soft lights blossomed around us, people surged around me, some stopping to say, "Well done!" and, "Congratulations!" Gordi stood beside me with a genuine smile on his face, his white shirt illuminated with a blue tinge every time a flashbulb went off; his unruly hair was slicked down to a tidy version of its normal haystack look. It felt like a dream, my gown, with black sequins scattered over metallic silver material, glistened like oil under the flashbulbs. My dream had come true, but it was hard to believe it was happening, it felt so surreal. Everything was in fast mode, now I wanted it to slow down, to savour every last minute of success. I had worked for this it was mine to enjoy with all my senses.

My heart heavy as I knew my decision to part from this heavy relationship would be full of drama, I knew we were at the end.

The party was in full swing once we had arrived in the casino lounge, the film company that I was associated with was assigned a small table in the middle of the floor. Once again I was congratulated by several people as we made our way through the crowded room. The noise of society partying was deafening, mature age women like myself were out on the town, the older men – the silver fox brigade – were eyeing up younger fresh wannabe actresses. The younger set was lined up by the bar or bouncing around the dance floor, giving off the vibe of pack animals wanting to party big time. We were shown to our table which was surrounded by deep plush crimson couches. The glass table top was covered in an array of glasses and bottles. Already seated was the producer Dylan and his partner Helena, who I'm sure was only eleven, with all that makeup on and the dim lighting she looked like a beautiful doll.

Gordi and I were introduced to the investors, a German couple who could not speak a word of English. I thought, *This was going to be an interesting mix for the night,* my sense of humour kept interrupting any logical thought. Helena looked up into Gordi's eyes like he was a god, Dylan sat with his arm draped over back of the seat, his legs open, with his other hand tucked into his cummerbund. His body language spoke volumes to me, this man was very sure of himself. His face red as he knocked back his brandy, he slurred, "Babe, casino treating you alwight?" I hid a smile, the image of this successful wealthy movie tycoon disintegrated; to me he was just another drunk who could not sound his consonants.

The German couple channelled their messages through Helena, who understood their broken English, as an intermediary. The woman wanted to know how I got my ideas, they loved what I did with the story and asked if I could show them some more. Gordi's chest grew three sizes on realising that Helena was flirting with him. Her large blue eyes looked into his, her voice was husky, with little flutters of her amazingly long black spiky eyelashes and pouting her red full lips, she purred, "What do you do for a living, Gordi?"

I thought he was going to choke, his bow tie that had looked so neat caught on his Adam's apple and bobbed up and down like fish on a line. He cleared his throat and replied with an unnaturally deep voice, "Oh, this and that, I mainly travel, seeing the country, you know, camping, fishing, looking after this one." As he patted my knee, what I actually heard was *I'm a foot stomping wood chopping full-on bloke.* In fact, the image of the ram with huge testicles slid into my mind, Gordi was mirroring Stuart's body language, draping his arm over the back of the seat, snaking his hand inside his cummerbund. It looked like the two of them were protecting their private bits.

What do you say to your partner when he is in his element? Don't flirt with her, she's only eleven? Dylan was not much help; he was about to slide under the table in a self-inflicted haze of booze fumes. I excused myself. "I'm off to the powder room."

The powder or the ladies' (as its often called) room was stunning, I'm sure it was styled from a bathroom in some Hollywood magazine. It certainly had the wow factor, next to the toilet (with a warmed seat) was an armrest with a console built in, with buttons to push for a bidet, as well as 'refresh', 'flush' and an intercom. There were also buttons for a TV channel; I could have sat in the cubicle and played with the buttons all night, but Helena found me; calling me in her purring voice: "Tara, you in here, honey? Gordi wants to know if you'll be long." Damn, I was enjoying myself, finding out what the buttons did. So far, I had made the blue neon lights in the toilet bowel flash to mauve. Changed the flushing tune from *Memories* by Barbra Streisand to *Take Me Home* by John Denver, I again pressed flush and the soft musical tinkle of water splashed into the bowl, John Denver began to serenade me and as it did the water changed to a glowing green. How clever!

Transitioning myself from Aussie nomad to professional scriptwriter, I walked out to greet Helena with what I hoped looked like a genuine smile. Her next words took me by surprise.

"You're not one of them, are you?" My pretence at sophistication was blown, this kid saw right through me. It was a relief just to sit down on the red velvet seats that were shaped like open hands scattered around the palatial rest room, they were so soft, the hand felt like it was hugging my bum.

"You are so right, it has been fun, but now all I want to do is pack up and go home." Admitting to this girl child, "I don't feel comfy at all."

Helena giggled. "I knew it, I knew it the moment you said powder room, that's so antique." She nearly got a slap, who was she calling an antique? "Aren't they an awful lot?" she asked.

"Then why are you here?" I asked.

Her answer was incredibly honest; "I'm here because I make a shitload of money just keeping those crappy sods happy, they love my big boobs, taut arse and the way I flirt with them. When I'm not here I'm in Darwin helping my dad on his stud farm."

Now my interest was caught, the picture of this very sexy female as a stud farm worker did not jell with me. Helena took my arm; "Come on, Tara, let's show our faces to those boozy schmucks then piss off outta here!" The high-pitched girly voice was gone, instead she sounded like my Rae back in Perth, a normal person, not like a young child.

"Helena, tell me, just how old are you?"

"I'm twenty-eight. This is all smoke and mirrors, Tara, in my job you learn to play the game, or you don't have the job, it's great money, it's that simple, this is what I do to help my dad with expenses. It can be fun, especially when I get paid to dress up and have a night out on the town. It can be a problem, though, when the boss gets creepy and his hands start to wander, or when his guests think I'm an escort that tends to all needs, and I have to fend them off. It will do till we have the mortgage on the farm paid off."

I had to ask, "So, where's Mum?"

"Don't know, and I don't care. She could be out there right now, and I would not know her, she dumped me as a baby, took off with a city guy. My dad does not like to talk about it, so that's all I know." She summed it up quickly, through being hurt and feeling abandoned she was playing at being a grown-up in high heels, make-up and slinky evening gowns. We walked out arm in arm, both of us chuckling at our hidden personae, knowing it was for tonight only, then normality here we come.

Helena sat down next to Dylan; by now he was incapable of focusing his eyes. Gordi's face was pale, his hands clenched by his sides. He looked like he was in pain, or maybe he was about to cry. I had not quite made it to the couch to sit beside him when he tried to stand, the glassware on the table clinked together as the table rocked dangerously.

"Tara, I have to go back to New Zealand as soon as possible, my brother Ryan just rang me. It's my Mum, she's dying." I looked at Helena, she had not said a word about this, we had been chatting like old mates while Gordi was in limbo with this news. "Shit, sorry, Tara, it completely slipped my mind." was Helena's excuse.

My thought was, how could you forget that piece of news? Dylan slurred something unintelligible; I grabbed Gordi's hand. Let's get back to the room where we can make plans in private."

The lift took forever to reach the penthouse. Gordi was gulping tears as he stood beside me; two other people in the lift gave him withering looks, 'another drunk' was written on their faces. I swiped the card and the door clicked open. The room had a stillness about it; our beds, two doubles, had been turned down, rose petals and chocolates lay on the pile of pillows at each bedhead. I made us a strong cup of coffee each, making sure Gordi got out of his hired suit and into a comfortable dressing gown. Then I did the same, it felt heavenly to relax, but I was watching Gordi carefully to make sure he was okay. I packed our beautiful clothes into the bags and boxes they had been delivered in and called reception. Within minutes they were collected.

Gordi had started to shiver with shock. Adding two teaspoons of sugar in his drink, I sat down beside him. His hands trembled; hot coffee sloshed over the side of the cup into the saucer. Suddenly, his face scrunched up, tears slid down his face once again. "My Mum!" he gasped. Wrapping my arms around him I rocked him like you would do a hurt child, I had been here before, I would have given anything for someone to hold me when my folks or Russ had passed over, just someone to hold me as my heart had squeezed tight from so much aching pain.

"Gordi, I'm going to make some enquiries with Cairns airport. Maybe we can get a flight out today." It was twelve-thirty in the morning; hopefully, someone was at the airport to help me make a booking. The phone was answered by a tired male voice, I asked about flights out, there was nothing. I explained it was an emergency, he could not offer much assistance, until I had a pure light bulb moment – I dropped the film company name. Suddenly, the service was magic, nothing was too much trouble, I was offered flights which I grabbed , they were booked and paid for, courtesy of the wonderful 'no expenses spared' card. It really is not what you know, but who you know, in the game where being famous is what counts.

CHAPTER 22

Gordi and I were booked to fly to Auckland, New Zealand, with Qantas leaving at two-thirty in the morning, and from there, on to Christchurch. Gordi looked numb; he just nodded when I told him the arrangements. I used his phone to redial the last phone call he had received and spoke to his brother Ryan, giving him our flight details. It was useless trying to sleep; I turned on the TV and found an old movie, *The African Queen*. Gordi had nodded off on the couch. Going into the bedroom I opened my laptop. Checking for emails that I needed to respond to, I also needed to cancel the next round of author appointments.

I received an instant reply from Elsa saying that she'd be able to cancel the South Island engagements, but not the cruise. What cruise? I knew nothing about a cruise. There was no response to my question, I thought she must have made a mistake. I emailed Rae and the family; it was much too late to phone them; they did not get enough sound sleep as it was with Shauna teething. I explained to Rae in detail as to why we were not coming home immediately. Now all that had been seen to I settled on the bed and nibbled the complimentary chocolates. The room was very dim with just the soft bedside lighting.

Why is it when you only want to snooze you seem to fall into a deep sleep? The reception desk rang: "Ma'am, your taxi is waiting." After a Herculean effort from us both, we were soon checking into the international airport at Cairns for our flights to Auckland. I slept on the plane the entire flight, waking up as the wheels touched the ground. Gordi was instantly up, pulling out our overhead luggage, not caring who they banged into on their way down, telling me to hurry up. We rushed through customs, Gordi becoming confused, normally you would walk to the domestic airport. Now you boarded a bus to be driven across the tarmac and straight to check-in for domestic flights. For that hour in the morning, it seemed super busy; I guessed this was what airports were like in the modern world, busy no matter what the hour.

We had only just arrived at the waiting area to board, when I heard my name being paged; we had ten minutes to get up to the flight attendants' desk, who checked our tickets with a frosty smile, then rushed onto the plane, up the aisle to two vacant seats. The doors were being closed as we were shown our seats, this flight was packed, there was not a lot of choice when I had booked, so Gordi had the window seat and I had the aisle, with a woman sitting between us,

The folk around us were giving us strange looks, but there was no time to worry about that. No sooner had we buckled in and settled back than we were taxiing down the runway, and off into the air on our way to the Christchurch. Gordi settled back with a sigh; his face relaxed. He was going home, whereas I was fidgeting, I was trying to get my head around where I had just been, dressed to kill, and right now here I was in leggings, a long jumper, scarf and sneakers. The book I was trying to read was boring me, my laptop was in the compartment above us, I was itching to get it down and start writing. The woman sitting between us was large, she needed an extra seatbelt, her body overflowed onto my seat, adding to my discomfort. I mentally ticked myself off. *Get a grip, Tara.* I was praying that I would fall asleep, but my bladder disagreed. I tried to cross my legs, but the passenger in front of me had her seat set right back, so even though I was in the aisle seat my legs were trapped.

Gordi has a repertoire of night noises, including a light snore that is more like a popping noise, often accompanied by a sucking noise, or at times, a full-blown roar. This time he started with the pop and suck. Beside me, the woman was snoring as well. Her head began to roll towards my shoulder, where she drooled on me, then it slid slowly forward facing her lap. Her face turned puce as she slowly strangled herself, at which point her gasping grunting noises became scary. Twice I pressed the consul button for the hostess to assist, as I could not move. A lone hostess eventually came and woke her. It was not a pretty sight; they asked her to stand up. This was tricky as she was sleepy; she overbalanced and staggered backwards taking the flight attendant with her, and they both ended up on the floor. It took three of us to lift the passenger off the hostess who was partially trapped underneath her. I guess it's true when they say many hands make light work. Gordi slept through it all.

There was no way I was going to sit back in that seat, and the crew kindly acknowledged this, first they settled the women who had now sleepily settled into my empty seat, it had left an empty seat between her and Gordi. If I sat there, it meant I would be in the middle of these two snoring, No! I had taken off to the toilet, once I returned, I was offered another seat, one that flight attendants used during take-off and landing, which I gratefully accepted. It was not comfortable, but anything was better than sitting between those two. Soon the commotion died down and all lights were switched off, peace took over. As I looked through the window, I could see the clouds above us with a gap for the moonlight to poke through and reflect in the water. The kind hostess offered me refreshments saying we were halfway to Christchurch; I could see the moon shining over the midnight blue Pacific Ocean.

As I replayed the scenario in my mind, I got a fit of the giggles; it could have ended up being much worse. The crew could not do enough for the passengers who had complained; light refreshments had been offered to those of us who were woken. A cosy blanket and pillow was offered to me, along with an egg sandwich and a lovely hot cup of tea. I was happy.

The next time I looked through the window, the South Island of the Land of long white cloud had appeared, tinged by an orange and pink sunrise. New Zealand was a wonderful place of fond memories. I wonderd how my friend Margi and famiy were getting on. I had met these wonderful people on my first trip to New Zealand. We had become family then and the realtionship was still as loving and rewarding as ever. My other friends from the North Island had seemed to disappear as the years had moved on, but so had I. I had not told Margi of my arrival; if I had the opportunity, I would certainly take it, for now I would see how things panned out, as I would with Gordi. Now was not the time to tell him I was not the one to make him happy. I slipped the silver ring he had given me off my finger, popping it into my coat pocket.

Hopefully I would feel when the time was right to tell him. Right now, I was here to help if I could.

I looked up to see Gordi was awake; he was surprised to find me missing, his head poked upwards like a turtle from its shell, his hair was going in all directions and his glasses slightly askew. I waved, but he could not get out; the lady on the end was blocking him, Gordi was now the trapped one. I waved, smiled, and continued to watch the sunrise as the lights went on and the intercom crackled into life.

"Ladies and gentlemen, this is Captain Tyson, thank you for flying with Air New Zealand, welcome to the land of the long white cloud, Aotearoa."

I was back; I always knew I would one day make this journey once again, there had been such a huge connection between Margi, Tom and I on my previous visit. This trip was out of the blue, and undertaken for a sad occasion, but I was very excited at being in this mystical land once more. After waiting in line to disembark, we moved on to the baggage carousel; Gordi, wishing the carousel would go faster, whipped his bag off and walked away, leaving me to grab my own bag. I was only minute behind him as he walked through the doors when Gordi spied Ryan, his brother. Much back thumping, hugging and hand shaking took place.

"Bro, I can't believe it, you're home!" Gordi looked so happy. He suddenly remembered me.

"This is Tara, my partner," said Gordi.

I held out my hand in greeting, but Ryan walked away, flinging over his shoulder, "So you're Tara," he looked me up and down, "we meet at last!" There was no smile in his eyes or on his face, and it was very clear I was not welcome. We were ushered into an very old station wagon that sat three across the front, I decided to sit in the back seat with Brutus the farm dog, giving the boys some private time to catch up. It turned out to be a bad idea; Brutus quickly decided I was his new conquest. I was fending off the animal that had latched itself onto my arm, its haunches quivering in anticipation of sexual release. When Gordi recognised I was in strife the wagon screeched to a halt, Brutus was tied up on the tray of the ute, and once again we took off to what I had been told was home, the family farm, but first to the hospital to check in on their mum.

So far on this trip I had been part of and watched so many interactions from many people, and now an unwilling love match for Brutus. I was itching to write everything in my notebook. If my time in New Zealand was anything like the last time, it would be an interesting experience; however, if I had known what was ahead of me, I would have stayed on the plane. On the way to the city hospital, Gordi and Ryan discussed their mother, what was being done to help, the medications, treatments she had been given that had so far proved unsuccessful. The news was not good, her blood pressure was too high, plus while Gordi and I had been in the air, they thought she may have suffered some sort of ministroke.

The hospital seemed to be empty, night lights were only just being turned off in the corridors as Ryan led us to a private room. On a single bed was the matriarch of Gordi's family, his mother; the formidable presence lay quiet. Her skin had a yellow tinge to it. Gordi sat beside her, his love for her written over his face.

"Mum, I'm here." Gordi whispered softly.

One brown beady eye slowly opened. "Son," she wheezed, then that beady eye widened just a little as she saw me. "What's she doing here?" I knew as soon as we made eye contact that yes, she was ill, but not at death's door, this matriarch had brought her oldest boy home on a whim.

I tapped Gordi on his shoulder, "I'll wait for you in reception." This was his family time, I was not welcome, nor did I want to be here, in that unwelcoming environment. An hour had passed when Gordi and Ryan appeared, Gordi's face a mirror of mixed emotions.

"Tara, I'm sorry, but you're not welcome at the farm," he looked miserable.

Ryan stepped in. "Sorry, lovey, but I'll find you a really nice motel close by, you can see each other every day and sort out where things go from there."

What else had I expected? I was not surprised or fazed, I simply picked up my bag and said to Gordi, "You have my phone number," and walked away.

Gordi followed me. "Tara, don't walk away; we'll work something out." I'd had enough; he was here to see his mother, which was fine with me. What he did not understand is that I had no need or desire to see his mother or his family; they had made a unanimous decision a long time ago, that I was not who they wanted for the prodigal son, and I was not welcome here. Fine, so be it.

I signalled for a taxi and asked to be taken to a motel. Gordi insisted I ring him soon as I was settled in. I couldn't get past the feeling that the whole thing shrieked of my first time in New Zealand, of being deserted by a person I had called a friend. Well, that was five years ago; a lot of travelling and growing up had happened since then. The cab pulled over at the first sign that flashed *Vacancy*; as I paid him and got out, he said, "You alright love?" His words bought back memories of my very first visit to New Zealand, except that time I had flown into Auckland, and when I had hailed a cab I was in tears.

This time a huge smile lit my face. "I'm just dandy, thank you."

I signed the motel register and took my key. I entered the room with an idea, one that I had spied in a travel brochure on the plane. It made me smile, it would not go away. Once settled I was going to book a motorhome. I had not finished my trip around the South Island that I began when I was last in New Zealand, but this time I had the money, the time, and adventure was surging through my blood. But first I needed a hot shower and a comfy bed for a much-needed sleep.

When I woke up, I felt so much clearer, making myself a hot cup of tea I Googled the information I was after. It took around thirty minutes to find the Wayward Motorhome Company and booked myself a small one-person motorhome. It was delivered two hours later; the owner/driver and I checked the contents: pots, pans, dishes, winter bedding and bath towels. I signed the papers, showed him my licence and passport, paid with my credit card, he handed me the keys and the contract to return the motorhome in four weeks. It was that easy. I was of on another adventure.

CHAPTER 23

My plan was to get as far from here as possible, but first I wanted to ring Gordi and tell him I was taking off for four weeks, and then to call home and tell them of my decision and where I was heading.

"You fuckin' what? What about me?" was Gordi's reply to my phone call. I reminded him he was here to spend time with his mum, and as I was not welcome at their family home, what was I to do, sit and wait for him to call in? I promised I would phone regularly, to keep him posted, and when he was ready, if he wanted to, we could head home together. It was always better to give Gordi options. He had to agree, as it was the truth, it was up to him to deal with his family. I was not going to play the role of victim, simply because his mum said so. They had not been prepared to offer me a bed; these people had some serious issues to sort out, but at least I could now see that Gordi had inherited that tendency towards anger and those opinionated outbursts. His family handled their emotions with anger, loud opinions and deceit, I had seen it happen in Bali, when they rushed to his side, and I was not wrong this time either. I would not encourage or allow rudeness or abuse from any of them.

Rae's reply to my phone call was, "You're what? He said what? What the hell's going on, Mum? Do you want me to ring Gordi and sort him out; are you going to be okay?" It took a while before she understood that I was okay.

"I was fine with my decision . Gordi and I needed some space, this is perfect, I'll be home soon enough." I intended to enjoy this trip; I was relaxed, excited and busting to get on the road, with no dramas, no arguments, nothing but the hum of a motor, the radio on, and the wind in my hair. *South Island, New Zealand, here I come, what have you got to show me?*

Before I turned the key to fire up the motor, I rang Dylan from the film company to tell him I had left the company's credit card with the concierge at the front desk at the casino and to offer to reimburse them for the flights I had booked on the card. He did not answer so I left a message, which was all I could do until he contacted me.

I had two more phone calls to make before I left Christchurch. The first was to my mate Margi. I had met this fabulous woman on my very first trip to Auckland, in fact she had been my saviour, we had been become closer than friends, we considered each other as sisters. Margi screamed down the phone from Auckland, "Bloody hell, shut up you lot, it's Tara, she's back in Aotearoa!" I promised her that once I had seen what I wanted to see I would do my best to fly to Auckland. I looked forward to catching up with, Margi, my mad Māori mate, and her family. Her offer per-normal so generous.

"Got Whanau [family] everywhere, Tara, if I can help ya, I will, ya know that, don't ya?"

Then it was time to contact my agent Elsa; she should know where I was and what I was up to. She calmly informed me I was free to do whatever I wanted for the next few weeks or so. "However, I will warn you now, do not be late for your cruise to Singapore, you leave in four weeks, from Wellington harbour. You're booked as staff; your job description is in the email I sent you two days ago. You will be assisting with the arts collection. There will also be art auctions, so you will be posting a description of each piece to those registered, as well as running creative writing and journalling classes. Enjoy your holiday, please, Tara, it's important we stay in touch."

Holey Moley! "Wow, are you sure? Me? Thank you!"

My hands shook as I opened my email account, searching for her company name. There it was, a ticket for one; I was on a cruise to Asia for two weeks. The excitement ran like liquid gold through my veins. Then I thought of Gordi; should I tell him now or wait till after his mum showed signs of improvement? I decided it was best not to disturb him; he was already upset with me for taking off on my own. To add this to the embers of his anger would create a bonfire, it was not worth the drama.

These duties done, my blood sang at the thought of travelling alone once again in this beautiful country of fire and ice. By 3pm that day I was behind the wheel of my new abode, my first stop a grocery store, not too hard to find on the outskirts of Christchurch.

I had not been on the road long when I began feeling fuzzy in the head. The last twenty-four hours had been a whirlwind, and the time difference wasn't helping. It was time to pull over and switch off the brain if possible. I needed to find a caravan park and try to have a good sleep, now that I was officially on my new adventure.

The Kimihia caravan park on the outskirts of Christchurch was empty. It was low season, so they weren't taking guests, kindly I was offered a spot for the night for my own safety. I was fine with that, all I needed was inside the little motorhome. Once in my little spot for the night, sleep claimed me, it was a restful, calming sleep, just what I needed after all the dramas. When my alarm trilled, it was just on dawn; my head still felt fuzzy, my throat was a little sore.

I was having a lovely hot shower when I started sneezing, I knew then that I had caught a virus of some sort. It must have been the aircon in the plane, long flights did it every time – a day or so after the flight I always got an aching head and yucky sinus, and sometimes a sore back. I had packed Vicks my ever-ready go-to for sinus and chills, I literally smothered myself in Vicks VapoRub: my throat, chest, feet and lower back all got a huge glob of this wonder cream rubbed into them. I had also heard it was great for headaches; we would have to see about that.

My lower back had never been the same since I had had to jump from a slow-moving road train in Kulgera, I had spent many weeks recouping after that painful experience, since then if I sat or stood for more than an hour or two my lumbar region would click, giving me a painful twinge. It was nothing too serious; I had been for X-rays once I was back in Perth which showed I had the start of arthritis in my lower back caused through injuries that had occurred both in the distant past and more recently. This did not worry me too much; I took the odd painkiller if it got to sore, massage always worked a treat, but I was only too aware of the crippling migraines that were a constant threat, I had found hemp oil worked wonders for these crippling headaches at times, but was not permitted to bring it through with me to New Zealand. So today, to hedge all bets, I downed two painkillers. The Vicks felt wonderful and warming, as did drinking my hot cup of tea with some warm toast with honey, which was not all that appetising, but it filled an empty spot before I got on the road. This was the smallest motorhome I had ever been in, but it had all I needed. No mod cons, no bathroom, but it had a queen single bed, lamp, small wardrobe and kitchen. A heavy brown curtain divided the cab from the bedroom part; what made me laugh was that the driver's seat could be turned around to face the teeny kitchen that contained a small sink, ring gas stovetop and a microwave. If I took five steps I was sitting on my bed.

On turning the key in the ignition, the motor sprung to life with a purr. I noticed the name 'Mattie' on the dashboard, so faint it was almost invisible. A previous owner had obviously named this little home on wheels, so Mattie it was, off we purred, blending into a long line of cars on their way to work. The one small cupboard was now full of tinned food, the tank full of fuel, the Hema map, courtesy of Wayward Mobile Homes, was programmed to where I wanted to go. I was off to see Akaroa, a good two-hour drive from where I had stayed the previous night.

What a beautiful place Akaroa is! I pulled into a spot right on the foreshore, the visitor information centre was almost in front of me, the sun was weak, the wind cold. I felt invigorated even though my nose had a distinct pink tinge to it, the sneezing had stopped but that determined drip that perched on the end of my nose was a dammed nuisance, no sooner had I given it a good blow than it was back again. Once out of the warm cab, I knew a scarf, beanie and warm coat was needed. I needed to sort out some heavy winter gear, the clothing I had packed in Cairns was not going to come even close to keeping me warm. The price of each piece was astronomical! Beautiful garments made from both llama and sheep wool adorned the shelves, the plain sheep wool ones next to them looked mundane and ordinary. "Beggars can't be choosers," my wise mum used to say. I chose a scarf, beanie, leggings and a suede jacket lined with sheep wool at a price that made my eyes water, but it was so warm once I popped it all on, so on it stayed.

The sales lady had noticed my interest in the llama wool; she informed me that camping spots were available at the local llama farm. I could park there for as long as I wished to stay, for a minimal fee.

CHAPTER 24

There are art trails and eateries dotted all over the hills, that is part of what I love about New Zealand. My home in Perth is almost flat, apart from the Darling Ranges, and the further north you go, the redder and flatter it gets. Here in the South Island, I was surrounded by the green hills, mountains and the Southern Alps, everywhere I looked was a magnificent view. I could even see Mt Cook's glorious snow-covered top way off in the distance.

I have always found if you want to get to know a place, talk to the locals. Akaroa is definitely worth a visit, it is so beautiful; all the buildings have a French influence. It sits right on the waterfront, a peaceful harbour of blue and green. The French were the first settlers here, and the children had honoured their ancestors by keeping the tradition alive. It was inspiring. I rang the number for the llama farm, and yes, I was able to stay for a few days, which sounded great to me.

I turned the key in Mattie, her engine sounded just as keen as I was to get back on the road. I had a long drive; the skies had turned from sparkling to dark grey, a mist was rolling in from the ocean. Sea mist was something you don't often see in Rockingham, but here it was part of the normal. Hopefully I would miss the storm that was coming in from the sea, I did not like the idea of being in the thick of it. As I drove over lime green hills around tight corners, the sheer drop beside me took my breath away, it was a very long way down. My headlights were on full beam as the mist rolled in, enveloping Mattie in a pale ghostly light. Only two cars passed me, it seemed that the sensible people had stayed indoors.

Finally, I saw the most welcome sign: *Llama & Goat Farm Stay* two hundred meters to the right. I turned in and drove very slowly up the driveway. A sign guided me to the reception area, I could hear dogs barking and a weak yellow light shone through the office windows as the first huge plop of rain hit the windscreen. Just as I pulled up, the heavens opened up. It was torrential, water hissed across the driveway for maybe half an hour, then pitter-pattered to a light shower, which gave me time to escape into the office and find out where I was going to be parked for the next few days.

The smell of wool was the first thing that greeted me, I went to the counter, rang the little bell, waited; no-one came so I rang it again. The face that poked around the doorway made me think of a picture postcard from the early nineteenth century of the old village woman. She had chubby apple-pink cheeks and her steely grey hair was tied up in a bun. With a welcoming smile, she looked every bit the iconic blue-eyed friendly baker's wife in a typical English village. Then I heard another voice say, "Mum, sit down, I'll see to it." This voice brooked no nonsense; out stepped a fashion plate from *Vogue* magazine, her long knitted jumper in vibrant green hung over fawn jodhpurs tucked into brown riding boots. Her blonde hair was tied up in a short ponytail that bounced from side to side as she walked towards me. Emerald earrings matched the green top, her nails and make-up were immaculate. Her steely-blue, almost grey eyes looked down her nose at me. Her name tag said Diana; the dot on top of the 'I' resembled a small golden crown.

"Are you the person who rang to book a place here at the farm?" It was not so much a question but a command. Her long nails tapped on the visitors' book, then pushed it towards me to sign my name and motorhome registration.

"You're over there on the concrete pad beside the large shed, Site 8. The power goes off after ten at night, we have extra blankets and pillows for rent if you require them. Do you need milk? We have a small freezer with essentials in it, if you run out; the price of all food is taped to the wall."

I thanked Diana for the hospitality and left the office. I would wait until tomorrow to see which way the wind blew, with the weather and the reception I just had, it felt very unwelcoming. Then the thought struck me that perhaps this is what the South Island was like, unhospitable and unwelcoming. Or was I being oversensitive? Hopefully, Gordi's rude family had not set the scene for my adventure here. But this woman had certainly filled the mould of inhospitable.

Life on this farm was nothing like the Quaker family I had stayed with two years earlier. These people were in a business, the farm had nothing to do with a love of living-off-the-land. Everything within sight was shiny clean, tidy and orderly, even the llamas looked clean and orderly; some of them displayed golden cream coats, some of them a deep rusty brown, and one or two of the cream ones had smidges of brown patches. Llamas have such an attitude about them – rather haughty, as they raise their long necks to stare at you, the intruder.

The day had set into gloomy grey, drizzly, and a bitingly cold wind blew, it was a good day to stay inside in the warmth, I still had a touch of a cold, once more I lathered myself with Vicks, and thought it was time I got out my laptop to make notes for my next novel, send some emails, and possibly make a few phone calls. First of all was a visit to the bathroom, which was not ten feet from where I was parked. Mattie was tucked under the long protruding eaves of what looked like shearing shed. Apart from the wind which blew in every direction, I was quite warm and safe inside.

Once outside I almost ran to the bathroom, the cold wind edged me on to be as quick as I could. Like everything here, the facilities were perfect, as clean as a whistle; paper towels were folded by the basin, there was liquid soap for washing hands and a soap dispenser in the shower which, when I turned on the taps, had boiling hot water gushing out the shower head. I was super impressed when I stood under the hot water, letting the heat soak into my body, allowing one huge, relaxed sigh to escape me, I felt my muscles soften. I had become very tense since my recent conversation with Gordi.

I had rung him as soon as I had parked at the llama farm to assure him there was no rush to return to Perth, to take his time with his family, he had been friendly and calm. I left my cruise news till the end of our conversation, I told him I was booked to go on as staff and that I would be leaving once I had returned the motorhome.

There had been a long silence then a quiet, "Are you kidding me? What sort of crazy are you, Tara? We are a couple; you just don't flit off whenever you feel like it. Now you listen to me, you cancel your lovely cruise, finish up your tour in your camper, then get back to Christchurch, immediately. I forbid this sort of behaviour." My reaction to this was to switch off my phone. I was speechless.

From the majority of camping places and ablution blocks I had experienced, once you turn off the hot water, you feel the cold – unless it's summer. I expected this to be the case here, but to my delight it was cosy warm. Inside the room was a small wall heater, the door fitting so snugly no cold breeze streamed in. I took my time getting dressed, revelling in the heat, and the fact I was nowhere near Gordi at the moment, being told that he had forbid me to go anywhere. I was not his property.

I thought about my response to Gordi. There was no answer, not really; he knew by now who I was and what my goals were, so I was not going to encourage anger and accusations. A thick hot Milo was needed. I looked at my laptop and phone, but I was feeling restless, so I went back into the office to ask what there was to do, see, or take part in. Ringing the bell on the countertop, I heard it echo somewhere in the background, once again there was no answer. I could definitely hear someone in the back, so I poked my head around the office door that Diana had disappeared behind; still there was no-one to be found. Then I heard it once more, a whirring sound. Between that sound and I were two swinging doors, each with a smoky glass insert; I tried to peer through the glass, but it was no good, so I opened one door just a little, hoping with all my heart it was not private quarters.

The apple-cheeked lady I had met on arrival was sitting in the middle of a mountain of fleece. She was using a spinning wheel that reminded me of a child's toy top. She was deeply involved in her task; there were so many gizmos rattling around in cooperation with each other. When she finally realised she was being watched, she gave me a beaming smile – this was the first genuine smile I had seen since arriving on the South Island. It felt like a bright ray of sunshine was given to me. The lady beckoned me over, not once missing a beat in her spinning; her hands worked quickly as they flicked and twisted the fleece. I followed the production, she carded the wool then spun it in to thin thread, which then ending up around a spoked wheel; the end result looked to me like grey and cream strands of wool you would buy from a shop. How clever.

"Welcome, how are you today? Awful weather for you to arrive in. I would love a cup of tea dear; would you mind?" Her head did a little sideways jig towards the shelf that held the jug and cups. I made two cups of strong tea and took one over to her. Finding a spare stool beside her, I sat down and my lessons on llamas and their wool began. The only thing I knew about these animals till now as that they came from the Andes Mountains, but there was so much more to learn.

CHAPTER 25

I spent the rest of the day here, drinking tea and learning how to use a spinning wheel. Ira, who was in her eighties if she was a day, taught me some facts about these graceful, haughty animals. I learnt that meat was high in protien, with little or no fat in their bodies. Llamas are very susceptible to a certain native grass which gives them facial eczema. Every six months they are herded together to be examined for foot rot, they have split toes so their toenails overgrow and can cause pain. Older llamas have their teeth filed back as they outgrow their soft mouths. Depending on the weather and abundance of fleece, they are shorn perhaps twice a year, their fleece has a little amount of oil but is silky to touch and very light to wear. It was, once called 'the fleece of the Gods' by the Incas, I was fascinated.

The rain had stopped and a weak sun did its best to shine through the clouds, Ira asked me to walk with her to the gates that faced the rolling green grassy fields. After calling out in a high-pitched voice, "Millymilly!" a large brown llama loped gracefully towards us. Ira placed oats in a feeding tray for this beautiful animal. She patted it, then hummed to it while she pulled the fibre apart and showed me the length and strength of the fleece, and its creamy colour closer to the skin. Millymilly batted her long eyelashes; her eyes seemed to be full of love for Ira. I think the love affair was mutual; as Ira cooed and patted her, I looked at the llama's huge protruding teeth and asked the question I knew must have been asked hundreds of times.

"Ira, do they bite?"

She pondered my question. "They can do, but like a camel, they will spit or give you a good kick, and believe me," she gave a chuckle; "no matter what they do, spitting is nasty and kicking, well, their aim is spot-on and painful." Ira saw me looking at the stout wooden rails that stood between us and the llama. "Yes, even though I think she returns my affection, I'm now too old to take that risk." The farm dog Todd joined us, his lolling tongue dribbling saliva over my boots. Ira snapped an order, he wriggled through the wooden bars and stood panting beside the llama, ready for action, his eyes full of happy excitement, the llama's eyes now focused entirely on Todd. "We use Todd to herd them into a holding pen when it is time for shearing." Todd's ears pricking up at the mention of his name. "Take her back, Todd," Ira called out, but there was no need. Sensing our meeting was over, Todd and Millymilly casually wandered back to join the herd, quite happy to be in each other's company. Ira went back to her spinning wheel, and I wandered back to my motorhome.

I wanted to make my reply to Gordi perfect, with no mistakes; there would be no 'he said, she said', I needed to let him know how unhappy I was with his recent behaviour. Perhaps this was the way to say I no longer wish to be with you, I began writing my thoughts down in an email rather than trying to have a conversation. Maybe he would see the harm he was doing when he read it. I was deep in thought when a sharp rap on my door made me jump. "Diana here, may we speak?" Good lord, she sounded like she was requesting permission to approach a royal presence.

"Of course, Di!"

Her beautifully arched eyebrow went up. "My name is *Diana*; I believe my mother-in-law has shown you how we raise our llamas. I nodded in agreement, "Well, Tara, please wait for us to book you in for a tour of the farm, we have dangerous animals here that may harm you. Ira is not an employee; she is my mother-in-law and is not to be disturbed."

Was it me, or was I finding insults were part and parcel of the South Island? I wondered if I should fling a few about myself, to see how they felt. What a snobby cow! To explain what a pleasant informative morning Ira and I had together to this woman was as good as talking to an iceberg, I apologised; "It won't happen again," literally slamming the door in her face. I began to wonder if Ira knew that her daughter-in-law was warning people not to converse with her. I knew then I would give this farm another day and most likely find another farm or campground to stay in;

this sort of rude behaviour towards a visitor was not acceptable in my eyes. Diana certainly needed some education in the art of being farm stay host. I just hoped Ira was okay and had not been given the telling off I had just received.

The day dragged by, I felt unsettled by my decision to have a farm stay way out in the country, there was very little to do, and I felt unhappy about the way I was spoken to. My reply to Gordi was only half written. I buoyed myself thinking about all the tomorrows I was looking forward to, then I had an epiphany – *why stay even for another hour? Let's find another adventure,* I said to myself. I packed away the laptop – Gordi could wait. Put my lunch dishes I had been about to use in the cupboard and made my way into the office. Passing Diana my credit card, I said, "I would like to pay for the one night, I'm leaving."

Diana threw down the book she was reading, snatched my card and jammed it into the machine, keyed in a code then passed the machine to me for me to key in my code. The machine blinked into life for a second, then beeped twice and died. Diana's eyes became slits. Through clenched teeth, she said, "Either your card is faulty, or we are having a power cut." I offered to give her cash; the electric till gave off a merry ting, the amount of what I owed lighting up. Diana looked at me with a sneer; "It looks like it's your card that's ... shall we say ... faulty."

My eyes looked into hers; my words made hers change from slits to shock: "Really, I thought it was the ice in here."

I walked out of the office, got into Mattie and drove off. As I passed the side barn door Ira waved to me, it was between them, nothing to do with me. At the first chance I stopped and pulled over to check my bank account. My intuition was saying perhaps Diana was correct, maybe it was my card. There had been just over two thousand dollars in credit when I had paid a deposit on the motorhome yesterday. Where had it gone? My gut was saying one thing, my head was saying another. I reached for my phone and, with a sick feeling in my gut, logged into my bank account. Sure enough, the balance confirmed my fears; nearly two thousand dollars had disappeared; I checked the withdrawals, the money had been transferred and I knew exactly where it had been transferred to. Only one other person knew my details, and it wasn't Rae. I rang Gordi. Not waiting for a greeting, I asked, "Why, Gordi? You only had to ask." His reply left me wondering if he had lost his mind.

"Someone had to stop you, Tara, you can't keep running off when you're not happy with a situation, it's about time you shouldered some responsibility, especially where we are concerned, so I have stopped you the only way I know how."

I felt like I was going to throw up. "How, by stealing my money?" I knew this was not just Gordi, his family were part of it as well. I had not been the obedient girl and done as I was directed, so I had to be punished. "How dare you! I've had enough of this, Gordi, you either pay it all back within the hour, or I will be laying a charge of fraud at the nearest police station."

My body shook with rage, I screamed my frustration into the air, straining my throat as I did. I started the motor and aimed the wheels towards Mt Cook, which rose majestically above everything else around me, its bright sunlit snow-capped tip inviting me to come closer. A picture postcard photo shoot was right in front of me; I should have felt a whoop of exhilaration, a sense of adventure, but instead I felt deep sorrow and anger. I had trusted Gordi, and he had tossed that away in favour of his family. I had entrusted him with my bank details, and he had screwed me. I was bitterly disappointed in him. It was not so much a case of *how* he could have done it, it was more that I had, despite my misgivings, put my trust in another man, even making plans to marry him. He was way out of bounds, there was no way I would consider marriage to any man that treated me like this. My thoughts buzzed: *What should I do? Am I brave enough to report it as fraud? Maybe I should say to Gordi, 'You can keep the money, but I no longer want you in my life.' Should I tell Rae, who I know, without a doubt, would explode with anger?* That was not going to help matters. For now, I was going to keep this close to my chest, the township of Methven was in my sights.

Two hours had passed by the time I reached Methven. Had he returned the money? I was still having problems digesting the enormity of what he had done, the nerve he displayed, his claim of complete ownership and control of me. I was insulted, humiliated and incredibly angry.

CHAPTER 26

Methven. It was the advertisement that enticed me here, I felt the thrill of adventure start to stir with the heading on the brochure: *The Lord of the Rings*. The rest of the information compelled me even more: *Nestled in the Hakatere Conservation Park on Mt Potts station sits Mt Sunday – a sheer-sided hill in the middle of an expansive plain in the Rangitata River valley – a hill made famous by Peter Jackson's Oscar winning trilogy script wriitng.* Hopefully, I would stay here overnight, first I had find a park to make a phone call to my bank to change my PIN, then I would check my bank balance, yes, it was all paid back. and finally, I would call Gordi. He owed me a proper apology, and an explanation, not some gibberish implanted by his family.

The first two items took maybe fifteen minutes, the last took an hour. Gordi had replaced all the money he had taken and sent me an email. He had decided it was best all round to leave our relationship. He asked me to send his personal belongings to him once I was back in Perth. In addition, he considered our mobile home in Perth half his, he wanted me to repay him his half. He apologised! For his and his family's behaviour, asking me to forgive them and remember him with fondness. There was a PS at the bottom – would I also return the opal ring he had bought me. I remembered the story of opals I had read up on, it was called the magicians' stone as it had all the colours of every gem stone in it, later on in history it was called the misfortune or unlucky stone. I had to agree, I decided no-one, well not if I could help it , would wear this ring again.

I must admit I felt shocked, the one thing I had learnt in our relationship, Gordi did not apologise. He never left things alone, always picking them apart, he was never to blame no matter who got hurt in the proceeds. Then I felt enormous relief, as I would no longer feel pressured by his demands to do and be what he expected – obedience and permanent commitment by marrying him. I no longer needed to put up with his petty jealousies. To be honest, at times it was great having another person to travel with, to chat with and share experiences with, to become more than friends, but the battle of wills with Gordi was wearing me down, I felt no matter what platitudes I made it would make no difference in the end, we had each given it our best.

The truth was, Gordi would never been able to have a long-term relationship, not without his mother's approval, even though he wanted it with all his heart, anyone could see that. I, on the other hand, had known such a relationship, which included family and friends. My path had already taught me some valuable lessons that Gordi had yet to learn, and there lay the problem. I wanted an equal, someone I could admire and look up to, not a partner who sulked, or who had tantrums when I received public attention, or did not agree with him, whether it was through publishing a book or showing a piece of art, Gordi and I had always butted heads. I needed to think carefully about my reply, so as to leave him with his ego intact, I was not going to stoop to his level of insults even though I dearly wanted to. Hopefully finish our relationship with good memories of our time together. I found a café still open and ordered some lunch, even though it was already late in the afternoon.

The hot coffee and toasted cheese sandwich smelt amazing. As I waited for it to be served, I read the little notices that people had stuck in the window. There were dogs, cats, goats and sheep for sale, as well as kids' toys, trikes and clothing, old books, old furniture. Right down the bottom was a faded yellow handwritten ad for Cave Cottage. The photo showed a hobbit house built into the side of a hill. Scribbled in fading ink I could make out, *Tours available*. This was more like it. I rang the number; the voice that answered was masculine and cheerful. I said I had read the ad and asked if there were any tours available today. Sadly no, he had just come back from one, the weather was not looking good but there was another tomorrow, all going well. I immediately made a booking for the next day.

He explained the meeting point at a designated road sign. Excitement filled my chest, tomorrow I would go on a tour! My meal was served, it looked so yummy, the melted cheese squishing between the crusts of golden bread, bright red slices of tomato jostling for attention between a creamy mayonnaise. Also encased within the heart of this golden sandwich were some green pickles, you could hear the crunch as my teeth descended onto it. The mug of coffee was so rich and aromatic, swirls of dark liquid lightened with a splash of white milk. Heaven!

I leant back in my chair, completely satiated; the hunger, frustration and anger had all gone, and in their place was tiredness mixed with a glow of happiness and a sad quiver of finality. As I wrote to Gordi, I thanked him for returning the money, and apologised to him, I too had been at fault. I had expected him to fill Russ' shoes, at least to some extent, which realistically was too big a task. I wished him well, saying I would ask Rae to store his personal gear, and of course once I had the money in my bank account, I would reimburse him half of the mobile home. We had bought it as a couple in Coober Pedy, therefore he owned half of it. I thanked him for his care and attention to me on our road trips, I thanked him for all the adventures as my partner. I almost wrote, *The End;* instead, I signed off with, *Regards, Tara.* I did not ask that we stay in touch, I simply ended our life together with, *Goodbye, Gordi,* I was stepping into the future. It felt like I had literally jumped off the side of a mountain, with no support whatsoever, scary and exciting at the same time. I had one more thing to do, leaving the cafe, walking to the side of the road, reaching into my pocket I took the ring of silver and opal and threw it into the snow-filled valley before me, as it sailed through the air, I sucked in a huge lungful of air then let it out a *whoop* which echoed around the hills. I was free to do, say or be wherever or whatever, at last.

It was getting late, time to find a campground for the night. I found one on the map. It had no phone number so I took a chance, the chains across the gates were down so I drove in. Once I found the reception, the sign said closed. However, there was a sign pointing to the back of building. As I walked to the back, the snow crunched under my boots, the wind was making my eyes water my throat had begun to ache; it was really freezing here. The manager appeared at the cabin door as I knocked introducing herself as

Tanby. She was most agreeable, a small block beside her cabin was vacant, then showing me where the ablution blocks were, the kitchen and wash house. Everything was super clean and compact, everything I needed. I paid for two nights.

"Right, you're the last one for the today," Tanby announced. "I did have a convoy of grey nomads due, but they have not arrived." I looked around me, wondering how she was going to fit in a convoy, the camp looked full already. As we walked back to my motorhome, two of the permanents came out to say hello to her, then joined us. We became a gang of four trudging through the deep snow, their opinions flowing as to where I should camp and why. I was happy I had chosen the small concrete pad that was right next door to Tanby's hut.

I felt safe, and once I had plugged my power cable into the outlet and attached the water hose, stomped off snow from my shoes and gave my coat a good shake, I started to prepare my own dinner, grumbling to myself. I should have bought a small fan heater to warm my home up, when I heard, "Whatcha doing, Tara?" outside my door, "Wanna join us for dinner?" Tanby was there with the two other campers. "It's baked beans night," I looked hesitant, she added, "the bonfire will keep you warm." I could see the orange glow of flames, why not? Dressing once more in my damp coat and shoes. Very soon I was adding my tin of beans to a large pot that was simmering over an open communal fire pit. The night was black, there were no stars in the sky. It was so cold I wanted to jump in with the baked beans to warm up. A mug of mulled red wine was offered, I gave it a quick slurp, feeling the warmness inside me as it slid down. Everyone was really friendly; I could feel my body and throat relaxing.

A canvas chair was offered, then a paper plate and plastic spoon; soon the four of us that had wandered the camp grounds that afternoon were sipping warmed wine and munching baked beans. After we had all finished, they built the fire to a sky-reaching roar. Thank heavens, I was freezing. They asked me to tell them about me. I love story time! I told them I was a writer and a traveller, and that I was collecting stories for my new novel; I felt that was all they needed to know. Tanby gave off a hoot of laughter. "You came to the right place here, Tara; we have a million of 'em for you!" They told me a little about themselves, the two semi-permanents were seasonal workers, possum hunters, and occasionally, fruit pickers. By 8pm I had listened to many tales, some rang true, and others, well, as my Irish father always said; "A ripe imagination never hurt a good story."

My eyes were gritty with tiredness and a slight headache was forming over the back of my skull. I begged off for the night, weaving my tired, slightly tipsy, body into Mattie the motorhome, the two cups of strong mulled wine had proved potent. Clumsily stripping off my clothes I groaned my way into bed; it was lights out in every way, immediately. I woke to my body complaining loudly. My mouth tasted like dirt and my head thumped like a tin drum as I sat up, then my stomach rolled. I grabbed a plastic basin off the bench and heaved, red fluid shooting out of my nose and mouth and foaming like red lemonade as it hit the basin. Getting up to throw the red mess outside when cold chills began running down my spine.

CHAPTER 27

My backside let me know it was about to explode, there was no time for niceties. I grabbed the basin that had just been emptied and filled it with a painful rush of dysentery. Knowing I was right on the verge of throwing up again, I grabbed my dressing gown and pushed my feet into my sneakers, plunging through the doorway I ran to the camp toilets, only just making it. Once again, the pain in my stomach alerted me, I needed to sit immediately. I threw up on the floor of the cubicle, and whatever was in my tum exploded into the toilet. Whatever was in the wine, or perhaps it was the baked beans, had a horrible effect on me – once again, both ends exploded.

My sneakers soaking up the pink winey vomit spattered over them. I tried to clean myself up as much as possible. Somehow, I had to have a shower before I went back to my motorhome. I did something I had not done before, while I was in the toilet another camper had come in to the showers, leaving her towel on a peg outside on a wall hook. I stole the towel and literally leapt into a shower cubicle. I stood under tepid water, shivering until the other camper turned off her shower, when my shower changed up a gear, almost scalding me.

"Bloody hell!" She banged on my shower door; "Have you got my towel? This is not funny; I'm going to clobber you when I get hold of you!"

I did not say a word, I let the water pour over me in surges of hot, very hot then freezing, I had never wanted to go home to Perth so badly. I folded the wet towel up, leaving it in the changing rooms. With my dressing gown wrapped tightly around my shivering body, I only had the energy to crawl slowly back to my site, where I swallowed two painkillers, fell onto my bed and slept. The black hole of dreams I fell into was full of nightmares, people were calling me, there was loud banging, then I was being shaken. I woke to find Tanby, the manager standing over me, "Tara, you okay? Someone call an ambulance; we have another one down."

The churning hole of blackness once again engulfed me, I was on a silver road of noise, being pulled and pushed, anger was in the air, there was a sense of pure animosity at my presence. From within the foggy inkiness, I heard *You,* soft as thistledown was breathed against my cheek, *you don't belong here, you're not welcome, Scribe, go back.* I cringed in terror, too scared to move. Shades were all around me, silent, unseeing grey ghosts, no movement, nothing, they hung there, seemingly threatened by my presence amongst them. My hands reached out, brushing the ghostly strands of shadows around me. Whatever these things were, they were hostile, I was surrounded by them as the chant continued: *Go back,* rolled as surf onto the shore. I was too ill to fight, if they did not want me here, then where was I to go?

My body lay on a white hospital bed, face up. The blankets pulled tight up to my chin. I looked so pale and peaceful. I was looking down at myself, yet it was not unpleasant; I had no pain and no fear. Soft lights, or chakras, as I knew them, flickered on and off over my body. The light over the heart was the brightest of all. It reminded me of the worn and fading lights my parents I strung around our Christmas trees a lifetime ago. My body was attached to tubes and a heart and blood pressure monitor, a slight crease appeared on my forehead. Was I in pain? Or was I annoyed by those dammed beeps the machines made every two or three minutes. Was it the hustle and bustle of the people around my bed?

I sat beside my body and scanned it. So, this was what I looked like without that essence of life. It felt like I had simply unzipped my body and stepped outside while repairs were being made. I soon realised there was nothing keeping me here, I was free to move around, there were no bars or orders, and nothing to hold me, so while my body lay inert, I decided to see what was happening in this room. In the cubicle next to me lay a very old man; his body was grey with age, his deeply lined face told of a life of hard work. His eyes were closed, his heart had not quite stopped according to the heart monitor – it sluggishly beeped – but his spirit had fled. His wife sat next to him, knitting needles clicking furiously; clearly frustrated and angry, it felt to me like she was willing him into an argument.

"Stupid old bugger, you had better get well soon, we have a farm to take care of, sheep to feed, they will be lambing soon," she rasped through age-purpled lips. Her veined and mottled hands certainly told the story of hard work. If I could have communicated with her, I would have said, *He's under the bed.* There he sat, a cherubic smile on his face, reminding me of a small boy who had been caught out doing something naughty. I had the feeling there was no way he was going back to his body; he did not appear to have a desire to haul that old sick carcass around with him for one minute longer. I felt, rather than heard, his deep chuckles; his form was fading, the heart monitor gave off a godforsaken shriek, in a twinkling of an eye, he was gone. His wife rolled up her knitting, and stood aside as the hospital staff ran in; ready to revive, could they not see the body was lifeless? I moved on, there was nothing anyone could do.

In another cubicle was a young mum, her pregnancy was not going well; she looked distressed and unhappy. Her spirit, though, was well, the aura she gave off was in the tones of spring – yellow and gold, and from her protruding tummy, the glow of pink, a life of love, telling me she and her baby would survive.

I moved on into the next cubicle, a young thirty-something woman whose spirit hung like a grey raincoat on a coat hanger beside her. The sadness it felt at leaving her body was traumatic. Her face, arm and leg were a mangled mess, a car accident, perhaps. Yellow fluid oozed from deep abrasions, the bandages and sheet could not hide the blood and fluids escaping her body, I could feel the pain of her spirit mourning the separation from its earthly form, it was up to the spirit now and the decision it was prepared to have with the body, did it live or did it leave.

I was about to pass through closed doors when I was summoned back to my body. Tanby stood alongside me with her hands circling slowly in the air above my body, occasionally stopping so her right hand would ring a small silver bell. Then she looked at me and spoke, which gave me jolt. She could see me.

"Tara, you need to step back into your body, otherwise you will die." To be honest I was enjoying being able to see the other spirits, watching the soft pulsing glow of their chakras; to see the other side of life was amazing. Tanby clearly did not agree, she was insistent; the bell rang again, and she repeated my name over and over, until I felt a deep longing to become one with my body again. However, if I thought all I had to do was pop back in, I was mistaken – there was no way I could find a way. Tanby watched me circle my body, my frustration growing as every entry point seemed blocked.

She took a crystal from a pouch that hung from around her waist, pulling the blankets back she placed it below my belly button; it bobbed up and down with my ragged breathing. Chanting, Tanby began to place the crystals one by one, around and over my body using their names: "Red jasper for the root chakra, yellow apatite for the navel, rose quartz for the heart, sodalite for the throat." On my forehead she placed a lilac lepidolite, to protect my third eye; she then placed a small grey stone above the crown of my head. White pebbles were placed around the outside of my body. Finally, she looked right into my eyes and said, "Follow the path, Tara." I was feeling anxious; if my body was closed off to me, I knew what the diagnosis would be. I had to make a choice; maybe it was just easier to move on, but to where?

The white pebbles glowed in the semi-darkness. Tanby quickly pulled two white pebbles from my left side causing a small break in the pattern. As I began to slide into my body another presence harshly pulled me away. I tried once again and I was blocked by an orb of anger. Tanby began blowing a melodious tune on a small silver flute, and the presence that had stopped me melted away. I quickly slid into the gap Tanby had created; she replaced the two stones as my spirit settled back into my physical state with a huge sigh. Pain rushed into every crevasse of my body as liquid fire, the agony of once again becoming human again was intense. Tanby placed a crystal on my navel, again chanting; "An ametrine for protection and power," and waved new signs in the air above me saying sternly, "Now stay there!" She collected her white pebbles and placed them in small jar filled with water; as I watched her, my eyes felt heavy and sore, but clear. Slowly she removed all the crystals on my body, except for the ametrine which she left in place, gently bobbing up and down with my breath.

"Have fun, did we? I'm leaving the power stone where it is, can't have you escaping again." I was too scared to even think about it; I had almost died, tossed away my earthly body, to do what, exactly? I had definitely felt hostility when I had been returning to my body. Salty ears slid down my cheeks; I knew without Tanby's interference I would have joined the spirit world.

Once I was fully awake, I took stock of where I was, I was lying on a single bed wrapped in a white blanket, bright lights shone overhead, a deep blue curtain was half-drawn across the cubicle, a ballooning bag of yellowish liquid on my left arm was dripping its contents into me and a nurse, who had been recording my vital signs, was speaking with a doctor. He turned from her to me.

"Tara, you're awake – that's good, how's the tum feeling?" He snapped surgical gloves onto his hands, and proceed to gently probe my stomach, his fingers gently exploring all areas, muttering 'harrumph' each time, he moved to a new position. He checked my eyes and ears, his hands probed my neck glands, then under my arms he checked my throat then asked me to cough while he listened to my chest, the nurse assisted in rolling me over, the doctor apologising for the cold stethoscope on my upper back.

"You have been really ill; we believe you caught some form of campylobacter."

The nurse explained: "Food poisoning, lovey."

I knew exactly what the doctor had said, I had been a victim of this sort of virus before, and it had also been in New Zealand. Maybe I was not supposed to be here; I had not enjoyed the experience then, and was not enjoying it now.

Tanby sat beside my bed holding my cold hand tightly in her warm ones. Once the medical staff had left, she explained, "You're okay, your spirit got a tad confused that's all, I'll stay till you're feeling okay." I was really grateful as I had a million questions. Tanby stopped me by placing her forefinger to her lips: "Wait till you have strength, rest, Tara, we can talk later.".

I slept like never before. You know that saying, 'to sleep like the dead'? Well, I now know how that feels. When I woke up, I remembered everything. Tanby was sitting in the chair next to me, her head bent forward in sleep, her woollen cloak was wrapped tightly around her, the small silver flute hung from a leather string around her neck. Whatever Tanby was – witch, crone, healer, herbalist or wise woman – she had saved my life. I was so grateful to this woman for bringing me back into my body. Our hands held each other's, I could feel an energy coursing between us as I lay in bed studying this woman, still trying to figure out what exactly had happened, and whether it was a delirious dream or an actual experience. However, deep down, I knew, and it was this knowing that scared me, as I had been very willing to walk away from this body.

Where was I going to? I had no idea, what I did feel with such clarity was if I had of gone, there would have been no return.

CHAPTER 28

Tanby's eyes opened like a sleepy owl's; large, more golden than brown. While she had slept I was offered a very weak warm tea, which I had gratefully excepted.

"Oh boy, I could use one of those," she said, peering at my empty teacup. I pressed the little buzzer; a frazzled-looking nurse popped her head around the curtain.

"May I have another, please?" The empty cup was whisked away, and another was plonked into my waiting hand. Tepid tea sloshed into the saucer; the curtain billowed out in the nurse's wake. I offered it to Tanby, who uncurled herself from the chair, took the offered cup and drank it down, issuing a huge sigh as she slapped the cup back in the saucer.

"Damn that was good!" Tanby stretched her lean body, then extended her arms upwards and outwards, I noticed a small blue tattoo on the inside of her wrist, carpe diem. Her cape of green fell softly away from her body. It reminded me of an advert I had seen of Moses in the film *The Ten Commandments*. For the first time in a very long time, I laughed out loud; it was almost painful. As I slapped both hands over my mouth in an attempt to silence myself, Tanby smirked; she knew exactly what I was thinking. Her weirdly coloured eyes lit up; "Tara, you're a knob!" Again, I shrieked with laughter, I had not heard that word for a very long time.

"Now, let's see about getting you out of here," she said as she got up. After she had left the cubicle, I lay back, trying once more to sort out what had happened. A doctor, nurse and Tanby appeared, the drip needle was taken out of my arm. I was given a small packet of antibiotic pills and instructions on when to take them and what to take with them. All they needed was my signature on the bill; now, that was a shock. I was so glad I had insisted on traveller's insurance for myself when I had booked the flights from Cairns. As Gordi was a New Zealander, he did not need travel insurance in his own country. After he received the news that his mum was dying, he was rattled enough not to argue as he would have done normally; he believed in flying by the seat of your pants, and if something happened, worry about it then. I was the opposite, I was the one who always prebooked and prepaid for everything; the comfort that came with feeling as safe as possible when it came to insurance was worth it, even if I hadn't needed it. I was doubly thankful to myself now for taking the trouble to organise it.

My mind flipped back to a day when Gordi and I had a huge row after I had paid the insurance on the house and contents, the mobile home, my car and all the family members life insurance bills. It left a real dent in the finances, but I took comfort in knowing everything had been attended to. Gordi bellowed his displeasure at my silly spending for days; I reminded him of the Bali fiasco, when he ended up in hospital there without travel insurance and relying heavily on his family and I to sort it out for him. My argument was called stupid, he had lost it completely, accusing me that it was all in my mind, a lot of women's rubbish. He then proceeded to ring every insurance company possible looking for cheap deals, becoming obnoxious when I refused to switch to a cheaper alternative, I pointed out that it was *my* finances keeping us afloat, if I wanted to insure us with a well-known reputable company, I would. End of story.

"Tara, come on, stop daydreaming, time to go home." Tanby hurried me along. I left the small country hospital in a wheelchair; the nurse almost tipped me out at the door, the wheels becoming snowbound as outside the warm hospital, a blizzard was raging, the windswept snow sucked the breath from me, the ice on the footpath made it difficult not to slip over. Tanby and I held onto each other, doing our best not to skid and go down together. We almost gave up, but sitting down in the grey wet sludge did not appeal. I was never so glad to see an ambulance, it was our ride back to the camp.

Once we were back at the camp, Tanby put me to bed in the camper and left me to rest, occasionally waking me to give me a cup of tepid water and to make sure I was warm. Each time she entered the mobile home ,cold snow-filled air blew in with her. By nightfall, the wind had gone. I slept through it all. The morning was bright, there was ice everywhere and it was below freezing point. Mattie's windows were iced up on the outside, she looked like a huge white puffball from where I stood, I was rugged up to the hilt, I had wrapped my doona around my clothes for my morning rush to the camp toilets, my breath forming a constant stream of steam as pure cold air filled my lungs. I was still trying to convince myself that what I had experienced was caused by food poisoning, I was beginning to feel a little better, my head and tum had lost that sick feeling, my legs had lost their shaky feeling – that is, until a snowball hit me in the back.

"Morning, Tara, how are ya?" Tanby was dressed for the weather, only her eyes showed above the thick woollen scarf covering her lower face, while her green cape hid the many cardis and jumpers under it. We both resembled multicoloured snowballs. "Come inside and sit with me, I have a fire going." I did not need a second invitation, we stamped off the snow on her porch, I followed Tanby in, my eyes getting used to a dimly lit room, which was a cornucopia of mystery and magic. The smell of hot vegetable soup went straight into my nostrils; saliva poured into my mouth, I craved a big cup of that wholesome goodness.

If Tanby had not offered me one immediately, I swear I would have helped myself. My hands curled around the old tin mug; its warmth extended through my mittens to my icy cold fingers, the heat of the liquid warming my insides. I settled into the one old comfy armchair covered in a patchwork of yellow and orange crotchet squares, Tanby was nestled into a pile of large cushions that she had dragged off her bed, each a faded version of maroon and green velvet. She gave the open fire a good prompt with the poker and added more wood; it flared into a bluish flame, its orange centre dancing to an unknown tune, hypnotising us both. We sat in companionable silence sucking on lumps of juicy carrot and potato from the tin mugs of creamy soup.

I was warm and comfy, and once again lulled into dream-like state when I was woken from my semi-trance by Tanby's voice.

"Okay, Tara, spill!" I was bought back to the present with surprise.

"You first," I replied.

"Nope, I rescued you, so you first, tell me why you're here." I was too warm and comfy to argue, so I told her about my life of writing and travel, also my life and family in Perth and my little slice of fame in Cairns. As I spoke, she nodded in understanding, when I told her about Gordi and of my meeting with his family, how he had decided to call it a day, and I had agreed to end our relationship.

She sighed. "You made the right decision."

"In short, Tanby, I'm footloose and fancy-free."

She held up her tin mug, I got the hint and refilled both mugs from the pot of soup that was simmering away by the foreside. "Don't sit down yet, it's your turn to bring in more firewood." Tanby excused herself saying, "Ladies' room first, then it's my turn to share my story."

I did as requested, pulling on my damp coat and boots, it was so uncomfortable, gladly shucking off my snow-covered clothing once back inside the cosy warm shack she called home. Once I had settled back inside, the armchair still warm from my body, I relaxed, I took the opportunity to get my bearings. This was an old hut; its walls were thick stone; this small one-room building held Tanby safe during this season. Everywhere I looked I could see faded colours, handmade crafts – woven gods' eyes made from a variety of coloured wools hung from the ceiling, there were bunches of hanging herbs, jars of various sizes were aglow with beeswax candles. A big round wicker basket now filled with the pine firewood I had just collected sat in the corner; the sap from the pine scenting the room giving off a nice fresh smell, not a closed-up and musty winter smell that most small cabins have. This little hut glowed with peace, harmony and life; I did wonder if, somehow, I had made it into the world of hobbits without realising it.

There was a small alcove-come-kitchenette, a miniature wooden dresser with an assortment of mugs and plates on it, and a large single bed that still had several coloured pillows and woolly throws scattered over it. There was no television or wireless, but drab and cold it was not; Tanby had made this one room her home. Everywhere I looked bloomed soft colour. The one small window was covered in snow, a grey light shone through, the fireplace was made from grey and white river stones. On the dresser sat ten or so books. Two large brown cow hides adorned the wooden floor. This place represented Tanby's life, and from what I could see, it was an ordered, peaceful, a room that one could happily hibernate in till spring shone through.

Now it was Tanby's turn to tell me her story. We resumed our positions in front of the fireplace, me snuggled up in the chair and Tanby curled into her big pile of cushions. The fire had burned down to hot embers, the soft heat keeping the room toasty warm. Memories flooded back of Rae and I staring into the flames at our family camp fires; it was our night-time thing, cuddling up together and describe the castles, dragons, ghosts and fairies dancing around, leaving sparks of light floating in the air in their trail.

Tanby cleared her throat, bringing my attention back to her as she said, "Okay my turn."

CHAPTER 29

I settled back into my chair and listened to what turned out to be a cryptic story. "So, where do I start? For many years I have travelled wherever I was called, always knowing when it was time to move on, I asked for the universe repeatedly to give me a clue. I saw an advert for a management position at these camping grounds for the winter months. I was in Canada at the time, I felt called to apply, had a phone interview, and I got the job; I can stay here for six months of the year, and am free to do as I wish for the rest. The hut goes with the job, and to be honest it suits me to the ground, as during the autumn and winter they hardly have any visitors; it's too damn cold!"

Her quick flick through her life did not jell with me at all; it was all too smooth, too practised. When she had finished, I had questions.

"What do you mean you were called to?"

Tanby gave me a searching look. "Are you sure you want the truth, Tara?" We stared at each other. "I guess you do." She took another big breath, "Okay, here goes. It is my belief that we are all spirits having a human experience. I practice the ways of old, including, as you can see around you, the power of herbs to heal, to cure. I believe that there is a cure for everything in nature; we just have to find it. I also believe that we are all here for a reason, but the choice is ours as to whether we follow our true path. Wherever I find myself, I love to wander the hills amongst the crags and valleys to find the untold stories."

I had to stop her. "What do you mean, finding untold stories?" Her tale intrigued me. Again, I got the golden stare from the eyes of an older women in this young woman's body.

"Tara, I come from a line of woman who practiced the old ways of druidism." Now, this was more like it, my attention was completely focused – but her next words floored me; "But you, Tara, are the first person I have ever guided back to the physical. My purpose here is to guide a lost spirit to the other side."

"You mean, you help lost spirits?" I could not get my head around it.

Tanby sighed, "Tara, I'm a conduit, as you are a catalyst."

"Whoa, back up the horses," I cried, "what on earth do you mean, catalyst?"

Tanby carried on. "I help those that either can't or won't go to the other side, or who do not understand that life for them, on this planet, has stopped. I guide when I can; if they refuse my aid they wander, some causing mischief, others pain; my main work here in this world is finding the lost ones, and guiding them to the realm of the spirit."

I was aware that my mouth was hanging open long before she had finished her story; now I knew with the utmost certainty that what I had experienced in the hospital was no dream. Tanby stood up, my head was reeling, first I was called *Scribe,* when I had been very ill, now I was a catalyst. What was going here? Tanby was acting like everything was normal.

"I need to check the ablution block and the kitchen, want to join me?" I dreaded going outside, but I also needed to move around some more; I had not realised we had been chatting for hours. Dressed in several thick layers of clothing; it was a wonder we could walk at all. It was so cold outside, my bones were aching even though I had on an alpine singlet, two jumpers, my suede wool-lined coat, beanie, scarf, gloves, and under my fleecy track pants, long winter underpants, another pair of socks that Tanby had lent me, and a pair of someone's gumboots. We trudged through the calf-deep snow, wind and snowflakes clinging to our eyelashes and eyebrows; the camp was ghostly white and very quiet. The people with whom I had shared that deadly meal with when I first arrived had gone, there was no-one else here; once she had checked everything and had taken a final look around, she made sure all doors were locked tight. It was midwinter, we were iced in, snowbound – for how long, nobody knew – yet I knew that I was meant to be here. An adventure I was very unsure of.

We trudged back to Tanby's little hut and bade each other goodnight.

Even though it was only early in the afternoon the weather was dark and oppressive; I closed the door on the snow-filled winter sky. Inside it was like a freezer; I pulled off the layered coat and jumpers, stripped off the wet track pants but kept my winter underwear and one pair of socks. I scrabbled under two winter-weight feather quilts and a warm woolly rug before flicking off the little bedside light. The eerie glow of snow was now the only light in my motorhome. As I thought about my last conversation with Tanby, it occurred to me that it was weird how we went from talking about spirit to going out and checking water systems, like it was the most natural thing on earth.

I was itching to know more, I had so many questions. The *whys* kept popping into my head, one more important than the rest – why had I been addressed as *Scribe* when I had been in my spirit form? That would wait, though; sleep was what was needed now. Soon the warmth of the quilts took over and my muscles relaxed as I slid into a world of symbols and glowing colours.

I was woken by my stomach making huge rumbling gurgling noises. I needed a bathroom, and fast; there was no use trying to contain it. It seemed the hospital medication had temporarily eased the dysentery, rather than curing it. I felt weak and shaky as I made my way to Tanby's door; her little room had the only toilet around that was open and working. When she saw my face, she insisted I stay with her inside the cabin. I already knew where her toilet was. The first time, I fully expected it to be an outhouse, so it was a nice surprise to see the toilet was an earth care system; a small cedar box where you did what you had to, then covered it with sawdust or ash. This time of the year the water pipes for any washing were frozen; a pot of warmed snowmelt was waiting on a stool by the fireplace, next to it a sliver of yellow soap that lathered up smelling of fresh lemon.

I made myself comfy once again in front of Tanby's glowing orange fire; the room was a honey yellow in the firelight. The hot spicy tea passed to me was bliss; the first cup warmed my hands, the second one warmed my insides as it slipped through to my sore stomach. The tea was sweet, almost creamy, I do not usually like sweet tea, but this was pure manna. Tanby saw me look into the cup as I sipped. "Too sweet for you?" I shook my head. "It's not sugar I've added, it's condensed milk, a war remedy for any sort of tummy ailment, and believe me, it works. And the ginger and chamomile is good for tummy problems." My body sucked up the fluid; I enjoyed every last drop.

Tanby now sat beside me. "I think you should stay with me till this is over, you're not at all well; not yet." I nodded, the thought of going outside to sleep into the freezer box I called home was not exactly appealing, and I certainly did not feel all that well; my head ached, so did my back. I settled back into the comfy old armchair and Tanby pushed an old brown corduroy-covered pouffe under my feet. She took a blanket off her bed and gave it to me. "Wrap yourself up well and warm your bones." She went to the alcove she called a kitchen and I snuggled down. I had already begun to snooze when Tanby nudged me, there was a hot water bottle in her hands. "Here, put this on your tummy." I felt my tummy muscles relax immediately. The snow and wind screamed around the house, rattling the single window and the heavy wooden door; but I didn't care, I was peacefully cradled in warmth and safety, my body doing its best to heal itself.

I was woken by the smell of fresh baking. Tanby sat by the fire opposite me munching on what looked like hot bread. I could hear the crunch of the brown crust; there was also another smell, one of spice – cinnamon and nutmeg. It reminded me of raisin bread, my mouth watered; I was really hungry. Struggling to an upright position, my back let me know that sleeping in a soft lumpy chair was not the best thing to do.

Tanby chuckled. "You're in a bit of a mess, aren't you? Come on, let me give me you a hand." Once I was standing, the world seemed to calm down, the headache was gone and slowly my back muscles eased, my stomach stopped cramping. In fact, I was feeling a whole lot better. Tanby suggesting she whip up a herbal smoothie to help with my digestion, then she saw me eyeing the fresh bread. "Well, you could, but I wouldn't. Soft foods only; doctor's orders, remember?" I heard her using a wooden whisk; over the rattle of wood and plastic she informed me there would be no power till the storm had passed. The smoothie was the best I had ever tasted, it was sweet, creamy, and had an aftertaste of flowers. Then it spread warmth down my throat into my chest; what was left had a pink foamy look to it. I held the empty glass up to the firelight, remarking on the taste and colour. "What was in that? It was yum."

She rattled off a list of ingredients, "Among it was honey, yoghurt, white willow bark, a pinch of yarrow root, and a fistful of dried lavender."

CHAPTER 30

The light was already gone, there was no telling the afternoon from evening. We decided to strip the camper and bring what I needed into the hut, mainly the bedding. Encased in our outdoor clothing, we made a dash from one door to the other, the wind doing its best to blow us away, its white fury screamed as I pulled open the motorhome door and launched myself inside. To say it was cold was an understatement. I tried the engine; after a couple of turns of the key she tried to turn over, gave a stutter, then stopped. I was not going anywhere; once I turned off the engine it was instantly black; it felt like I had been swallowed by snow. Aiming the large torch around, I found what I wanted. I grabbed the blankets and Tanby took charge of the foam mattress; I filled up a bag with goodies from the small cupboard and I closed Mattie's door, knowing I would not be on the road till this storm was over.

I was never happier than when my hand reached out and touched the doorknob of Tanby's hut. The wind whipped away my breath and buckled me at the knees, it felt like I had a lead belt on as I struggled to remain upright. Was I scared? Damn right I was, I had never been in anything like this. I knew my family in Perth would be worried about me; it had been days since our last contact, but as maddening as it was, there was not a thing I could do about it. I was in the hands of the gods, as I'm sure Tanby would have put it.

For days we stayed cooped up in the small stone hut. The fire never went out, my bed was always warm, even though it was made up on the floor, Tanby had placed a large cow hide underneath the foam mattress to keep the cold out. Hot soup was made every day with what we found in tins and packets; I made small pikelets to go with our soup in the morning as there was not enough flour or butter to make a loaf of bread. My supply of treats from the motorhome – the biscuits and chocolate, and my large tin of Milo – was dwindling fast, as were Tanby's stored foods.

I settled in to write about my snowbound experience; my notebook was crammed with pieces of information I had gleaned from Tanby. We had discussions on philosophy, religion, her druid faith, her world of spirit verses life in physical form; there was so much I wanted to learn. We discussed what I wanted to achieve on the South Island tour, about using my blog to write about my experiences here. We attempted going for a walk once but ended up sunk hip-deep in snow; it found its way into our gumboots and instantly soaked our socks and track pants. My mobile phone and laptop were of no use out here; to be honest, I was not exactly thriving in this harsh climate, I was a Perth girl, accustomed to warm sunny skies the majority of the time, with golden sand and blue sea. The towering white southern ranges that surrounded us often boomed with avalanches; at times, a pale lemon disc would try to shine in the grey-bruised sky, and the snow never ceased to fall.

Tanby's company was amazing. We had some incredible discussions and debates; I discovered so many things about spirituality, and how its roots reach back to the time of mankind's birth. Tanby's opinion was not so much related to a religious mindset or a Sunday lip service, but came out of a heart that was full of wonder and love for everything. She celebrated this winter storm, its arrival meant new growth would soon start peeping from the buds, newborn babies of burrowing animals would emerge, nests would be built, and eggs laid. The new birth of nature would not happen if winter did not give it a chance to sleep for a while. She advised me to look upon my time here as a much-needed, important time in my own growth; to see it as a spiritual sabbatical. As I let go of my world, I felt a healing happening, not just for me, but for my family, and for Gordi, who we discussed in detail. The words of wisdom I had seen in Cairns repeated in my mind: it made sense, I was meant to be here, to experience what was happening; hopefully, some of Tanby's wisdom would rub off on me, and perhaps, vice versa.

Countless days passed before the snow stopped. By that time, I had learnt so much, our discussions became personal lessons on alchemy, and I examined my spiritual beliefs. When wrapped up in the cocoon of her hut, time was not an issue – we slept when we were tired, and it made me realise just how ordered we are as humans in a life outside these walls. As we sipped hot barley broth, Tanby really opened up; "I don't believe in curses, but I do believe that we all reincarnate with a karmic lesson, one we have not learnt in a previous life. Then we punish ourselves, adding layer of hurt and betrayal, instead of forgiveness and healing. When a wound is not healed, it's not about what you did or did not do, it's about your need to feel the pain, no matter what the truth is. If we do not begin a journey of enlightenment, each new encounter will reconnect us to that pain. We both heard you called *Scribe*, and I saw fear and denial in your eyes. Why was that, Tara? Why does that word scare you so much, when that is what you do for the living?" That was a jolt of insight I was not expecting; she was right.

I handwrote recipes from Tanby's notes, and documented her collection of herbs from the mountain. We plaited wool and made an Aztec god's eye in the homemade bronze wool she had spun and dyed, and together created a beautiful piece of artwork. In my country, we call it craft; Tanby called it protection. When I mentioned craft to her she went into a long discourse on the meaning of craftspeople, how today it had degenerated into meaning something less worthy. She pointed out that the prophet Jesus was a craftsman with wood. I had no argument there, I had never understood the arty clique, as I myself enjoyed making a diverse range of products and called myself an artist. It made no difference to me as to which label it wore; whenever I came across a well-crafted piece of art, if I thought it attractive I took a photo then would add it to my blog.

Tanby claimed she arrived on this planet in the early 1900s, her story staggered me. To think she had been guiding spirits for over a century. I did not say anything it sounded a bit far out there, if it was true, she would have been older than my folks. However, I would not have survived without her kindness, and for that I was incredibly grateful. We shared stories from our past, rocking in laughter as we recalled the outcomes of bad decisions; sometimes a tear would spill over with love. While I knew mine were factual, I found some of Tanby's memories a tad unbelievable.

One night I carried two full baskets of wood to the door. After I had dragged one inside with me and flopped it down around the hearth to dry, I realised I was over it. I seemed to be forever floundering about in the snow, making soup, carrying wood and helping Tanby with her herbal infusions. I fell asleep in front of the fire and had dreams that were unsettling; ghosts stood in line, beseeching me with outstretched hands to help them. I was trapped in a grey world of dark cold fear. I woke as Tanby was stamping snow off her boots. She held a large pot of ice in her hands; "Bugger, it's frozen solid!" she yelled at me, "Why did you not bring this with you when you came inside?" Her outburst of anger made me feel like I was five; had I been living here to long? Was this a little bit of disrespect creeping in? She grabbed another pot, flung open the door and filled it with snow. "That will have to do for now." She settled it over the embers, and soon a steaming of pot of green tea was served, I added big slices of dried ginger. We shared a couple of pieces of the now sparse remains of the dark chocolate I had brought. Her apology for her outburst was sincere: "I'm over the cold," was her explanation. I just noded and moved some wood around to dry.

"Okay, so what's worrying you?" Tanby commanded an answer, so, I told her of the recurring dream I was having. As I described the line of spirits calling me Scribe, she sighed and pushed a small chip of chocolate in her mouth, then closed her eyes in pleasure as it melted on her tongue. She swallowed, her golden eyes now looking at me: "I was wondering when this would come up, and I have a feeling you're not going to leave this bone alone, are you?" She was right; my stay in hospital had been replaying in the back of my mind. I settled back and also popped a small chip of dark chocolate into my mouth, slowly sucking on it until it turned into a sweet liquid, coated my tongue and slid down my throat. It was a feeling of pure pleasure.

CHAPTER 31

There was a sense that I was about to be told something that could not be shared with anyone outside this hut. Tanby's eyes became more owl-like. *Here goes nothing,* I thought.

"Okay, Tanby, what happened in the hospital?"

If I had expected a lengthy explanation, I was very wrong, "Tara, you have to understand this; if you leave a vessel – your body – they will use the opportunity to seize it and settle into it, to live once more on earth. You, my friend, were being followed by such an entity; the only way I could get you back into your body was by playing tricks on it. As you passed by, I made sure you saw me open the stone gateway, but an entity tried to block you. I sent it off with a few notes of the purest of sounds. The rest you know."

The soup soured inside me. "They? Who are they?" If I was scared before, now I was super scared as Tanby went on with her explanation.

"In the world of shades, most wait quietly to be reborn, choosing a new soul, a new body, to start out in a new life. There are others that do not want to, shall we say, stand in line; they stalk the hallways and corridors of the dying, seeking out the very ill, waiting until there is barely a flicker of life left in the body's heart, then they move in. I have seen the spirits of those who have only just left look back with horror to see their earthly body taken over. I have seen the bodies respond with shock and disbelief as the brain tries to restore a personality to what it once was, but more often than not they become what we call 'possessed'. You were fortunate."

The thought of that happening horrified me; all the ghost stories I had called rubbish over the years might actually be true. Unfortunately, her words made sense, I had never questioned the process of death, so I knew nothing about it. I asked another question.

"Can you explain why they feel animosity towards me, and why they called me *Scribe*?" A new pot of tea was ready; my focus was on the steaming liquid being poured into cups, it seemed like the bubbling water was the only sane thing in this room.

"Because that's what you are, Tara, a scribe and a catalyst, in this world and on the other side. Can't you see that? When you wrote your film script, did you not wonder how the idea came to you? Did you think it was pure genius? You called it your creativity. Did you not stop and think, even for one little second, how did I get this idea? Was there not a niggle of how? Let's examine the meaning of scribe or, more to the point, your fear of the word. You already are known as a storyteller, yes?" I nodded. "Well, what if another were sitting in this room wanting to tell you their story, I'm sure you would sit and listen." Again, I nodded, agreeing, and she continued, "and what if I said there was?"

My back stiffened, I furtively scanned the room looking into the darkened corners, I felt fear travel through my body. Tanby continued, "When you yourself became a spirit form in the hospital did you feel fear?" I shook my head no, admitting I had enjoyed watching what was going on around me. I had enjoyed the feeling of no boundaries. "Then why do you feel fear now? You must learn to trust, Tara, there are many like me who walk between two worlds, it's no coincidence we met and no coincidence you experienced what you did. It was to show you that there are some stories that need to be told and have not been. I can make you a promise now, while we sit here in the warmth of each other's company, you will be called until you decide to answer, there comes a time when we must all fill our chosen destinies, this is yours, the *when* is your choice. However, once you decide you are ready, you will never be on your own, for I am the conduit that will bring them to you. In this you will simply have to trust me.

"As for being a catalyst," Tanby stood up and placed both our soup mugs on the bench, "just look into your past. You have the ability to open one's personal Pandora's box by asking questions, then you become upset when people react in anger or accusations. From what I've heard today, you question, prod and search until you get an answer you're happy with, and if you're not then you argue the whys and wherefores. Maybe your Gordi was right in a way, maybe you asked too much."

By now I was horrified; she seemed to be stripping away my power of reasoning. My reaction was swift: "What a lot of rubbish, you're having me on. Spirits entering bodies, scribing for the dead, that's crazy talk. And I'm no catalyst, I can tell you that."

Tanby stood up; there was a flicker of dislike in her golden eyes; "And this is why I enjoy isolation, it's why I roam the hills in summer, because humans annoy me, people like you, who ask for the truth and when I tell them, just like you, they cry rubbish. I'll be glad when the storm is over, and we can get back to our normal lives."

You're not wrong there, I thought. Tanby and I barely spoke for the rest of the day. She busied herself whittling wood carvings of the winter animals and I wrote in my journal. The weather, it had quietened down a lot, the wind was no longer fierce, the snow was coming only in short gusts, the sky was even showing a touch of blue. When Tanby began to make that night's soup, I moved all my bits and pieces, including my bedding back into the motorhome; I would sleep in my own space. Although I joined Tanby for an early dinner the once friendly conversation was now strained; we knew our time together was coming to an end, both acknowledging it silently.

"So, what are your plans once you leave here?" she asked as we sipped our vegetable soup.

"First, to buy some fresh fruit and veggies. Living on this sort of soup can't be that good for you." Sarcastic, yes, rude yes, but I was still feeling angry. "Then I will head back to Christchurch, I guess, and deliver the motorhome back to her owners. I will think about what else I may want to do and see. I might go to Mt Cook, take a look at Otematata or Twizel, calling into Timaru on the way. I guess I will just see what pans out for me. What are your plans for when this is over?"

Her answer tumbled out, "I'm out of here soon as possible, I have cabin fever, I just want to get back to wandering the hills and doing what I do. I feel what has happened was meant to be, so I intend to leave as soon as the snow plough arrives and cuts a road out of here and you have safely left."

Before I knew it, despite kicking myself mentally, I had invited this confronting person to travel back to Christchurch with me. The dishes were washed in silence; I boiled two big pots of snow water for an all-over wash in Tanby's small alcove she called a bathroom; the water was still frozen in the pipes. Stripping off layers of clothing with just the firelight casting an orange glow on the walls, I washed every part of my body I could reach. It felt so nice to stand there in the nude, giving myself a hot sudsy wash in the warm air, with no harsh lighting, no mirrors, nothing of the modern world to distract me, just a soft cloth, tepid water and some lavender soap I had found in my motorhome. Drying myself off quickly made the blood flow, I left the second bowel of water along with the lavender soap for Tanby to use. Wrapped up again in my layers of clothing, I wished her a goodnight as I left the hut. Tanby's last words were, "About your offer – I'll let you know in the morning." I knew that by the time I was in dreamland she would be consulting her crystals and casting her runes in search of signs. No matter what her answer was, I knew my time here in Methven was over.

As I settled down to sleep I recalled my experiences here: I had had a near-death experience, I had seen a little of the other world, and learnt so much of another's world from their perspective; it was a whole new way of thinking, I had made soda bread scones by the ton and countless pots of nourishing veggie soup using local herbs and spices. And, I felt, an weird friendship had been constructed. If Tanby was correct about my being a scribe, then so be it. In the meantime, all I needed was the smell of a sandalwood tea candle drifting through my small home and a bed that was warm and comfy. All my aches and pains disappearing as my body relaxed and I drifted into a warm cocoon of sleep.

When Tanby offered me a mug of leftover soup for breakfast, my stomach rolled over. I had had enough soup. I opted instead for a stale pikelet. As I took my last bite we both heard the snowplough chugging its way up the pass to the camp. We met the driver at the gate with huge grins on our faces; it was time for me to go. Tanby had decided to stay for another month, "Then I will see where the wind blows me."

It took another three hours for the snowplough to clear a safe exit from camp to public road. While I waited to leave, I helped Tanby replenish the stack of firewood in her hut, then I handed her everything that was left in my pantry. All I could think about was getting to Christchurch by nightfall. Tom the snowplough driver called out, "Glad to see you both alive, I guess you're Tara." I nodded, knowing in my gut what he was going to say. "Your family thinks you're dead, mate, what a bloody palaver they've been causing. We knew there were two females stuck out here, one of the semi-permanents heard an announcement on local radio for you to contact them, so he called in to say he had met you out here. We all know Tanby, don't we, lovey, so we figured the other one was you. You've been missing for ten days."

I was shocked, correcting him, "No, four days!"

I looked at Tanby but all she said was, "Remember when we talked about time? Well, Tara, time stopped for us both for ten days, we once shared all the time in the world."

Tanby walked me to Mattie. As we hugged goodbye, her words made me feel sad. "We will meet again, Tara, when we do it will be your choice, this time, shall we say, was our introduction," we both smiled at her quip. Always the mystic.

I hugged her one more time. "Bye, my friend, thank you for helping me in more ways than one." Tom helped me get Mattie started with a jumper lead, the motor was too cold to start by just turning the key. I took one last look back at my snowed-in hideaway, suddenly it all seemed so unbelievably small, the word 'unbelievable' stuck in my mind – maybe the next title for a book. Yet had been a major lifeline for both Tanby and myself. Gratefulness swelled in my heart. As I followed behind the plough, snow was once again falling softly, silently, but deadly for those like me, who don't know this country. I drove back to Christchurch behind the snowplough with the utmost care, I was certainly not used to roads topped with ice, Tom waved goodbye as he turned left, and I turned right. I was now in the outer suburbs, small parcels of snow-layered farmland looked like the perfect Christmas card. Once on the main road, cars began to whoosh past at great speed, flinging grey sludge onto my bonnet and window. A couple of hours later I finally pulled into the yard of Wayward Motor Homes.

Their questions exploded around me. "Where? How? What? Why?" I was four days late for the next payment. I explained what had happened, and once they had checked the motorhome they eventually asked if I was okay. I collected my meagre belongings and was bundling up the sheets, blankets, towels and pillowcases for the laundry when my hand touched something hard. As I turned the pillow over, I found Tanby's small silver flute. I had to sit down; I knew how much this meant to her. It was her guide to the other world, and she had gifted it to me. This was precious, I would treasure it always.

I tucked it away, safe inside a zipped pocket of my track pants. I paid the owners for the days I owed and asked if there was a motel close by. I planned to contact everyone by email and have a meal that did not include soup; then I would phone my family. They offered to call a motel that was a good fifteen minutes walk to see if there was a room. Unfortunately, the All Blacks rugby team were in town and all the rooms were booked. They tried two more hotels and I did the same. Everywhere was fully booked. While I pondered my next move, I noticed there was a phone message; it was from Dwan from the film company. I had a light bulb moment. I called and told him of my predicament; he said he would fix it. Ten minutes later he had located a small single room still available at the Christchurch Casino.

By this time, I did not care; I booked it for one night. A solid meal was next on the list; I was dressed in a black track suit which was now baggy at the knees and needed a good wash, definitely not something I could wander into a good restaurant wearing. I passed a fish and chip shop on my walk to the casino; it stopped me in my tracks, the odour of fresh fried salty chips made my tum gurgle. The small package kept my hands warm as I walked towards the casino in the freezing cold air. I could not wait, eating everything in the bag, delightfully munching a piece of golden flaky fish and a handful of crunchy chips. It tasted wonderful. However, presenting myself at the reception desk was another story; one look in the glass entry door told me I did not look my best; I looked more like I had been on the booze for weeks. The receptionist stared at me as I showed her my passport, then my credit card, thank heavens it worked.

CHAPTER 32

As I held out my hand for the key card, I did not recognise my own hand, with its chipped nails and a little Methven dirt still attached, along with work-roughened knuckles and calloused palms.
She dropped the card into my open palm from a distance. I guess if she knew I had not showered or bathed properly for days, she might have asked for the key back. It's always confused me how we make assumptions about one another; even I was at fault there. If someone does not fit into what we think they should, we make assumptions about them. I entered the lift and clicked the floor number on the brass panel, to find it was descending; not a good feeling at all. The room was as small as a broom closet, with a single bed, a small shower and toilet and the smallest bedside table I have ever seen. It felt like such a massive swing from the Cairns Casino many weeks ago. I sat on the hard, unforgiving bed and thought about how I ended up here.

A few weeks ago, I had been among the rich and famous, buffed, polished and fabulous; what a ride it had been. The hot shower was lovely, the white, if not too fluffy towel was just big enough to wrap around me. No fluffy white cotton dressing gown, no comfy matching white slippers, no warm aircon, the heater on the wall was a one-bar, and I was cold. Wrapping the quilt around me I plugged my laptop into the power point. Thank heavens the wi-fi worked. I skimmed my emails; two needed a reply as soon as possible, the first one was to Rae, the next one was to my lawyer, others could wait, including one from Gordi. I dialled Rae's number.

"Mum!" was all she said. She sobbed until I thought her heart would break; my tears flowed as well. Eventually she stopped crying for long enough to say, "Where have you been? We thought you were dead."

I almost replied with a joke about having just about done that but held back. It was not time for my humour. I told her the story, finishing with, "I am sorry, sweetheart, I knew you would be worried, it was impossible to ring or even get a message out to you."

It was Jess' turn; his voice sounded so manly; I had missed him so much. I told him that if we had been together it would have been such a big adventure. Jess had such a charisma about him. "Aww sounds so cool!" was his reaction each time I related a new part of the story.

"Where to next, Nana?" he asked, as if everything I had just told him was perfectly normal and everyday. "Mum and Kane were freaking, but I knew you were okay."

"I will have to see, Jess; there is so much to see and do here."

Jess held his little sister up to the phone. "Say hello to our nana, Shauna." I heard all sorts of squeaks emerging form from the other end, I started to feel homesick, I had had so very little to do with this baby.

Kane, my son-in-law, took over the phone, speaking in his gruff voice "Jess, put Shauna down, homework time for you." Shauna disagreed, giving out a wail.

Kane was abrupt. "You had us all very worried, Tara." He then fired a barrage of questions. "Have you and Gordi agreed on the sale price for the mobile home?" "Have you spoken to him recently?" "Are you alright?" "Is Gordi okay?" "Do you need financial help to get back to Perth?"

"Kane, I'm fine, financially and health-wise, I'm great." I knew Gordi and Kane had become good mates, should I tell him the truth, that Gordi and I had split, and that it was Gordi's decision? Now was not the time; I knew if I said anything my son-in-law would have sorted Gordi out in no uncertain terms. If there was one thing I trusted about Kane, he lived by a motto of family first. It would be best to remain silent and let Gordi tell him, so I suggested he ring Gordi on his mobile. I ended my phone call with as much love I could push through the phone to my daughter. Her tearful goodbye left me feeling guilty, maybe I should fly home immediately.

There was one more phone call to make. I really did not wish to speak to Gordi; I felt we had said all we needed to when we parted. Against my better judgment, he immediately made a big deal about me not being in any sort of contact. I explained everything again; even I was getting tired of repeating the snowstorm story. I really wanted to tell him about Tanby and about my time in hospital, about the llama farm too, but it would have fallen on deaf ears, it felt like all he wanted to hear was that I was okay and about the state of the bank account; specifically, when was he getting his share of the motorhome.

Gordi asked to meet me in the city, offering to take me to lunch the next day. I was wary but agreed to meet him as a friend. For now, I needed to shut down the laptop, turn off my phone and get a good night sleep. I lay in the dark for some while, missing the flickering flames on the wall in Tanby's hut; I tried to imagine what she was doing right now. My mind's eye saw her face just for a second, it was lonely and a little sad; her body seemed weary.

The alarm on my phone beeped; it was 7am but did not feel like it. It was still black as night outside. After I pulled the curtain across to look through the window, I discovered why this room was the last resort room and had not been booked. It had no window; I faced a brick wall.

My tum growled; it was in desperate need of decent food. Once dressed, I peeped through the doorway into the corridor. There was no movement, not a sound to be heard. I made sure my key card was in my coat pocket, quietly walking to the end of the hallway. I faintly heard voices, as I approached a set of swinging doors the voices grew louder. I opened the doors and came face to face with machines giving off loud steamy gurgles, and perhaps fifteen faces of all nationalities looking at me in surprise. A large man of Asian appearance started walking towards me, telling me to get out; I was in the laundry. I backed out quickly and scuttled back to my room. What a bloody nightmare! There was only one option, to pack up and leave. In the lift, I pressed the reception button and headed up to ground level in my wrinkled, stained tracksuit. My hair looked dreadful, it had grown considerably from the short spikey hairdo I normally had to what looked like the old-fashioned basin cut. I looked even worse in the elevators gold-tinted mirrors that were meant to flatter, my skin and eyes looked Jaundiced.

The overture of the movie *ET* was filtering through the loudspeaker as the lift rose, at last the lift doors opened with a soft ping, and a velvety voice said, "Foyer." I was suddenly back in society, there were so many people all going their own way. Broad daylight shone through the windows; it was 8am and I had slept for twelve hours, which was a first for me for a very long time. I signed my name on the bill, collected my receipt and escaped. My first stop was Farmers, a department store very much like Myer in Australia. At The Bra Bar I bought two pairs of navy blue knickers and bras, then I was off to the ladies' clothing department. I chose mustard-coloured slacks and a matching jacket, a smart navy blue T-shirt, a pair of brown leather ankle boots with a small Spanish heel, and a matching carryall. After placing all my worldly goods into the brown carry bag, I happily binned the tracksuit, along with my nylon backpack. The only thing I kept from my adventure was Tanby's silver flute. Just like Myers, they had it all; a little make-up and a visit to a decent hairdresser would complete my look. When I arrived, there were two ladies ahead of me; when it was my turn for a wash, trim and dry, I almost ran to the basin.

There is no price you can put on being pampered. While my hair was being dried I enquired about the special of the day, it included a mini-facial, manicure and pedicure as well as a light makeover. In no time at all I was done. I bought the face creams, the pencils for lips and eyebrows and hair-spray. As I was paying, I spied one of my favourite perfumes, White Linen; it was a fair sum of money. I paid with my card and as the receipt was handed over the saleswoman purred, "Madam, would you like these gift-wrapped?" I shook my head and popped the items into my newly purchased holdall. Walking out of that department store, I felt like a million dollars; there was a spring in my step, and the outline of a new book was running through my head. Tara was back! This was confirmed by Gordi's whistle, and the look of admiration in his eyes as his arms opened wide and I stepped into that familiar circle of his aftershave.

"Tara, I've missed you!" he whispered against my ear.

"And I you, Gordi," my heart was saying but my head was saying, *Have you?* Linking arms, we wandered towards the city centre. On the way he told me about his family, how sorry he was for the rude reception I had been given, apologising for the money incident. He told me his news: his mum was not responding to medication, the farm was thriving, but he still wanted to get away from all of them with the constant sniping at each other: nothing had changed. Gordi was not a country farmer in any way, shape or form, but he had enjoyed being part of a family, building herb boxes, mowing lawns and planting small gardens. He enjoyed the small intimate dinner parties he attended with his friends and when approved of by the matriarch of his family. Most of all, his love of travelling. On the farm he went nowhere, saw no-one but family. Every day was the same – up early and look after the animals, the only exciting thing was when the farm dogs had a litter.

I told him about my experience in the snow, about meeting Tanby and our amazing conversations. I mentioned the llama farm, but not my out-of-body experience or the world of shades. He asked about the mobile home in Perth; had I put it up for sale? Yes, it was and as soon as it was sold Rae would let me know, and once the money was in the bank, I would forward half to him. Again, he apologised about his treatment of me, and for helping himself to my bank account. I told him about the family in Perth and mentioned that Kane had been trying to contact him. We stopped to admire the steel chalice in the city square, an amazing piece of silver architecture.

I took some photos, then a little way on Gordi showed me around the new cathedral that had been erected in honour of the old one that had been destroyed in the big earthquake. It was stunning, contructed from chemically treated and strenghthend, huge rolls of a carboard mix, the sun streaked through the amazing stained-glass windows. It was a place of silent beauty, a place where a person could sit and gather their thoughts. I could almost hear the angels sing inside this beautiful building of light and glory.

Outside on a grassy patch stood an eclectic mix of chairs, each one depicting the death of someone who had died as a result of the earthquake. I was deeply moved as I read the names and ages of the deceased; my head spun at the thought of this beautiful city being plagued by such brutal energy, and there was not a dammed thing anyone can do about it. For the ones who had died in this tragedy, I wished peace. Gordi put his arm around my waist. "Let's have that lunch." Neither of us wanted to go into a noisy restaurant or café; instead, we found a food van selling waffles and hot coffee.

Buying our food we walked across to a nearby park to sit on grass that was so green enjoying the weak spring sun, taking delight from small bunches of daffodils clustered around weeping willows. The magnificent trees trailed their long green budding fronds into the Avon River that swept slowly past us. Soft birdsong added to the ambiance as we sat amicably, discussing family, our holidays, even laughing about Cairns and our 'dress-up night', as Gordi put it. Everything seemed so right between us.

CHAPTER 33

It began to get cold; I did not intend for this to go any further than meeting up as friends. I knew if I told him of my intention of resuming my travels, going as far as Mt Cook, his answer would be the same as every other time: "I want to go with you," or when I wanted to do anything a bit unusual, "You're too old to be doing that sort of stuff," so I said nothing. I was on alert, waiting for the cruise to be dropped into the conversation, but it was not mentioned.

By 4pm I had spent most of the day with Gordi; he had shown me his city and now I was ready for a hot cup of tea. "Leave it to me," he said, getting his phone out and pressing numbers. He had a quick conversation with the person on the other end, then asked me if I could wait for another half an hour, I could see no reason not to, but I stipulated that I also needed to find a room for the night. Again Gordi said, "Leave it with me."

I heard the clip-clop of hooves; soon a horse and carriage stopped in front of us. Gordi opened the carriage door and whispered to me, "Close your mouth, sweetheart, you'll catch flies." As I settled into the warmed seat, Gordi sat down alongside me and placed a tartan rug over our knees. The driver pulled up the canvas hood and our ride suddenly became very private. Gordi reached under the seat retrieving a cane basket with thermos and cups and food; what a lovely surprise ending to my day!

How had Gordi done this? He knew what I was thinking: "I've been networking, Tara, with the woolgrowers in the area. See, I did learn something from you after all." It was true, I had often said to him, *It's often not what you know, but who you know.* The horse slowly clip-clopped his way through the city streets, we drank our tea that was lightly laced with brandy. The warmed fruit mince pies were light and delicious, and the kiss we shared, was perfect.

Gordi paid the driver and slapped him on the back, then escorted me into a small B&B where I was to spend the night. This place was so pretty, the garden was softly lit, we were surrounded by hanging baskets filled with ferns and flowers. A small chalet was nestled at one end of a winding flagstone path; a soft hazy light shone over the front door. Gordi picked up a stone that was strategically hidden amongst the potted plants; underneath lay a silver key. Gordi used it to open the door and ushered me inside. Two slim, elegant stemmed glasses stood beside a bottle of chilled champagne, a bowl of dark chocolates sat alongside them. Steam from a spa on the outside veranda rose up and drifted away on the slight breeze.

I gave Gordi a withering look, meaning, *The answer is NO,* but Gordi was busy stripping off.

"Come on, my old girl; where is your sense of adventure?" Where had the 'my old girl' come from? He had never called me that before. In his mind had nothing changed. "Come on, Tara, jump in. I'm not going to ravish you!"

Soon, I too was immersed in the hot bubbling water. I could feel the tightness in my lower back dissolving, my shoulders relaxing; even my jawline felt relaxed. Gordi and I faced each other as we sat in the spa, steam was drifting up into a sky heavy with snow-pregnant clouds.

"Welcome to Christchurch, Tara, it's not all doom and gloom." From where I was sitting looking out into the night, with hot water splashing and bubbling all around me, a cold glass of champers in my hand, I had to agree, right now it was perfect. What made it more perfect was it began to snow; soft fat flakes fell into the steamy water. I knew this man, I knew he had something in mind apart from sex, and I was right. It took a while before he could say what he wanted; my being spoilt stopped with the next question:

"Well, are we back on?" So, this is what he thought it was all about. I had only agreed to meet and enjoy his company, while he thought I was indicating that we were a couple again.

Perhaps I was the one who had changed; 'live each and every day' was what Tanby had advised. Gordi insisted on drying me down in an enormous towel; he then wrapped me up in it, picked me up putting me down on the heated double bed. He began to feed me rich dark chocolate strawberries.

This was a first, and I was thoroughly enjoying it. Gordi was now lying next to me; he still had a great body, and I was still attracted to him very much. I felt that little flame of desire flare as I ran my fingernails lightly down his chest onto his stomach. There was no question, Gordi was ready to finish what he had started with that kiss in the horse and carriage.

I was going to enjoy every last minute of our lovemaking, secure in the knowledge that this was all it was, two good friends making love to one another; the freedom that thought invoked was amazing. Our hands explored what was familiar territory, his tongue circling my nipples, then my belly button; as we became one he whispered his need for me, the soft words curled around my ear into my hairline and shivered down my spine. I arched to meet his thrust.

A rooster crowing nearby made sure we were awake at dawn. Gordi was only too willing to make us both a cup of tea. We had just finished watching the news when we heard a discreet knock on the door. Gordi pulled on his jeans and opened it; sitting on the step was a breakfast tray. Boiled eggs with funny miniature knitted hats perched on top of them sat in a row, the toast had a colourful cotton towel wrapped around it. A golden pot of honey, a dish of butter and a saucer of marmalade were laid out on the tray, what was very sweet was a small vase with one tiny pink sweetheart rose. I did not realise how hungry I was till I smelt the toast.

As we ate, Gordi asked what I had planned for the day. His face fell when I replied, "I'm off to the tourist office or the local backpackers' to see what there is to discover today, and hopefully to find a tour and be away from here by tonight."

"But what about us?" His face had begun to set in anger.

"Gordi, there is no us," I touched his face, "you are a wonderful friend and that's the way it's going to stay, no commitments to each other, no pining for what might have been. You asked for your freedom, Gordi, it's yours, enjoy it. Let's part as the very best of friends, and once I'm back here, if you want, we can meet up again."

The angry mottled face that looked at me now did not belong to the same man I made love with the previous night. Gordi's fists kept clenching until his knuckles cracked under the pressure and turned white. His voice was brittle, his eyes, that I had once thought were a pretty cornflower blue, were now angry slits. His anger erupted, spitting words of hate and venom at me so fast he could not stop, ending with, "Fuck off, then, see if I care. You're just another bloody user, don't ever contact me again. We all hate you; you need to be stopped from hurting people." Had he just threatened me? He pulled on his jumper and grabbed his jacket, jammed his feet into his shoes as he slammed the door that shuddered in its frame. I must have sat on the bed for a good five minutes not quite comprehending what had just happened, then I bolted for the door and locked it, doing the same with all the windows and the glass door that led to the spa.

So many questions raced through my head: *Do I shower first, ring someone for help, dress and run, or call the police and ask for assistance?* I was a shaking mess; my tears came in gulping sobs. I knew he was unhappy, unforgiving in many ways, emotionally unsettled, call it what you like, this was the first time I felt in danger of Gordi harming me. I knew if I had tried to stop and/or reason with him, he would have physically harmed me. My hands shook as I packed my holdall, dressed and left the motel; I had a strong feeling that Gordi was waiting somewhere, and that I could possibly be in physical danger. I became wary of every sound.

I walked to a little shopping centre; although the winter sun was warm on my face, I felt cold and scared, my crying had stopped but the fear had not gone; every shadow was Gordi watching me. My mind repeatedly went over the last scene between us. Wondering why it had ended so badly, I corrected myself – there is no us. I kept repeating, *There is no us, from now on there is me my family and friends.* It felt right, and I felt lighter having acknowledged that, finally, I was done with Gordi's mood eruptions. I could no longer make excuses for him; he needed psychiatric help. A taxi cruised into a park opposite me; I hurried over to it and gave the turbaned driver the name of the place where I wanted to go.

CHAPTER 34

He was an expert at dodging the buses and trams, we wove our way onto the city and within a half hour I was standing outside the tourist bureau. Once inside I collected some pamphlets and went into the little coffee shop attached to it, ordering a hot chocolate. Just the smell of it seemed to calm down my frayed nerves. I was still reeling; this was the first time I had felt physically unsafe with Gordi, and this was as close to abuse as I ever wanted to be. How could a person who slept beside me and said he understood, needed and loved only me, go from treating me with such tenderness to treating me so badly? It was very confusing.

I sat in a bright shaft of sunshine reading about tours on the South Island. The amount they charged was a little scary, but common sense also told me it was the same back home; if you wanted an escorted tour you paid for it. Did I want that? The other option was to re-hire the campervan and toddle off on my own. No! being with a crowd was a far safer option. I chose the two-week escorted tour to Mt Cook, which should give me enough time to see some of the island I had heard so much about, before boarding the cruise ship in Wellington. There were two tours I was interested in; one bus tour, it left Christchurch to Kaikoura, Nelson, Greymouth, Hokitika, Fox Glacier then to Milford sound, Queenstown so many more places, I knew the South Island was small next to West Australia, our tour was zigzagging across the South Island, but here you could do it in two/three hours, and as an option I could change tours and go experience Mount Cook on a one-day flight tour.

I was looking forward to this tour, I did not have to drive, the package contained all I wanted including overnight stays, meals, and touring; it sounded great. I walked up to the sales counter and asked whether the east or west coast was more interesting to see. She was not able to assist, so I chose the west. I added the optional scenic flight and she totalled it up, her fingers tapping over the keys as she looked up at me as if to say, *Anything else?* I gave her my credit card and the itinerary was printed. She inserted it into a cardboard folder, smiled her thanks and I smiled mine. The most painful part was done, in three hours I would be on a tour coach, heading for a night in Kaikoura.

I had one more thing to do before we set off. I really needed some warmer clothes; the brochure did indicate that the weather at this time of the year was unpredictable. I asked the same lady I had just purchased my ticket from where I could buy winter clothes, she pointed out a discount clothing store on the street map, a good half hour walk from there. It felt great to stretch out in my stride, with no-one else saying 'wait' or 'hurry up', I could choose my own stride in all ways and that meant everything to me. But my anxiety about Gordi would not go away; my hands still trembled, and a migraine was forming at the base of my skull. I scrabbled around in my purse for two painkillers, so grateful when my fingers found the two small pills. I bought a large bottle of water from a street stall and two small bananas to settle my tum; fingers crossed I was not too late to kill the head pain that had now settled in behind my eyes.

I found the discount store; how appropriate, it was an army discount store. I came out a good hour later with two woolly jumpers in army green and two pairs of long pants in navy blue. I still had my old beanie and scarf, however a pair of fingerless gloves in a same interesting shade of army green caught my eye, as well as a puffer jacket with removable sleeves. I added them to the growing pile, along with two winter wool cotton mix singlets and four pairs of woolly socks that were on sale. The salesperson showed me the authentic 'most essential pair' of army aviation glasses from the USA which were also on sale, still in their plastic wrapper. 'Made in China' was stamped on the back. The last thing on the list of essentials was comfortable solid walking boots; this took a while, I firmly believe in the adage, 'happy feet, happy camper'. I tried on four or five pairs, strutting up and down the aisle till I found the pair I liked, the sales assistant obviously thought, *She's a nutter, but I'll take her money anyway.* He took my card and tapped it against the money machine.

A receipt rolled out; I was now the proud owner of NZ army discount clothing. I could not fit the socks, gloves and boots into my bag. I waited for the man behind the counter to stop cleaning his ear with the pen before asking if he had a plastic bag to pack my gear in. With a sigh that indicated he was about to make a huge personal sacrifice; he wiped the pen on his pants and produced a much-used Woolworths food bag; inside it was his sandwich for his lunch. He carefully placed the brown lettuce and what smelled like vegemite sandwich on the counter; it was not the most pleasant of smells. He pushed my socks and gloves into this bag and passed it to me with a regretful sigh. For some reason we were both hypnotised by the lonely sandwich that sat on the counter, drooping its insides onto the grubby counter. I wanted to pat it better, he obviously wanted to eat it. I needed to leave before I said something outlandish, which was always my undoing; I seemed to always see the weird funny side of things that others did not.

On my return from the store, a queue of grey nomads were already lined up outside the tourist office. Suitcases littered the walkway. I was a bit breathless from my walk, carrying my used plastic bag and new carryall. I found the public toilets and changed from my city clothes into travelling gear, feeling much like a sergeant major as I clomped outside in my new army boots. Everything about me in this outfit screamed army; people stepped aside for me. I was obviously considered important, or weird, I could not tell quite which. And I did not care. The driver checked our tickets and placed the suitcases into the baggage compartment under the bus. I had nothing to store; everything I had with me fit into the rack inside the tour bus. The driver appeared to be surprised at my refusal of assistance. It was obvious I did not have that much, everyone else seemed to have one or two suitcases.

We still had half an hour to wait before the scheduled departure time. My seat was at the very back of the bus. After settling my bag into the overhead rack, I grabbed my phone and sent text messages to everyone important saying I was on a tour but contactable by phone. I also left a message at the shop in Methven for Tanby with my phone number and a message to please stay in contact; hopefully, she would receive it. Rae responded immediately: *What's up with you and Gordi? He has rung demanding his half of the mobile home immediately.*

I texted back, *Things turned to custard, Rae, please don't worry. I'm okay, keep it on the market for me, please. I will ring you tonight and tell you all about it.* My phone beeped once more as we inched out into the afternoon traffic. I turned it off and slipped it my pocket, the silver flute was also tucked into the pocket; these navy pants were amazing; they had hidden pockets all over the place.

I had the whole back row – eight seats to myself, unless someone else got on in Kaikoura – I was going to stretch out. I was sleepy, my brain felt tired. The headache had settled but anxiety still crawled around my body. I rolled up the puffer jacket and stuck it behind my head. Before I snoozed off, I saw the driver giving me the thumbs in the rear-view mirror.

"Ladies and gentlemen, we have arrived in Kaikoura. We have a two-hour stop here, please be back at the bus depot in time." There was the usual mad scramble to be the first off the bus, some dragged out walkers from the bag rack under the bus, other rushed over to the local pub, and some hailed the mini tour buses. I had pre-booked my Watch the Whales tour, or so I thought; but as I was sorting which was my bus according to the numbers written on my booking receipt, my bus – number forty-five – took off. The driver of my tour coach shrugged his shoulders and shook his head as he walked over to the pub. "First in, best dressed my dear, best take it up with the main office." So, this was the way they played their game, okay, I was onto it.

The pub grub was basic, I ordered a pork and pickle sandwich, and a lemon lime and bitters. The locals were loudly rehashing their day's events, I was stared at with interest. A game of bingo started; the Country Women's Institute was raising funds for wool to knit beanies for the kiddies in South Africa. I popped an Australian five-dollar note in the tin that was being passed around and then took a walk outside while I waited for my meal; the cold fresh sea air was tonic to my blood.

My number flashed up on the small screen pub screen. At last, I was starving. I munched my way through the sandwich, which was not all that nice, I reminded myself why I disliked organised tours. There was no control over where you went, I knew fear had been part and parcel of this hasty decision plus my pride had been dented by being more or less told to bugger off by the minibus driver. Maybe I would.

CHAPTER 35

To be honest with myself, I preferred to travel on my own, so I could do as I liked when I liked. I enjoyed ferreting around local areas, hearing interesting stories; with organised tours you did as you were told, going where and when the clock struck. My inner voice said, *You can do this, it's seeing what you wanted to see, going where you wanted to go, it's only for two weeks.* Taking a big breath, I decided I would blog every detail of it all, that would make it more interesting for me; it could well be my next novel. This time I was asking for 'bestseller' status; my publisher said she was on to it. That's all one can ask.

While I was eating, a sea lion lying on the rocks in front of me rolled over, her clawed flipper rasping on her big fat tummy as she scratched herself, her huge limpid brown eyes looking at me as if agreeing with my thoughts, or else asking for my now discarded sandwich. A sign on the table I was sitting at warned visitors to not feed the sea life; I gave her a sorry look; thinking I'm sure she would enjoy it more than I was. I gazed out to sea and realised that, for once, I had absolutely nothing to worry about, everything was organised. I was already bored silly. I gave myself a good mental shake, telling myself to find my laptop, take some photos and start journalling my journey around this beautiful island.

Once I was back in the bus, I set myself up. I had great reception here, a blog site to continue, plus I needed to add my written thoughts from the logbook about Methven. I was itching to write about Tanby, but now was not the time. I checked my emails, Facebook, LinkedIn, Instagram plus answered some emails. I wrote a long-detailed email to Rae, adding the story about my misadventure with Gordi and how he had reacted. I knew there would be more questions to deal with over the phone, but by sending her this I hoped she could get a gist of it. I did not add anything about the near-death experience, by the time I had done all that, we were about to leave for Picton. The bus bubbled with conversations between the passengers about what they had seen and done. The few who had gone to the pub were full of bonhomie. They did not converse with me, nor did they include me in their conversations; I watched as they made friends, sorted themselves into conversation huddles, and changed seats so they could become better acquainted: laughter and new friends made in an instant. I guess a 'do not disturb' line had been drawn when I commandeered the back seat; this would have to change if I was going to enjoy myself. I pushed my things to one side, looking up, I caught a fellow traveller's eye. Using sign language, I smiled and invited her to sit with me.

She was hesitant but made the move. I introduced myself and held out my hand. She introduced herself as Darlene; I could see her attention wandering over my laptop, notebooks, camera, iPod and phone. I explained I was an author and that I ran a travel blog site. To my delight, she said she was an avid writer herself. Her first question was, "What's a blog site?"

I showed her on my phone. This information spread like wildfire; from a simple blogger, I had become a filmmaker. Chinese whispers can do wonders. By the time we had arrived at Picton the back seat had been transformed; six ladies, all creative writers, had joined us. Some had joined writing groups in their hometowns, which lead to interesting conversations about editing and publishers. Some wanted to learn how to blog. Two American ladies, Delta and Fran, had joined us; they loved to blog, sending off photos and newsy bits to their mates back home. The two 'Yakkity Yanks', they called themselves, were baby boomers like me. They had me in stitches with stories of their escapades, both were in their late seventies and game for anything life threw at them, I felt right at home as the back seat was now the place to be, the eight of us were perched like crows on a fence line, with no agenda, just enjoying ourselves, and a mutual interest in writing and blogging.

I offered to tutor the ladies who did not know what blogging was all about. Delta offered her skills on using photographs on the blog site, while Fran was the expert on photography, owning up to managing a small business back in the States that was once affiliated with Kodak. Before getting off the coach in Nelson, where we would be staying for the night, we agreed to meet after dinner. It's so very true when they say birds of a feather – Fran, Delta and I had formed an instant bond that went much deeper than sharing our knowledge; the three of us made sure we were seated together for dinner as well. We chatted about our trip, why we had chosen it and what we wanted to see during this adventure. Delta, who was the more outspoken of the Yakkity Yanks said, "It was meant to be, it was written in the stars for us to meet."

Fran gave her a nudge in the ribs saying, "Quit the BS, honey, it is what it is, no big deal."

Fran's dark eyes had a glint of humour; "Can you tell we've been together for a very long time?" There was no need to answer her, I dug into my dish of spaghetti and meatballs, it was delicious. I certainly got the drift of what she was saying, these two were a couple.

"I think we can trust her," Fran said, nodding in my direction.

"It's a bit late for that," Delta replied, "Tara's got the drift." Steamed fruit pudding and hot custard was served and Fran ordered three cups of strong black coffee, then dug into her little bag and produced a silver hip flask.

"Want a hit?" she offered as she dosed hers and Fran's cups.

"Why not?" I replied. The dark liquid packed a punch; first in my mouth, then it caught the back of my throat. I gave a little cough, then exploded into a hacking, spluttering mess as the full force of alcohol hit my chest. Even my eyes felt like they were on fire, the barman was concerned and asked if a glass of cold milk would help. Once I had calmed down and was back to breathing normally again, I croaked at the two of them – who I might add, had sat in what seemed mild surprise as my insides had turned into liquid fire, "What the hell was in that?"

Fran looked surprised; "It's nothing, honey, just a little rum we picked up in Jamaica."

They looked and were acting quite normal, so why was I feeling like I had molten lava in my chest? Delta leaned over to Fran, whispering loud enough for me to hear, "Maybe it's the eighty-five per cent proof." I could not believe what I had just heard, my throat felt like I had swallowed drain cleaner. Feeling very sorry for myself, I headed off to my room. Since I had arrived in this cold god-forbidden island I had been abused, stranded, insulted, and lied to, not to mention been robbed and nearly died; plus, that stupid bloody word *Scribe* kept haunting me. Geez, all I wanted was a peaceful life, was that too much to ask for? Now these two ladies had thought it was fun to add almost pure alcohol to my coffee.

Once the pain had subsided I decided to ring Margi. Hearing her ever cheery voice, I poured out all my woes out to her. She responded to my sorry tale with a deep chuckle.

"Why are you laughing, Margi?"

Her answer was simple. "Tara, my advice is to find out what the spirits mean when they call you *Scribe*, then go from there." Finally, it was out in the open, that one word *Scribe* that had been rolling in the back of my mind since it was first whispered to me.

"So, how do I go about it? It's not something I know how to do; I have no idea how to '*scribe*'."

"Of course you do, silly!" she argued, "you're a creative writer, an author, these are the words used to describe you in this world; in the spirit world they call you *Scribe*. What makes you think that all you have done has not led you to where you are right now? Ask for guidance, remember this, you are now in Aotearoa, the islands of the old gods, Celtic and Māori; ask them to show you. As for Gordi? Poor sod, he's really screwed up, well, pet, you're better off now than before. Now get a good night's sleep. It sounds like you're on quite a journey."

The advice from my Māori sister took hold. Those two words, *spirit* and *scribe* shook me, they were so alien. Did I want this? No. I looked at the time, it was one in the morning; good heavens, in my rush to talk to her I had forgotten the time. That's what I loved about Margi, no matter the time or place, she always listened, she always had time for me. If I thought that in my late sixties, I would have gathered a large font of wisdom, one I could draw on whenever I had a problem, I would have been wrong. I still needed a sisterhood of wisdom, in fact I welcomed it; a circle that could guide me when things became awkward. As I drifted off to sleep I saw their faces, my circle of sisters, we lived all over the globe. How blessed was I to be one of them; we had built up a solid relationship over many years, and within this circle each and every one of us felt safe to be who we were, the masks we wore for everyday life were dropped whenever we met online or in person. We knew each other well, respecting each other's gifts of nurturing and healing, no matter what form they came in. There is no better way to fall asleep than knowing you are loved and listened to by the few who count in your life.

CHAPTER 36

I could hear the burble of conversation coming from the breakfast room; some of my fellow travellers stopped to wish me a good morning; Delta and Fran, my two dining room buddies, looked sheepish. Now, I could respond to their bright greetings with a smile or act churlishly and ignore them; I could also refuse to sit with them. Instead, I waved to them and headed for the buffet and helped myself to porridge with a huge dollop of honey and a pile of creamy yoghurt. It looked soothing, just what I needed; my throat and chest were still a little tight.

Sitting down, I snapped the napkin from the table onto my lap, as I ate, I felt it helping any remaining soreness in my chest go. Asking in a somewhat husky voice, "So, what have we planned today?"

Suddenly the tension eased out of the room, Fran and Delta started chirruping like two old budgies about the options: a tour around the township of Picton, or a harbour boat cruise before leaving Picton to head off to Nelson at 2pm. Both tours sounded good to me.

Back in my room I gathered my laptop and camera, I had decided on the road trip around the city of Nelson, two of the others in the blog club would accompany me, while the rest wanted to go on the day cruise. Before we split up we made arrangements to meet back at the coach. The first stop on the mini coach tour was the shoreline, I took some great photos, especially of the coastline, with its man-made structure of huge boulders. Then we visited a couple of art galleries. The first had an exhibit of abstract art using the foreshore as the focal point, there was also a display of the use of the flotsam that had been flung onto the shore from far-flung places by the ocean currents of the Pacific and the Tasman. The other gallery had a display of post-World War II artefacts and photos of members of the local community who were in the Vietnam war. I could have wandered around the displays for ages, but the tour bus was waiting to drive us to our lunch spot.

At Elm Tree Park Tea Rooms a blackboard menu hung outside the cottage with all the typical fare: fresh scones, hot beef pies and fresh Anzac biscuits, as well as tea, Irish coffee and hot chocolate. After the previous night's debacle, and porridge for breakfast, I stuck to a large pot of tea, my throat still a little tender.

I watched and listened to my fellow diners discussing their families, homes and gardens; they appeared to be mainly New Zealanders, as when I popped in a comment about how fresh and green everything was in comparison with some draught ridden places in my homeland, one old dear spoke up and said, "Yes, but you're an Aussie, you won't understand what we are talking about." I had been put in my place, my opinions not welcome, so I decided to retreat to the minibus, ten closed faces against one that asked questions was not good batting odds.

That night I gave an introduction to the small group about blogging, covering the differences between a website and a blog, how to use hashtags, and the value of Facebook, LinkedIn and Instagram accounts. I set up my laptop and showed them my blog and pointed out the ways that I kept it looking fresh and interesting. I showed them the stats that let me know who had read each post and the country they came from, pointing out that in three years I had over a quarter of a million visit my blog; all it took was one viewer to recommend it, and within the first week I had ninety people following my travels. From there it had grown rapidly, it was great way of keeping in touch, discussing my points of view, and using Zoom I could start a group debate. It was like watching magic happen as they created pages or blogs for themselves. Delta and Fran were very capable when it came to digital networking and helped the others discover their own digital talents.

That night the dining room buzzed with a new topic: 'I can blog now, can you?' the pleasure they all took in learning a new skill was certainly a boost for those of us who were showing them how. One small group was blogging about the Ngutukākā, or as it was commonly known, the kakabeak tree. I soon learnt this was a small native tree with bright red flowers, and food for the amazing New Zealand bellbird, it was now running at number one in the debate of this tour of the South Island. It was an early night for me, wishing everyone a goodnight I made my way to my bed. A small cosy room with a very small window that allowed winter moonlight to spill silver across my bed. The next morning, a bain-maire breakfast was offered, a lovely array of hot food on offer, and quickly downed – most of us keen and eager to hone our new digital skills. I did notice as folks got on the lovely warm bus, they now had cameras hanging of necks, phones protruding from shirt pockets or an iPad ready to go. Best of all, most of us were smiling.

We headed to Greymouth, once a coal mining township. The itinerary provided for another sea cruise or an excursion down the Nile River on a raft which sounded amazing. I made sure my name was first on the list to do this one. It was advertised as *floating down the Nile;* I remembered Tanby telling me about this, and I had immediately thought of Egypt. What I enjoyed so much was there was no rush or hurry. A café with a walk-through garden was stopped at, the winter foliage was beautiful, blackbirds and thrush abounded, these birds are not known in West Australia, so they really took my attention.

We arrived early noon, a pub lunch was provided, I opted for a pot of ginger and lemon tea, I had a packet of these tea bags in my backpack so all I needed was a large pot of hot water, when handed a bill for five dollars I spluttered, "What for, hot water?" the waitress looked embarrassed, it was not her problem, so I paid and gave her a hefty tip which she refused, pushing the coins back in my hand.

"No madam, tipping is not allowed, but if you care to make a donation to our Christmas party, the jar is over there." Leaving the coins in the jar, I recognised that once again my shoulders and neck were aching, I could feel the signs a of a migraine forming. There are two options for these headaches that plagued me, there were times I could take a couple of over-the-counter painkillers and walk it off and I was okay, or there were times when nothing worked, and I was in a world of nauseous thumping pain until I could find a dark room and take the medication prescribed, which always made me sleepy. The other component to these damn things was to find a heat pack or even a hot water bottle to wrap around my neck, and the pain would quietly slip away. The accommodation was a ten-minute drive away; I decided to walk, I needed to clear my head, to make it more uncomfortable, I could still see Gordi's hands curl into fists.

We were booked into the local backpackers. It was dormitory style; it was one of those nights when no dinner arrangements had been made, it was up to the passengers, we certainly were catered for, small cafés were opening up everywhere. I was not hungry, nausea taking its place, we each had a thick doona placed at the end of our bunks, time for a nap. I was sharing with five other ladies, they were also ready for a nanna nap, one of them mentioning I looked very pale – was I alright? I was honest and told her I had a migraine and wanted to sleep. Suddenly the holistic healing brigade was on the scene, these ladies knew their stuff, their backpacks were opened, and a mini holistic chemist shop was on display, I was treated to a foot massage with a mix of warm lavender and almond oil.

A very hot cup of black tea with sugar from someone's thermos was placed in my hands, another took out of her backpack a bottle of hemp oil, hallelujah – this was what I had used back home in Perth. Ten thick green gooey drops were administered, to be held under the tongue for ten minutes. It was helping. But then another women pulled out what she called her 'magic pack', a small flat white plastic pack, she snapped it twice against the palm of her hand, placed it on the base of my neck and said, "Just wait for a minute, Tara," the heat I felt was pure heaven. Apparently, all skiers have these packs to warm their hands when on the slopes, this kind soul had a pack of them to warm her arthritis in her wrists and shared one with me.

I drifted off to sleep, the pain sliding away, I was feeling cared for in a way I had not for a very long time, in fact, I felt like I was in some sort of emotional challenge. As I slept, I dreamt of Tanby, her kindness and her wise words. I saw her golden owl eyes staring at me with a question in them, I knew what she was asking, *When will you accept your role in this life as Scribe?* It was not a troubled sleep; I knew deep down Tanby cared for me as a loved sister, there was nothing to fear from her.

Thank heavens only one of them snored; at around midnight her friend yelled out, "Bettie, put a cork in it!" That was the only disturbance; the next morning I woke with a feeling of a clear head supercharged and excited.

Joining these awesome ladies at breakfast I thanked them all for looking after me last night, telling them that if there was anything I could do to repay their kindness, to please let me know.

CHAPTER 37

I had never done raft riding; these rafts look just like tractor inner tubes. The previous day I had Googled and read up about it. The advert looked amazing adding in a postscript 'may see glow-worms but not guaranteed' I had already seen the Waitomo glow-worm caves, during that experience a tourist had sneezed so violently that the glow-worms stopped glowing completely. But from what I had seen for maybe ten minutes of that trip it was amazing. Fingers crossed we had no sneezers on this trip.

Three of us were dropped off at the designated pick-up point for the raft riding, I was tingling with excitement as we drove into the forest, then clambered onto a custom-made train that chugged its way through the rainforest. It felt prehistoric, and when the conductor of the tour announced that this forest was the one they filmed in the movie *The Lost World: Jurassic Park*, my mind instantly started to play tricks, I was soon seeing the shapes and shadows of dinosaurs amongst the shadows of the trees. There was a taste of fear in my mouth, I could sense without a doubt that around the corner a T-rex was waiting. Eventually we slowed down as we came to a bridge, then stopped. From there we walked across a shallow ford of the Nile and started a very short (so we were told) climb to the caves, the tour guide providing interesting commentary all the way, with bursts of, "Not too long now, folks." Most of us needed a ten-minute sit-down while waiting to breathe properly again.

At the mouth of the cave, we were kitted up with wetsuits, life jackets, helmets, and our personal massive black round tube, I asked if it was a tractors' inner tube. I was corrected when our guide said, "Madam, we refer to them as rafts." Descending into the cave involved a little scrambling amongst small rocks; the guide was very helpful to those of us who found that doing the splits between two large boulders a wee bit uncomfortable. We settled ourselves on the rafts, which looked amazingly easy, especially for two young blond Norwegian males who had joined us.

I watched carefully as one of our older members firmly wedged his large backside into the rubber raft and began to back into the water; to his dismay, he was stopped by the guide, who had such a huge smile on his face as he un-wedged the large black tube from the man's rear end. It was a struggle, the rear end finally gave up the tug of war, and with a squelch, popped out.

"Sir, we do it this way." Leading us down to the water, he demonstrated the process; first we needed to lie our rafts in the water, then settle into them by lying across them, and glide off with the current. Sir was first, then I was helped into the raft – talk about an awkward duck – once I managed to get into the correct position the guide gently pushed me into the slow current. I hit the opposite side of the cave, bounced off then picked up speed, the last thing I heard above the gurgle of river water was the beautiful call of the bellbird. I slowly ricocheted from one side of the wall to the other until the river decided to pick me up and take me along for the slow pleasant ride. Behind me followed other tourists. For an hour we floated on our backs, the silence, the blackness of the water all adding to the feeling of magic and mystery, it was surreal, our headlights picking up stalactites that had taken thousands of years to grow, then the guide instructed us to turn off our headlights so we could watch the glow-worms flickering on, then off, then on once again; they looked like small groups of pale fairy lights. I felt honoured to be part of this experience.

The guide softly calling out instructions to use our hands as paddles if we slowed down; sure enough we soon slowed to a crawl, and following instructions, I surged forward, my hands digging deeply in the water. I have no idea if the gentleman they had called sir in front heard the instruction or not, as he came to a stop. I lurched forward, bouncing into his raft then ending up with my feet over his shoulders. He tried to set himself free, thrashing about like a fish on a line. We were locked together until I pulled my feet up and pushed him away from me. I had caused a small raft jam, the recipient of my enthusiastic paddling was not happy at all, but it was soon sorted; I would definitely be adding this to my blog. It was a shame that I could not take photos, one thing I did do, however, was promise myself that one day, if possible, I would bring our Jess here so he could have this experience.

Suddenly we went from darkness into soft daylight, cloud-covered sunlight filtered down through the canopy of tree trunks. Massive silver ferns dipped their fronds into the water, before me was a curtain of green as I gently slid through birdsong and weak sunlight surrounding us; it was truly a beauty of nature, the Nile River glow-worm caves were quite an experience. Our guide was instructing us to paddle with our hands towards the pebbled shore. Once there, it was a race to the unisex changing rooms; fortunately, it had a curtained-off cubicles. I had no idea how difficult it was to pull a wetsuit off, I peeled mine off to the waist then literally need a shoehorn to get myself free. I could hear from the noises in the other cubicles that the others were having just as much trouble. This was silly, I began to chuckle, and was joined by a titter from my neighbour, then I presume the gent the river guides had nicknamed 'sir' started to chortle; it took us a good half hour to stop laughing and emerge dressed and semi-dry, ready to board the train, but not before I snapped some photos.

As we boarded the old train and chugged our way back to our pick-up point, we were told the story of how this cave was found; apparently a farmer was out hunting and lost his dog, he could hear it barking and followed the sound. The dog had found the cave, the farmer had reported it, and panned for gold in it. Not being successful, the farmer opted to sell this unusable plot of land. Then local government had seen an opportunity and bought it, and now it was used a training ground for entrepreneurs who loved the life of river or forest guides. It was kept as pristine and close to nature as possible, so that visitors could experience nature in its raw beauty, this wonderful piece of New Zealand.

Back at the pick-up point, refreshments were offered: a tasty chorizo sausage snack with goat's cheese and black pepper, fresh sourdough bread, and to wash it down, a glass of beautiful cold Marlborough white wine. Yummy, just what the doctor ordered for a chilled body. It did not take long to reach the tour coach, where Delta and Fran greeted me with hugs and showed me some amazing photographs that Fran had taken that day. Apparently, I had been officially adopted into the Yakkity Yanks club. They had heard through the coach grapevine I had been unwell, both sympathetic and happy I was feeling one hundred per cent. However, it seems that these two had become my new family, so I was told in no uncertain terms, if I had any more illness I should go to them immediately. I was still humming from my adventure; the smile on my face stayed there for a very long time. Plus, they did not have a supply of hemp oil, and I knew who did.

Hokitika here we come! It would be late afternoon when we arrived; I settled in the back of the coach – now referred to as the writer's zone; and arranged my iPad, connecting my phone to it. I then transferred all the recent photos I had taken since yesterday, that was all I could do today as winding around hills caused the back of the coach to sway constantly. I knew typing a blog post would be impossible until we reached our resting place for the night, so I closed my laptop down, seeing the photo of my smiling family in Perth on the screen as it dimmed; they were waving goodbye as Gordi and I had set off for Cairns. My heart gave a little twist; I missed them all incredibly. What a strange trip this had become, so many lessons, I decided I would Skype them that evening, once I was on my own.

Once again, dormitory-style accommodation was provided, four bunks to a room. Delta grabbed my elbow as we all shuffled into the reception area. "Let's find a room together. We can spend some time on the internet; I can't wait till you see what Fran can do." As our names and dorm numbers were allocated, Fran had a word with the owner and we were allocated a dorm room together, Delta let out a small whoop and Fran hugged my arm. With the three of us in a row, getting down the narrow hallway with my two new mates flanking me on both sides was not just difficult, it was darn near impossible. I saw the funny side; I had not quite got over my interesting adventure in the rubber raft with 'sir', now being squashed up in a dark hallway with these two were adding to the laughter that was bubbling up inside my chest; it had been forgotten in the chaos of all the recent events but now it was finally set free.

I was giggling so much I went weak at the knees; it was contagious. Delta had a laugh like buzz-saw; Fran's laugh was a tee-hee between her teeth. Myself? Well, I guess you could call me a quiet laugher, the shoulders go up and down and I chuckle. The three of us spilled into our room, each one of us beside ourselves with laughter; dear God it felt so good to laugh till my ribs ached. The poor woman who had the misfortune to be billeted with the three of us grimaced, put her duffle bag on one of the top bunks and left the room.

CHAPTER 38

Dinner was to be at a small Italian restaurant across the road from where we were staying. We had two hours to kill; Delta and Fran claimed time out for a nap, which gave me the opportunity I was waiting for to make that Skype call to my family. A fire was burning brightly in a solid river rock fireplace. After making myself a cup of hot chocolate from the dispenser in the lounge I dragged an old leather wing chair close to the fire. I also found an old leather pouffe and pushed it to the front of the chair; next to it I placed a small side table big enough for my drink. I shrugged my heavy boots off, my toes curling in pleasure, as the fire warmed them. I was finally set up.

I texted Rae to make sure they were all home; they were waiting for me on Skype, their dear faces blooming onto the screen; Rae had Shauna on her knee, Jess and Kane were beside them.

I feasted my eyes on them, I was so hungry to feel my arms around them all. I had worried that this beautiful baby was not going to know me as Jess did; she was almost two. Kane was still coming to terms that his mother-in-law was a nomad, as his folks were a settled farming family who only holidayed once a year at most. Rae's eyes locked onto mine; her first words were, "How are you, Mum?" I knew she felt the same way that I did. I had been away for a while, she missed me just as much as I did her.

My face lit up to see Jess, this young man always had the ability to make me smile from the inside out. As he got older he looked more and more like his grandfather. I asked him about school and got a simple response, "It's okay, Nana." His main interests were now acting and music; he told me about Alice, his new best friend. They had been to the movies together. Jess was growing up, he had been on his first date, more than likely had his first kiss! Where had the year gone? I felt that somewhere on my travels Jess and I had lost that tight bond, it had loosened as he now relied on his parents, which was a good thing. However, I felt at a loss as he had always come to me as a sounding board for his woes and his wonderful zany ideas; I recognised at that moment I was no longer the strongest figure in his life. He now had Kane to talk to about men's stuff – and that's the way it should be – but it still made me feel a little more removed from them all. Rae and I discussed the money she had received from the sale of the mobile home; Gordi had been paid exactly half of the original, and tomorrow she would transfer the remaining money into my bank account. I praised her for being so astute, I was happy enough with the outcome. Rae mentioned that Gordi and Kane still emailed each other, I was okay with the fact they were still mates, I'm not one for bitterness or family feuds.

One by one they slipped away. Kane took Shauna off to the lounge to watch *SpongeBob SquarePants* on the telly, then Jess wanted to call Alice. It was just the two of us left; Rae's face lost her smile her eyes looked sad. "When are you coming home, Mum?" she asked.

I had no idea why I said what I did, it was the furthest thought from my mind till it popped out my mouth: "Why don't you and the family use the remaining money from the sale of the motorhome to pop over to New Zealand for a holiday. My treat. Why don't you come here, and see me?"

Her mouth dropped open and her face beamed the biggest grin. "Really? Are you sure? When? Let me check with Kane. Mum, how exciting, wait there, I'll be right back." Soon the whole family was there once more, Kane was now in the front seat, with Jess on one side and Rae holding Shauna on the other.

Kane spoke for them all: "Are you sure, Tara? That's a shitload of money you want to blow on this mob!" I had missed our Aussie slang.

"I'm sure, Kane; keep the money from the mobile home. I'm due in Christchurch in about eight days, it may even be the start of summer here; you will love it, can you swing it with your boss? I could see Jess was holding his breath, waiting for Kane to okay it. They all looked a little stunned. Jess was then in the hot seat, asking all sorts of questions. I told him about my raft ride, he thought it funny, Kane and Rae were murmuring in the background, then Kane's face appeared back on the screen, his face stern. My stomach sank; it was going to be no.

"Tara, thank you; we would love to come over. When do you suggest?" I was smiling so much my face muscles hurt.

"Once this tour is finished we can make arrangements. How does that sound?" I said my goodbyes and promised to call as soon as I could, then I switched off my laptop, just in time, the peace and quiet was over.

The group I was with were straggling into the room, some standing with their backs to the fire, others sitting around the room. One of them came over asking, "Are you ready for an Italian feast, they say the chef is really good." I looked at my watch, it was 5pm, far too early for me to eat. I decided to wait for the second sitting if there was one, but the warmth and the company were also enticing.

"I'll see you over there."

I thought I should let Fran and Delta know it was dinnertime. I opened the door to our room quietly; it was in darkness; the curtains had been drawn, the windows closed; I could just make out two bodies curled around each other in a bottom bunk, Delta's arm was draped around Fran. I left them alone; a date with a glass of merlot was waiting for me across the road at the Italian food fiesta.

These folk seemed like they did not have a care in the world, is it because they have no further commitments to family? No mortgages to pay off? Whatever it was, these folks knew how to party. I sat back and enjoyed my wine. A trumpet fanfare resounded around the small room, then the music washed over us and through the restaurant, a small conga line of waiters appeared going around the room, the chefs enjoying it as well, their white-aproned bums swaying to the beat. I was invited to join in; I thought, *Why not? I can conga with the best of them.* By the time we had been around the restaurant once, everyone, including folk not on the tour, had joined in, so the line extended through the restaurant and around it.

By the third time around I was ready to quit. At my table sat Delta and Fran with scowls on their faces "Why didn't you wake us and let us know there was party going?" It seemed I had lost my spot of favourite family member, I was now in the hot seat.

I replied, "You girls were fast asleep." I was refilling my glass with a tonic water and ice at the bar when another table of seniors invited me to sit at their table. They all wanted to learn about blogging, websites, and the merits of LinkedIn, Twitter and Facebook pages. Their current levels of expertise varied widely: some of them already had Facebook profiles, while others – like me, at one stage – had no idea whatsoever.

By the time dinner was served I was famished. There was a choice of spaghetti bolognaise or roasted honey ham along with a red pepper and beetroot salad. The bain-marie was full of beautifully presented hot steaming food. This is where I learnt a valuable lesson. Each diner took a very large helping of their choice: I watched and did the same, thinking maybe the idea is to go back later for seconds. I found out that this was a thought-out system; each person took a plate of food for their table to taste, each of us was sharing with each other what we bought back. This way we all got a taste of what was on the menu but none of us was over-full, so we had plenty of room left for dessert.

I had a most enjoyable evening, which continued after coffee with a meeting – at first it was just our little blogging group. I showed them my updated blog, then helped them to navigate their own issues. This group quickly grew, though, as more people trickled in, soon Delta and Fran were asked to help with their knowledge of digital cameras, including uploading them to a blog or forming an album, or folder on an iPad or a laptop. Many heads were still bent over the devices they used to record their trip; my day had been a busy one. Wishing them all a goodnight, I was ready for my bed. In the morning we were heading off to do the treetop walk; I had done one similar in Western Australia and had loved it, so I was looking forward to another experience like this.

The mist that greeted us the next morning was grey and heavy; those of us who were booked on the treetop walk would not have been surprised if it had been cancelled. Yes, It was still on – we were shepherded into a minibus, the seats proving they were not that well-padded with each bump becoming a jolt up the spine, but we were through the forest in a matter of minutes. Each of us was given a hard hat and advised to hold onto the side ropes. For those who were afraid of heights, there were two lookout platforms, one about twenty feet up; the other I could barely see. I stayed on the lower one. What an amazing view! Right in the middle of this beautiful rainforest, we could see the mist far beneath us; the trees were silent sentinels that deadened the of chatter of folks behind me. These trees are the ancient Rimu and Kamahi trees, they are massive; below us were huge bushes of silver fern and tea-tree, and in front of us, the most majestic view of all: the Southern Alps, covered in purest white snow, dazzling us as the sun peeped through the grey clouds. To the west, the Tasman Sea was still mist covered; I was told if I listened carefully, I would hear the sound of rolling waves. They were not wrong.

CHAPTER 39

It took maybe an hour to complete the walk; there were several stops along the way providing photo opportunities. The smell of this forest was heavenly, thick with the pungency of leaves, brush and bracken that were now mulch for the undergrowth. As we filed downwards towards the minibus, our guide announced we could, if we wished, descend to the ground via flying fox. I had never done this before; the others in the group said they preferred to keep walking, but I was curious and asked for more information. The guide, who had looked quite disappointed at the lack of interest shown by the rest, became animated, and eagerly showed me where it was and what I had to do, which was nothing, really, except hang on. In front of me was a huge ledge of steel pipe from which riders must launch themselves.

A couple of young tourists arrived with smiles spread a mile wide across their faces. They eagerly waited to be buckled into some sort of halter around their hips, then buckles and ties were attached. The only support was a huge cable that was slanted across the tops of trees, ending up on the forest floor, I saw them leap off looking like a pair of great mythological winged birds, 'woo-hoos' echoing as they disappeared through the giant trees.

This was no time for the faint-hearted; I made a snap decision. "Buckle me up!" My 'woohoo', which was more like a scream, rallied through the forest as I sailed through the air. Landing was easy; another guide caught me, an 'oomph' escaping as I swung into his arms. The gear that was used to attach me was unbuckled, straps and helmet removed, but the grin stayed. Back at the tour coach, the others shook their heads at my silliness, except the smile that stayed reappearing every time I relived the experience in my mind. What a fabulous day! I made myself comfy in the writer's zone as the coach moved off. We were on our way to Fox Glacier, if the photos I had seen on Google and TripAdvisor were true, this place was going to be pure magic.

We drove for a couple of hours. When we arrived at the glacier the sun was glaring while the temperature was freezing. The coach driver drove us to the motel door, and we filed out into the freezing cold air. My ears, nose, fingers, even my eyelashes suddenly ached from the cold. We all wrapped scarves around our mouths and noses, and I added my warm coat to the jumble of warm clothes I already had on before I stepped down into ankle-deep snow. My mind went back to my stay with Tanby; I sent up a prayer, *Please don't let us be snowbound again.*

The motel was basic but clean, the staff ready with helpful advice. Our bags were loaded into a trolley and wheeled inside so we could find our own luggage. There was no restaurant in the complex, but from what I had seen as we had driven in, there were plenty to choose from in the township. Delta and Fran found me in line at reception, "Want some room buddies?" Fran asked, grabbing Delta and me by the arm. "Come on, chickens, let's find our room to roost for the night."

Lucky for us we had a choice, a main bedroom on the ground floor, or a garret at the very top of the building. I asked about a window, the receptionist smiled saying, "My advice is the garret it won't disappoint," and she was spot on. It had the most gorgeous view to the Alps. There were three single beds, two on one side and one on the other. Immediately Fran claimed the two beds on one side of the room, leaving me the bed on the side with the panoramic view. I pushed my bed as far as I could towards the window. I could not get enough of that view; tonight, I would go to sleep looking at the moon and stars and if possible, the silhouette of the snow-capped mountains.

Our next excursion was waiting; just about everyone had booked in for the helicopter ride. Four helicopters were standing by for us to board, each with a pilot in front of the open door. We were assigned our helicopters, which each took four passengers; a clipboard with our names on them indicated which one we would ride in. After the pilots had called all the names and assisted their passengers into the first chopper, four of us were left waiting. Obviously, our names were on the second flight. I realised it was late in the day, so if my timing was right, we would be on the glacier at around early dusk. Perfect.

When it was time for the second flight, my name was called, I was very excited. I had a helmet pushed onto my head and buckled under my chin; I was surprised to feel the pilot's hands were warm, while mine were frozen, even though I was wearing my fur-lined gloves. Once the other three passengers and I were safely buckled, the rotor blades began to go faster. Before we rose into the air, our door was closed. There was a small window to look through, and I could hear the pilot reporting his location and route, stopping to ask how we were doing. I gave him the thumbs up sign. Except for an 'Oh my God!' I was speechless as we flew over a small lake of pure turquoise blue, an ice melt that was cupped between long jagged fingers of white ice. Using a circular motion of his forefinger, then pointing at my camera, the pilot asked if I wanted to go around. I nodded, "Yes please, one more time.".

As we set down on the glacier we were surrounded by white. The door slid open, and I gasped at the beauty before me. It was everything anyone could ask for; the whipping cold wind had died down during the thirty-minute trip. By now I was on first-name terms with the pilot, Darius, from Motueka, who knew so much about the glacier. I was the first passenger out of the helicopter, as I took my first steps I was already taking in the wonderland of large and small crevasses, snow caves and ice sculptures. Darius and I helped the other passengers out; like me, their eyes were huge, like possums caught in headlights. Darius offered his hand to the first lady, telling her to step slowly, which was working well until the glacier gave off a loud groan. She shot back into her seat and belted herself in. She shook her head; "There is no way I'm walking on thin ice!" she cried. Her husband explained it was all a bit too much to take in, so he too decided to stay put.

Then the other passenger decided he did not want to leave the relative safety of the helicopter either, so Darius and I stood in the silence, he could not leave his passengers. His voice loud against the hum of the rotor blades. "Nowhere else in the world's temperate zones are glaciers so accessible as Fox Glacier." I believed him; it was hard for me to get my head around it; soon my camera was clicking away. I spied an ice monument about twenty foot from where I stood; the sun had gored a massive hole right through its middle. One droplet of snow water hung in the middle of the hole sending prisms of light into the pure air. It was truly beautiful.

Forgetting this is not stable ground but melting ice, I began to walk away from the safety of the helicopter to photograph the beautiful droplet when I was suddenly pulled backwards. Darius had grabbed the hood of my jacket and yanked me backwards. I got such a shock. "How rude ..." was all I got out, as he spun me around, not letting go of me, his voice harsh.

"For Christ's sake, lady, look where you're going!" I had not seen the smallest of hairline cracks between me and the ice sculpture. Darius told me to watch while he threw a large chunk of ice onto it. A small smattering of snow puffed up, then a small pin hole appeared, which began to give birth to a much larger and still growing hole. As the top cover of snow began to disintegrated before my eyes a tiny white gash yawned open: an invitation to certain death.

"Time to leave, now," said Darius. Now I was as scared as the three people who were sitting in the helicopter, within two minutes we were up and climbing.

Darius caught my eye, he pointed down, a long white jagged crack was opening up. It looked like a leering mouth with multi layers of pointed teeth ready and waiting for its next victim. While from where I sat it looked bottomless, the ice still crumbling inwards as we flew away, Darius added, "It changes every day, it won't be there tomorrow."

This is one of the most dangerous of places in the world; I found it hard to comprehend, but as we flew higher it once again looked like beautiful white castles in the snow to the tourist's eyes. The sun was sinking as we landed back at the heliport, the other three passengers scrambling out as quickly as they could. The other pilots were waiting for Darius to join them; I sincerely thanked him for a wonderful trip, then walked back down the track to join Delta and Fran at a local restaurant. It had been a great day, I knew I had some good shots on my camera, but at that moment I had no words to speak about my experience. Without Darius, an experienced pilot who knows might what have happened, I shuddered at that thought.

CHAPTER 40

Dinner was fresh fish and chips from a takeaway shop opposite the motel. They left a greasy feel in my mouth; I opted to go back to the motel for a hot drink while Delta and Fran stayed on in the warmth of the shop to chat with our fellow tourists. The reception foyer was closed inside the motel, but night lights had been left on for guests. A hushed atmosphere had settled, the busy day was over as I made my way up the gloomy staircase. Halfway up I met Darius coming down, genuine smiles were exchanged, I was really grateful, so when he offered me a nightcap to finish my day, I thought why not.

Darius knew this motel like the back of his hand; it was his 'home away from home'. I stood in the warmth of the fire, its soft light glowed on the wall and on our faces in the small private lounge room. One long couch encircled the room. Darius made sure I was close to the fire, then he lifted an old brass teapot that was sitting on the hearth. "Mulled wine?" he asked. How could I refuse? In the most romantic of places, where a fire glowed, fur-covered cushions scattered on couch and floor, the mulled wine tasted like Christmas in my mouth. Beside me sat Dariusa a tall, middle-aged, slim, handsome man with greying temples. The scene was set, I wished I had brushed my teeth. Darius's hand snaked around my shoulders; his wine breath brushed my ear. A hint of aftershave tickled my nose, and I leant into him a little.

"Excuse me, Tara!" The magic disappeared as he pulled back. In his hand was a large photo frame; he proudly said, "My family." I felt stupid, then I felt awful; I had fancied a married man. Then I giggled to myself at what I had thought was about to happen.

Darius was not sure why I was giggling, so I quickly admitted, "I have no head for mulled wine." It did the trick; it eased the situation. Admiring the photo, I learnt the age and gender of each smiling face as he introduced me to his beautiful wife, five children and three grandchildren. While I finished my wine, I told him about my family in Perth, then thanked him for a lovely evening. It had been some while since I had a chance to talk about my family.

Claiming I was asleep on my feet, I made my way to my room, where the two Yakkity Yanks were wrapped around each other once again. I realised how much I missed the feeling of another body pressed close to mine, of words soft and comforting at night, a soft kiss on my lips. I felt quite lonely as I fell asleep that night, tucked up into a ball with my arms wrapped around a feather pillow. There was only one way to get rid of the loneliness feeling, and that was to count my blessings, and that included Gordi, for without his commitment to my writing skills I would have never thought to enter a short story into a competition. I thought about how much I had achieved, where I had been, the people I had met; the experiences and stories I had been told to write about. There was so much to be grateful for, yet deep inside I still yearned for one strong pair of arms to hold me. I was not wanting the fairytale romance, I had already had that, and I had been in a volatile drama-filled relationship.

What I yearned for was a deep friendship – a partnership of like minds, a friendship that challenged and comforted, one that made no excuses or blamed others for mistakes. It irked me a little to think that maybe this was it, a life full of adventure, but on my own.

Lake Moeraki was on the itinerary for the following day, it meant we would drive across the island, if I was looking for adventure and a new book to write, well I certainly had it in spades on this tour. I woke feeling tired; in the mirror after a hot shower, I saw that I looked tired. There was no smile in my eyes, my hair had once more grown out of shape, and I had 'hat hair' from constantly wearing a woollen beanie. I felt like someone had given me bad news, I was grumpy and flat, and it showed.

At breakfast, the two Yakkity Yanks had saved me a seat at their table; my normal healthy appetite had lost its mojo. I buttered myself a piece of toast, slapped some peanut butter on it and bit into it, with very little enthusiasm. "Bad night?" asked Delta. I shook my head; I could feel the sting of tears behind my eyes.

Fran patted the hand that held the piece of toast, it bobbed up and down; her eyes held a look of empathy. "Missing someone special, sweetie?" I nodded, excused myself and bolted for the room.

I had no idea why I cried, maybe because I just had to get rid of all the crap that had been sitting around in my head, the constant, *Did I do the right or wrong thing?* When I returned to the table Fran pulled me to her and rocked me gently against her while Delta fetched a hot takeaway cup of tea from the foyer. On her return she said the coach was getting ready to leave, the passengers were starting to congregate with their bags. There was no way I could talk it all out now; it would take forever to tell them about Gordi, and my huge disappointment in the way it had ended between us, how we had all felt he was part of the family, and how I had finally come around to the idea of spending the rest of my life with him, just to have my heart broken. That would all have to wait till later.

As I boarded the coach it was obvious that I had been crying; large sunglasses jammed onto my face, my beanie pulled down, my face covered in oily suntan lotion. The Yakkity Yanks twittered behind me as I made my way to my usual place in the back of the coach. As we drove off I stretched out on the back seat, and while everyone else faced forward in anticipation of the day's journey, I finally acknowledged my loss and quietly wept away my grief for the man I had slowly come to love, despite the drinking, the attention-seeking, the temper tantrums; despite the jealousy and the put-downs, despite the constant negativity about everything I wanted to do; I missed our conversations, into which he injected his passionate opinions, whether or not they were justified. He had been a big presence in my life, and we had had so many adventures together. I had not given myself a chance to express any of this; I had driven it so far down inside me. His drinking I could not accept, but I had to applaud his efforts to overcome it. It was his multilayered personality that had finally pulled us apart. His bloody family added another impervious layer between us.

For one tiny instant I wished his mother had died, it would have been so much easier for us to get on with our lives the way we wanted, without him feeling the need to report to her everything we did. Even our wedding had been changed, designed around the travel and accommodation requirements of his stupid family. The tears dried up and turned to anger as it occurred to me how sad it was that a man in his late fifties was still controlled by his mummy – a man who had never left the breast, not really, anyway. It was time to put on my big girl pants and get on with my life.

Getting over the anger, the sense of loss, I resolved to move on with my life; I deserved some happiness. I sat up, put on some make-up, combed back my ratty hair, pulled on my beanie and got out my laptop. Very soon Lake Moeraki came into view, and what a stunning view it was. Picture perfect, with Mt Cook as the backdrop, and the sky was so clear. The lake mirrored the sky, reflecting the mountains and one small cloud that decorated Mt Cook.

People visited this isolated village for one reason: the Moeraki Boulders. I had clambered all over the Devils Marbles in Australia, they were a rich amber in colour. However, these boulders were also a contender for the title of Ginormous, these impressive grey giants were the remnants of a volcanic yesteryear when Australia and New Zealand were once just one joined land mass, known as Gondwana.

It appeared that I had been nominated as chief photographer for the day; couples and groups sat on or stood by the boulders with smiling faces as I snapped. Some posed, looking into the horizon like timeworn travellers, others slumped against the rock as if to say, 'Let's get it over with', a few men posed as if they had just tamed a wild beast, arms across their chests, or hands on hips, beaming at the lens – all that was missing was an old blunderbuss. When it was my turn, I climbed to the top of the very bottom boulder, whipped off my beanie and stood with outstretched arms. The cold wind caught my breath as I yelled, "I'm alive!" Delta thought she could do the same; it took a team of people to push her to the top; with a very wobbly stance and a hitching up of her jeans, she posed like a dancer with her hands above her head. I snapped her photo, then while she was helped down, I took a peep at the photo I had just snapped of her with a wide lens camera and realised I had taken the perfect shot. There stood Delta with her legs spread apart in a V, her arms forming a circle with the sun a perfect ball of yellow between them. She was holding the sun! I could not wait to show her.

Lunch was a picnic on the shore. As chilly as it was, it was lovely to be outside in the fresh air. We, each had a pack of three sandwiches, a muesli bar and a piece of fruit. My two roomies and I sat together; after finding a nice sheltered spot amongst the boulders, off came our hats, coats, boots and socks. We wriggled our pink toes in the nippy air. I had noticed that Delta and Fran had cast off the gold and diamond jewellery that they seemed to stack on every day, they had simplified their dress and where now wearing jeans and jumpers, like I did, and had started wearing socks and boots during the day. Today they sported one glamorous item each: beautiful, weaved, hooded anoraks that, they informed me, were made in Mexico. I had to admit the colours were stunning; so earthy and rich.

CHAPTER 41

We had an hour to enjoy time off the coach, and I was really enjoying their company. They seemed to enjoy mine too. It was here that I told them about my family in Australia; they also told me their story. They formed a close friendship while attending the same primary school; their parents were close as well, both families were immersed in the church. They went on to become college students, then honour students, Delta in science, Fran in literacy, this was when they broke the unspoken rule.

Delta was staying overnight at Fran's house; they had often done so but when they were caught cuddling each other in bed, Delta was marched back to her home; a meeting followed with both families and the church board in attendance. It was soon concluded that, as Delta seemed to be the more outspoken one, she was immoral company for Fran and would be removed to a boarding school two states away.

Delta explained, "We did not know what our bodies were saying that night as we lay in bed, I got all hot and steamy, Fran felt the same way. We kissed, and the rest just happened naturally. We were so young, we had no idea of what we were doing; all I knew was that I wanted something to happen, it was like a bubble of the unknown that was waiting to explode inside me. I was sent away; the next time I saw Fran we were in our twenties; she was married with a baby on the way. I was engaged to a university man; I thought we were happy. About seven years later, we met again at my mother's funeral. By that time I was divorced, a mum of three but still on great terms with my ex-husband. After the funeral I was exhausted and needed a quick nap. Fran came up to say hi, she put her arms around me. That was the moment I knew I still had the hots for my best friend. It took another year and many phone conversations, in the end we decided we had to try to build our relationship together. We arranged for my sister to babysit, and Fran's husband would have her kids; we told them we were having a catch up – a lady's night out. We booked a room at the casino, had dinner, had a drink, went upstairs and made love. I can honestly say it was bells and whistles for me; it was then we both knew we had been living lives that had been prescribed for us – fulfilling the American dream of the nuclear family, happy ever after was not.

"It's been a hard road gaining family acceptance, it was a difficult time for us both. It was hard to be in the public eye, maintaining my camera business and Fran hers, while wearing the label of lesbians. That's why we hide it from most people, but you seem okay with it?"

I had to stop and think about that one. These two had never offended me or been lewd in any manner or form in any way while in my presence. Sure, I had seen them cuddling in bed, I had not been offended, in fact, I had been a tad envious of the love between them. I told them about my first trip to New Zealand, of my experience with Gilly who had been my first lesbian friend; her bad behaviour had me wondering if that was normal, I told them of her behaviour on the plane and her disappointing treatment after we had landed, but also admitting in hindsight if not for Gilly I would not have met Margi and her wonderful family.

There would have been no adventure to New Zealand on my own, or all the discoveries I had made about me and my life. The experiences I had were all enriching. Maybe I should be grateful? Not for what she put me through, but where it eventually led. In fact, the more I thought about it the more I realised everything I had done, with so many different people, had connected me to this minute, right now. This experience of New Zealand I written about and had been published in a previous book, and yes, my experience with Gilly was definitely in it.

Our driver tooted the horn; It was time to get back on the coach. I packed away the wrappings from our picnic, while Delta and Fran helped each other with their socks and boots. Back on the coach we were off to Milford Sound, I showed them the photo of Delta on top of the boulder.

She was overjoyed. "Oh wow, that's really fabulous, thanks, Tara." This had the rest of the passengers checking their cameras for their own stunning shots at the Moeraki boulders.

The evening ahead sounded like it was going to be fun. We were booked into a small lodge by the waterside, dinner was to be held on a small steamboat circling the harbour, accompanied by a classical string quartet. It sounded heavenly, as long as it was calm enough for us to enjoy the cruise. I had decided that there would be no coach club get-together for blogging lessons, no discussion on the merits of the various social media platforms, I was going to relax and soak in the wonders of Milford Sound. After this last trip we were given a choice: we could swap coaches and continue to Mt Cook, or fly back to Christchurch from Milford Sound. The line up to see Mt Cook was long, and all seats taken by the time I was at the reception desk, my opportunity to get up close and personal with Mt Cook had gone. By all accounts, the weather conditions were perfect for it, and from whichever angle I had seen it as we twisted and turned around those tight corners, it looked amazing. The Māori name for Mt Cook is Aoraki and, as the word tumbled around in my mouth, disappointment sat heavily in my chest.

In a light bulb moment I knew what I was going to do. I was off to join the cruise ship. It was still hard to say it without the biggest smile breaking out; so, time to speak to my family and say they were more than welcome to come to New Zealand, the money was theirs to do what they wished with, but I would not be meeting them. If they wanted, they could make their own plans and tour as a family. I already knew the perfect motorhome company for them, for now, Milford Sound and my next adventure were just around the next bend in the road. Milford Sound is everything they say it is. It's magnificent in every way. We arrived early in the afternoon and checked into the lodge, very Swiss in design inside and out, it was incredibly pretty. Unlike the basic lodging of the previous few nights, this was no dormitory, we each had our own room. Mine was tucked away to the side; it was quite small but so inviting. Around the windows, the New Zealand native silver fern grew in abundance, while daffodils and jonquils in earthenware pots dotted the small courtyard outside my door.

The bed was so comfy; a deep green feather doona covered the brown cotton sheets. The room also contained a suitcase rack, a small wardrobe and a small bathroom with a shower with the obligatory pamper pack. It was all I needed.

We were told to be at the reception desk at 5pm pronto, or the minibus to the steam paddleboat would leave without us. This left me three hours to freshen up, have a nanna nap, enjoy my own time in my own room and check in with my family to update them as to my plans. I was disappointed when no-one picked up their mobile phones. I rang the house phone and left a message, saying I would call again tomorrow.

The itinerary specified the attire for this night was semi-formal, we were invited to have dinner at the captain's table. It had been nearly three months since I had last glammed up at the Cairns Casino; I had no evening wear, only the day clothes I had bought at Farmers in Christchurch for my date with Gordi. *I am going to have to be creative,* I thought, as I overheard the other women on the bus chatting about the attire they had brought along for just this night. I shook out my pants and jacket, then ran the hot shower till the bathroom was steamy. Hanging them both on the towel rail, I crossed my fingers that the wrinkles would fall out; they had not travelled well. I searched for my new city shoes, only to find they had disappeared.

Nothing for it: I could go barefoot or in what I had. Once I dressed, in my semi-wrinkled city clothed fluffed and tucked, put on a bit of make-up to add colour on my face, as for my freshly washed hair, it settled back down to what looked like a basin cut once more. I entered the hotel foyer. The entire group was in evening gear; I stood out like an odd duck in army boots. Some looked me up and down then ignored me, some nodded as I made my way into the room where my two Yakkity Yanks were waiting. They put their arms through mine and welcomed me with wide smiles.

I had always loved to dress up and look glam, catch an eye or two. And to be honest, I still did. Then I thought of the promised cruise and how I would enjoy some shopping before I boarded. I knew just how fortunate I was though; I had lived a good life and had some amazing adventures. I would make tonight a gratitude night, and not worry about the opinions of others; I was going to enjoy myself no matter how much I failed to comply with the dress code.

Delta and Fran both looked fabulous; in fact, everyone had on their best bib and tucker. Delta slipped her arm through mine; Fran smiled, and aiming her phone camera at me instructing me to 'say cheese'.

CHAPTER 42

I fell in love with this boat. As we glided along the dark water, fine droplets shone like mini chandeliers as they flew up in the air, reflecting the moonlight. We dined on fresh oysters and a dish made by our Māori chef called a Milford Waterfall, made with watercress and mountain herbs. The main dish was hoki, a white flaky fish, served with fresh steamed vegies and a white wine sauce. For dessert, we each received an individual Bombe Alaska. While we finished our wine, coffee was served, a Strauss waltz was played over the intercom; it was perfect. I watched a few couples move to the very small dance floor, thinking how I loved to dance. I must have looked a bit too longingly; a young crew member asked me to do him the honour; he held out his arm which I accepted. Not many can say they have waltzed under the Milford Sound moonlight with a good-looking young man, army boots and all.

The dancing was interrupted as we moved close to spectacular waterfall; plastic capes were handed out so we could see it without getting drenched. I heard it first; the drowning roar of water resonated in my chest, then I saw it, a wall of pure white foam against the darkness. We were mesmerised; the captain was on the intercom warning us not to go near the sides as this was a dangerous manoeuvre. At first the water sprayed gently over us as we passed by. No-one spoke and the music stopped playing, all we could hear was the throb of the motor and the thud of our hearts beating, then the crashing of the waterfall onto the rocks and against the sides of the boat.

On the way back to the wharf the music that was played was 1940s favourites. One was a song I knew well, my father used to sing it when I was a small child in his Irish accent: it was called *Are you having a little fun yet?* a real toe-tapper. Soon we found ourselves singing along to tunes from the fifties; Dean Martin and Frank Sinatra were definite favourites. As quickly as a candle is snuffed out we were back at the wharf, each lady was given a cream silk rose as we departed the beautiful paddle-steamer as a memory of this trip. I went to sleep with a smile; I had the best night: I had danced, dined on beautiful food, had great company with lots of laughter, and most of all, I'd had fun. The whole trip had been wonderful, would I do it again? Maybe, who knows where I would end up. Tomorrow, for me, was a flight back to Christchurch .

There are not enough words to describe Mt Cook; on such a clear day as today, without the constant cloud that covers New Zealand nonstop, in any case as my camera focused, I was speechless. I was up at dawn not wanting to waste a minute of my last day here. The kitchen staff surprised at my sudden appearance at the galley door to beg a mug of hot coffee off them, I took that and my camera outside. As the skyline changed in colour I took photos, till the Mount showed herself, perhaps she was shy? As the mist and clouds changed, it looked like wrappers of soft gauze lifting, the light surrounding her changed so slowly, like a slow heartbeat, I looked at the timer on the camera, I was watching the changes and snapping a shot every twenty seconds. I was so close.

While I was busily taking photos some kea birds decided to pay a visit. These are New Zealand's flightless parrot. They are not small birds; they are a bit like a large plump cockatoo in shape and size. They are very pretty, with iridescent green feathers, tiny red eyes and wicked-looking sharp beaks and claws. Two landed on the tour coach and within seconds were attacking the window wipers, and another two came really close to where I was sitting. I am a bird lover, but these parrots had such a mean look in their eyes as they strutted towards me, I had no idea if they meant harm or were just curious, but I was not going to wait to find out. I went inside and told the coach driver about the parrots; he spat out a few things he would like to do with them, which I'm sure is highly illegal, even in New Zealand, and rushed outside to scare them off, far too late by the looks of it. They had demolished one of the window wipers completely; it hung off its little hook and was swinging in the light breeze. The keas were now ripping holes in a canvas car cover.

"You little bastards!" came from the kitchen area. A bucket of hot water was hurled at them; for a flightless bird they sure move fast. For those of us who weren't dealing with the damage, this was quite amusing. While all the excitement was going on I pulled the tour driver aside informing him I was not carrying on with the tour. He was disappointed.

"That's a shame; you seem to keep them occupied, his head nodding at the other tourists. By now I normally have half a dozen unhappy campers." He asked me to sign a form saying I was leaving the tour which I did quite happily then informed me to report to the reception desk and enquire about planes. I was told to check with the airport to see if a private flight was available. I called but was only able to leave a message. It was only just 7am. Meanwhile the other travellers were gathering for breakfast. I was feeling hungry so I joined the tour queue, only to be told by the driver that if I was joining them for breakfast I would have to pay, as I had formally left the tour.

"You're kidding, right, that's a bit rude."

"Sorry lovey, them's the rules. I don't make 'em I only work for 'em."

It's funny how the universe shows its hand just when you think you're in control. I was at the reception desk when the coach driver was told there would be no window wipers delivered for two days, and no planes would be coming in or going out, due to a blizzard warning. I had noticed the white flakes falling; the driver and I looked at each other.

"Looks like we're bloody stuck here. Can't drive with only one wiper."

If I could have said anything it would have been, *Lord, get me out of here*. I could tell by their faces, the other travellers were not happy campers; they were just a group of growling, unhappy people. I felt sorry for the driver; it was not his fault. I had now come to terms that I would not be going anywhere myself; no-one had rung me from the local airport, so I immediately rebooked the same room for another night. I bought two oranges, a bag of chippies and large bottle of cranberry juice and took my bag in my room where I made myself comfy plumping up cushions to place around me, plugged in my laptop and watched a series I had downloaded onto a thumb drive some time ago: *Game of Thrones*, season one.

I backed the goodies and booed the baddies; it certainly was a very unusual show. I had almost finished the first episode when I heard Delta call out my name.

"Tara, you in, honey?" I wanted to say, *Where else would I be?* but I did not want to hurt anyone's feelings. Putting it on pause and opening my door I found Fran and Delta with three mugs of steaming Milo and huge chocolate muffins. "Can we come in? We brought you morning tea."

I pulled the door wide. "Of course you can!" then putting a finger to my lips to say 'shoosh'. *Game of Thrones* episode two was about to start. We all sat on the one bed with a blanket over us, munching and slurping our way through the series, till the last rolling edits had died on the screen.

"I hear you're leaving us." Fran said as I was about to press eject.

"I was, but by the looks of it won't be for a day or two now."

Fran patted my hand; "I'm glad; we love your company."

Delta was looking thoughtful. "Have you seen *Game of Thrones* before, Tara?"

I admitted I had not, and a phone call was made to her son for a password and a few buttons pushed we were able to settle back and watch the all the series. I loved it, this was where I knew I wanted to be, the one small taste of the movie world had wet my appetite for more.

I woke late the next morning. The snow had stopped falling; the room was chilly, so I turned the wall heater up then padded off to have a warming shower. Bliss! Hot water cascaded down my scalp then slid over my back. Once I had towelled off I did some back stretching exercises. I had not been keeping up with my yoga exercises and I had found that all the sitting around on the tour had not been good for my back. For days now it had been stiff when I first woke up; the cold seemed to affect my lumbar region. I could not understand why I had a sore neck at times; it was Gordi who had educated me about our body parts all being connected. "Too much sitting and leaning over your desktop, Tara! Learn to stand up and take big breaks from your desk."

I could certainly do with a massage right now, I thought as I stretched into another position. Breakfast was finished by the time I arrived at the dining room, so I made do with a cup of instant coffee. The day cook made me an egg sandwich, which, I was reminded, would be added to my bill. For some reason this niggled me; it seemed so trivial, so wrong. Yesterday I was the guru that kept everyone entertained, now I was paying for an instant coffee and egg sandwich. I was still eating when I heard a bit of a squabble, a lover's tiff by the sounds of it. I discovered Fran had lost her hearing aid, she had taken it out last night as she had gone to bed. She was rummaging through the many black sacks of paper rubbish looking for it, while Delta had the manager in deep conversation. Stopping Fran, I took one look at the mound of rubbish there was and thought, *Oh well, in for a penny, in for a pound,* and joined her in her search. We were halfway through the third black sack, both of us knee-deep in paper of every kind when the motel manager called my name. He was waving the phone at me; it was the airport saying the flight crew had found a small window in the weather, it was now or never, if I was ready, I had a flight to Christchurch, this was an opportunity I could not miss. Aoraki would have to wait, I was booked to leave within the hour.

The tiny airport was a twenty-minute walk from the hotel, no vehicles were leaving .Never the one to be defeated, I would have swum in the nude through the snow if that's what it took to get me away from this cold, seemingly endless snow-packed island. Thank heavens I did not have a suitcase to drag. Once I had packed everything up the manager presented me with the bill, which I still considered rude, but I reluctantly paid, while saying goodbye to Fran and Delta.

"You have my details to keep in touch; you never know where we will meet up once again." Tears fell between us; I had two new sisters who would be very hard to forget.

The coach driver held the motel door open for me; I pulled up the hood of my puffer jacket over my beanie hat and covered my eyes with my aviation sunglass. After making sure nothing was exposed, I took my first step into the soft snow. As I reached the end of the motel's driveway, I looked up and saw the arrow pointing to the airport. At that precise moment the snow stopped, the wind stopped howling; everything was thickly blanketed in pure white snow, the sun shone weakly. As I trudged along the road, the snow creaked under my feet; it was so quiet I could hear myself breathing, the exhaled air became huge white puffs of frost. Soon I could see the small dome of the airport, for one minute I stood completely still in the white stillness: no sound, no noise, no wind, just complete and utter silence.

CHAPTER 43

In the white quietness, I sensed the tiniest of whispers curling around me: *Scribe*. No! I was not ready, not yet, I started to run towards a block shape building, it felt like that word was about to involve me in something I knew nothing about. I literally threw myself inside the door of the building I was heading for, my breath coming in huge gulping gasps until I felt nauseous. I was greeted with, "Oh, here she is, I presume you're Tara, you're just in time, there is another storm approaching, no time for latecomers." I could not answer her, my pulse was so fast. "No time for niceties, hon," the lady said, passing me a takeaway cup of something hot and some sort of prepacked biscuits. I could hear the drone of a plane, then saw it in the azure blue sky. It was like looking at a small pinprick in the ice blue canvas; gradually it grew, first a thimble, then it was the size of a cup by the time it swooped down, coming to a stop right in front of the exit doors. The snow skiis scooped up the soft white snow and flung it around us as the pilot bought the plane to a stop. He cut the engine and the propellers whirled slowly to an almost stop. The pilot jumped out and handed a large post bag to a person who was obviously waiting for them.

Motioning me to join him, the pilot quickly resumed his seat in the plane and started the propellers again. Ducking low, I ran for that plane like there were demons after me; I really did not want to stay another night. I was determined to get to Christchurch and continue my journey. I strapped myself in, the pilot gave me thumbs up and pushed a set of headphones towards me.

"Hello, Tara." Darius, my helicopter pilot from Fox Glacier was my knight in shining armour once again. We taxied to what looked like a large lump of snow, then he turned the plane around and we faced Mt Cook as we gathered speed and took off, leaping into the air with a gut-dropping bounce. I was on my way.

"Feel like a quick look at the Mount?" Darius asked. I nodded; it had been one of the top things on my list and I had been disappointed in myself for not fulfilling that promise, but maybe now I would have that chance.

Darius was a highly experienced pilot; he handled the plane beautifully through the updraughts and downdraughts. I was in complete awe of his ability to keep flying smoothly; it was as if his hands were just an extension of this small dot in the sky. Her name was Becca, he was speaking to her in a low soft voice whenever she struggled with an air current; a few times, when he saw my hand tighten on the door handles, he used the same tone to soothe my nerves.

"It's alright, Tara, nearly there." His voice was almost hypnotic. We were flying so high with a world of blue ice beneath us: there was nothing but ice and sky for forever and a day. It was exhilarating and scary at the same time.

As we flew into a mile-wide crevasse, where white rows of jagged ice appeared ready to snap shut, trapping us like a Venus flytrap. It took my breath away. Darius slightly rolled Becca as he brought her out of that fissure of frozen beauty, then we flew over valleys of deep white snow. We went over a waterfall that was frozen in motion; it was so beautiful – the foam looked like lace. Flying lower, I could see an ice blue river rushing towards the land into already swollen rivers and creeks. My camera became an extension of my hand. What an amazing place, a prehistoric silent sentinel yet so alive, this really was nature at its best .

Darius spoke through the intercom, "Time to go home?"

I answered with a huge smile. "What time will we arrive?" I asked.

Darius checked his instrument panel. "Estimated ETA twelve-hundred hours." It's amazing how silent you become when you're with an almost-stranger, I had shared a glass of wine with this man, then I had met his wife and family through a photo, yet we were still strangers.

Darius seemed relaxed as we flew through banks of clouds, the currents of the wind making us dip and sometimes fly high. With his eyes firmly planted on the instruments, I relaxed; I was in good hands. I settled in to watch the changing skyline. As we flew over small townships Darius called out their names; some of them I had recently driven through or stayed in.

On arrival in Christchurch I did some quick mental planning: First, I had to confirm my intention to sail with the cruise ship company. I checked in for the night at the backpackers' across the road from the airport; I was allocated a bed in a six-bunk dorm, I paid extra for blankets and pillows. Setting myself up with pillows for a backrest and one across my knees to be my desk, it was out with pen and paper to make notes to myself. Once I was settled, it was time to ring my lawyer and have a conversation with him. There was no message from my family, I would chat with them later.

My lawyer answered his mobile straight away. "Tara, how are you? How's the holiday going?" I did not reveal a great deal, I told him I was tired of the snow and asked how my stocks and shares were doing. I heard tapping, then a whistle: "They're doing very nicely, might be time to look at another investment or two."

My lawyer had a good nose for investments. I had known him for more than twenty years; he had arranged a second mortgage for Russ and I and handled all the legal requirements when Russ died. He knew my financial status better than I did. I agreed with him. If there was a property investment he thought would be lucrative, I was happy to let him make that decision. I surprised him by saying I wished to make a slight change to my will. "I will send it off in PDF document, is that legal? Can I email it to you?"

There was a minute silence then, "As long as you have signed it and thought it over carefully, you know a signed document is legal tender, don't you?"

I did not add my personal thoughts to our conversation; he respected me as his client and I him as my legal advisor. "You will have it by tomorrow, then I'm away a few weeks on a cruise to Asia."

"Lucky you, Tara, enjoy, stay safe."

My next call was to Rae and Kane, "I'm sorry gang, I won't be able to meet you, I fly into Wellington tomorrow to join the cruise. Sorry it's such short notice but being snowbound and making it on time for this cruise certainly put a dent in my plans."

I waited while they had a family discussion, then Rae spoke again: "Mum,

I have another idea. We could wait till you come back, we could hire a mobile home and as a family travel up to the Ningaloo reef, we could go inland to Tom Price and I could see what Dad loved so much about the outback; Jess' school holidays start in two months, it would make it much easier for us all. That's if you don't mind."

"Of course I don't mind. That money is yours and Kane's, and I think that's a perfect idea."

My next call was to the cruise company. I spoke to the staff coordinator, Miss Marchant, explaining who I was. She sounded like a no-nonsense sort of person; sharp staccato answers that were very much to the point. I was expected on board at twelve-noon on Tuesday; today was Sunday, I was expected to complete staff training plus all the documentation, and present myself to the ship's personal officer once I had been cleared by security and was onboard.

That did not leave me very long to shop for some cruise-appropriate clothing; first and most urgently I needed to secure a flight to Wellington. My tum growled, I needed to find something to eat; there was a Chinese takeaway two doors down, egg noodles and steamed veggies were perfect. After a cappuccino I was ready to move on with the next stage of my adventure to find a flight, I found myself a small spot in a park that was out of the wind, taking my first bite of this lovely hot food I suddenly remembered standing still in the snow and hearing the word *Scribe*. Goosebumps creeped up the flesh on my arms. I shrugged it off, I would deal with that later, as another thought had scurried into my mind. Rae's suggestion that I join them on a holiday travelling up north once I was home in Perth, why not?

My fingers clicked onto Google and came up with the closest flight centre to where I was staying; soon after I hailed a passing cab giving the address of the Mid-City Mall.

CHAPTER 44

'Farmers, the department store in New Zealand that sells everything', according to their ads. I had to agree, there was even a very small Flight Centre tucked in beside the elevator.

"Scotty, the one and only," introduced himself to me, his bored, tired expression changing to one of animated delight as he asked me to take a seat, almost pushing me into the chair opposite his desk.

"I can have you there first thing in the morning, leaving on the Air New Zealand 5:30am 'red eye' flight. It is due to arrive in Wellington at 6:45am."

That would involve being up at 4am to get a taxi to the domestic terminal for check in by 5am. I asked if there was a later flight; anyone would have thought I had asked for the crown jewels. Scotty scowled over his computer. "I have just booked you a seat on this flight."

I could feel my temper fraying. Leaning closer to him I said, "Scotty, is there a later flight, or not?" It was obvious this cranky person was going to play games, and I was not in the mood.

"Okay, 5am flight it is," I waved my card over the machine, it blipped, then the word 'declined' appeared on the screen. My first thought was, *No! Bloody Gordi, not again.*

Scotty cleared his throat, "We are closing in a half hour, madam, perhaps come back tomorrow." He stood, ushering me out. What the hell? Closing time? I had not realised the time. When closing time arrives in New Zealand, it is non-negotiable, I had learnt that through past experience. Even Farmers was closing its doors as I made my way back out to the footpath.

Okay, Tara, I thought, *it is time for that thinking cap.* Walking to the backpackers' I passed an ATM. I would clear one mystery up first. My bank balance showed I was twenty-five dollars overdrawn; it was my own fault for not transferring money across. What cheered me up was the thought that I would book my own flight, at the time I wanted, or so I thought.

When I arrived at the backpackers', a group of young people were booking in for the night, they were staying in the same room as me. I was dreading my night in a room of party people, so I was pleasantly surprised that once they had found a bed each, they got busy playing games on their iPads and texting on their phones. I got busy checking out flights to Wellington. It seemed like everything was fully booked; God knows what would happen if I missed my cruise, my sense of humour taking over, as an old saying ran through my thoughts. 'Well, I guess you missed the boat'. My fingers were scrolling down the screen to look at all flights possible to Wellington.

A young redhead with cheerful blue eyes called over to me, "What up, Mrs? You look horribly pissed off." I was sure she looked familiar, however, on this trip I had not spent any time with any young ones, and I would certainly remember this one with carrot-red hair. But those eyes, I knew I had seen them before.

"I am. I've got to be in Wellington tomorrow, but I can't find a flight."

She walked over to me, holding out her hand. "Hi, I'm Larisa, Larry for short. What's the problem?" I explained about starting work on a cruise ship, and how it was imperative I be there at midday. I felt silly telling this young one my woes, including my error in transferring money.

"Let me make a call, I might be able to help," Larry said. I smiled. How sweet, and how on earth could a young teenager find me a flight? *But that's so lovely of her,* I thought. I went back to my search. Larry sauntered back to the dorm: "Hope your bags are packed, my dad's going to wait for you at the airport. He's flying over to Wellington tonight."

Then it clicked. I did know her – well, kind of. A week ago I was staring at a photo of her in a motel.

"Is your dad Darius?"

"Sure is! Hey, how did you know that?"

"It's a small world, Larry." I said I would leave that for her father to explain. I pushed on my boots and repacked my bag. I waved her goodbye and headed towards Terminal AO40, the same one I had walked out of a few hours ago, God bless Darius and his big heart. It was close to 6pm as I walked towards the small plane. The hangar lights were ablaze, Darius was doing his pre-flight checks. He shaded his eyes when I called his name. "Is that you, Tara? What on earth's going on? Larisa, my eldest, just rang and asked me to wait for a friend of hers, said it was urgent I get her to Wellington tonight. I had no idea it was you!"

It was nice to be welcomed by a huge bear hug by this pilot who had taken me under his wing in more ways than one.

Once again, he asked me to put on a pair of earphones and we buckled up. The crackling of the take-off procedure began, we got the thumbs up. The propellers roared, we rode down the runway – a short one but enough for a perfect take-off. I adore this part of the flight, and this was no different, once again I was in the cockpit and could see everything ticking over, clicking away as it should, I understood nothing, I just knew I was in safe hands. As we taxied down the runway, I heard the 'all-clear, mate', I had a front-seat view as the nose of this wee plane lifted up into the dusk of the South Pacific sky. I felt like I could have easily reached out and filled my pockets with stars.

"So, no more touring for you, Tara? Going home, are you?" He chuckled when I told him my next adventure. "A cruise? You certainly don't sit still for long do you, you should write a book, Tara!" Funny he should say that.

Seeing the lights of Wellington, my stomach did a huge flip. I had a feeling that this cruise was going to be very different; I did not know how, but I knew. Darius flew over the Wellington harbour he pointed out the ship, "I'm guessing that's your ride for a few weeks. I don't know if I should envy you or wish you luck, the ocean and I don't get on, believe or not I get sea sick." Yes, this was my next ride, as Darius had put it, I could just make out her name, the Pacific Princess was lit up like a Christmas tree. It was an amazing sight from the air, and tomorrow I was boarding her. I could not wipe the smile from my face.

"Now to find myself a place to stay," I thought out loud. Darius bought me to my senses.

"Tara, it's late. Did you not think to book ahead?"

I shook my head, "No, not really, all I was thinking was how I was getting to Wellington." It was a bumpy landing, Darius talking, coaxing his plane Becca. We taxied to a stop, the cold Wellington wind that blows forever and a day caught my breath as I opened the door, fighting to keep it in my hands and not smash against the side of the plane.

Darius rushed to help me off the plane, even taking off my earphones like I was a child. He ushered me into the hangar which was dimly lit and opened the office up saying, "Grab yourself a chair, I'm going to tie my little lady down."

Maybe if I was not an author, I would not have quipped, "Oh, chains, leather or rope?" He stopped in mid-stride, shook his head and carried on. I was worried that I had offended him. Oh well, it wasn't the first time I had opened my mouth and stupidly put both feet in it.

Once Darius had gone, the stillness of the room took over. More than once on this adventure I had experienced the sound of stillness. I could hear the blood pumping in my veins, my heartbeat, my pulse. I was still not comfortable with it.

When Darius returned, he was chuckling. "Looks like you're staying with me tonight, Tara, there's not much accommodation around here. I just spoke to my missus and told her I was sleeping with you instead." He saw my eyebrows shoot up, "Don't stress, I won't ravish you, well not too much, anyway." He walked towards me, I was ready to bolt, when his hands moved me aside, he pulled out a folding cot. "This is yours till 6am tomorrow. That's when I fly back to Christchurch."

He took my vacated chair and stretched his long legs onto a stool. With his arms across his chest, he promptly fell asleep. I was grateful, and despite being cold and uncomfortable I slept till the smell of coffee woke me. There's nothing like a rich brown wake-up shot of caffeine, it was so strong I could stand a teaspoon up in it, but it worked. I washed my face and hands in the bathroom.

"I've ordered a taxi for you; it might be a good idea to find a motel and clean up a bit before your appointment." I could see him looking me up and down. He was right, I had seen only half of me in the bathroom mirror, and what a mess!

CHAPTER 45

Hugging my pilot and silently wishing his lady love Becca kept him safe, I walked to the gates. A taxi pulled up, I turned and waved once more but Darius had his back to me, he was busy on the phone. For some reason, a feeling of acute loneliness washed over me.

"Where to, lady?" the cabbie asked.

I shrugged, "Do you know of any good motels or hotels around here? Close to the harbour if possible."

Within fifteen minutes I was entering the foyer of the Lambton Quay Hotel; it was not super plush but had exactly what I wanted. It was reasonably priced and very clean. The double bed looked so welcoming. I had re booked the taxi for eleven-thirty that morning; thankfully, this bathroom was fully stocked with all the goodies a girl likes. I placed a room order for one, eggs benedict, French toast and a large pot of English breakfast tea, it was now time to do what a girl has to do to feel fresh and clean. I had no sooner wrapped myself up in the supplied dressing gown when there was a discreet knock on the door.

"Your breakfast is here, madam." It looked and smelt divine. I settled myself on the bed and checked the time: it had just gone 8am. Munching on the glorious food, I pulled out my laptop and emailed Elsa my agent: *I'm in Wellington ready for the cruise*. Then I sent an email off to the family, *I'm in Wellington safe and sound, see you in a few weeks*. Wrote a long letter to my two mates in Perth emailing it to just one of them, I knew she would spread the news.

I had intended to find a decent clothing shop, I really did not want to turn up at the ship in my camouflage gear, so I was hoping there was a Farmers store nearby. Maybe it was the food, or the warm room, or just that I felt safe and clean – I don't know exactly, but the next thing I knew woken by the house phone in my room: "Reception here, madam, your taxi is waiting."

"Thank you, I'll be there in five minutes, please ask him to wait," I said as calmly as possible. I threw on my old clothes: army jumper and army jeans, ran a brush through my hair, made sure I had everything packed, and ran out of the room and down a flight of steps. My boots thumped on the staircase making it sound like the hotel was being invaded. The door swung open as another couple walked through, I charged outside into the waiting taxi and gasped, "City Wharf, Princess cruises."

The ship grew in proportion as we drove closer to the reporting office. She was huge, everything about her screamed 'holiday'. I knew it was only staff members who were checking in today, however a long queue was snaking down the wharf when I joined them. The smile never left my face, not even when a tired crewman in a white T-shirt and trousers shoved a clipboard jammed with papers under my nose and ordered me to check it over and sign.

I had to pinch myself as I looked at the itinerary, our first port Sydney – that is where the ship would be take on passengers, then Lombok, Singapore, Cambodia, Hanoi and Thailand. I had not been to the last three for many years, I loved Singapore and was there four years ago with a group of art lovers from my hometown Rockingham.

I signed many papers, most of them to make sure I was a legal citizen of Australia and advising I was to be insured by the cruise company but offshore it was my responsibility. I made a mental note to ring my insurance company to extend my insurance. I was given a name badge, I was now known as the arts supervisor, my employment contract was explained by a lovely Asian lady, her name was Geo. I was part of the team that kept the passengers interested and happy. My cabin was allocated and I was told I would be sharing. I was given a folder filled with instructions, Geo telling me to read it before I actually began work onboard. There were reams of paper to read and sign but in general it said:

I was not to accept anyone in my classes under the age of twelve, the children had playgroups and professional teachers to look after them. I also had a key to the portable stockroom and was asked once onboard and settled to give it a quick once-over, to write down what was needed and report to my supervisor. I had a meal schedule and was informed there was no association with the passengers. To disregard the last rule was immediate dismissal: no matter what port we were in, we would find our own way home. Wow, that was a lot to take in, especially all the reading paraphernalia. I was not permitted to take my phone to any workshops, I was allowed a small mic if deemed necessary. I was also asked to make myself available for talks on books and group meetings plus assist not only with a written description of art but to assist with the daily art auctions if the staff were unavailable in any way. My mind wandered to the recent auction I had attended with my friends in Rockingham. I had been impressed with the gavel-banging and the verbal excitement as the prices soared.

My wages had already been established; I was pleasantly surprised by the amount I was to be paid. Two hours later I was taken through a fire drill plus a fitness drill. I seemed to have passed, no-one asked me to leave. I was escorted to my cabin, deep in the dungeon of this mammoth, which I learnt I was sharing with three other staff members. There was to be a staff meeting at 3pm sharp: casual dress was specified. Little did they know I did not have a choice; I was standing up in everything I owned, except for my other grubby, wrinkled items that looked so bad I could not possibly wear them. I asked if I could do some essential shopping whilst still in port (it felt so weird to ask permission to go shopping); the answer was no, there were shops onboard with a staff discount. I found my way to the staff meeting wearing my boots, jumper and jeans, with a little bit of lippy and my hair brushed; some of the other staff were clearly thinking, *Who let her onboard?* One soft drink from the bar was offered, I had not realised how thirsty I was till I was through the formal introductions and meetings, the soft drink tasted like nectar .

After the meeting, my supervisor Geo offered to show me my portable stockroom. Again we walked through miles of corridors and down several flights of stairs into a basement area. Geo produced a key, opening up an Aladdin's cave of colour; crayons, paints, pencils, paper, stencils, rulers, chalk pads, and for each client a ships journal to fill out daily with every sort of decoration you could imagine, from little tubes of glitter to rolls of stick-on alphabet letters, each item was labelled and boxed, my job for the next two hours was to make it all was labelled and put away correctly, Geo beside me advising and helping me understand what was to go where. I tore off with cellophane wrappers of all descriptions and placing the articles into the waiting draws.

I fell in love instantly. I was going to be very happy showing the creative souls in my groups the many ways you could enjoy the art in my workshops. Geo walked me back to my cabin saying, "It's a lot to take in, Tara, but once you get it you'll be fine." We could hear laughter from my cabin. Geo commenting, "They're all old hands at this sort of thing, they will soon have you running around the ship, knowing what is behind every staircase."

I opened the door and was greeted by silence; three faces looked at me. I smiled and said, "Hey, my name's Tara. I'm the arts supervisor."

Gretel, Monnie and Lisa, who were all from Romania, relaxed when they saw I was not a big bad wolf, that I did have a sense of humour and I did not mind which bunk I slept in. When they saw the condition of my clothes, I explained where I had been and what I had done over the past three months. They decided I needed some help. These three girls shepherded me to the hairdresser's, who was only just setting up. "I'm not open, ladies" he bellowed, Monnie winked at me, and batted her extra-long eyelashes, purring something in his ear. I immediately found myself with a long black nylon cape around my shoulders, then seated in the huge marshmallow of a chair. My hair being washed with the warmest of water, his long fingers kneading deep into my scalp, heaven. Without consultation, he snipped so much hair that I thought I was getting a crew cut. When he finished, he slathered gel on my hair and blow-dried it. I was so surprised, the very short pixie cut made me look so much younger. Gretel, as it happened, was the ship's manicurist, she trimmed my nails and filed them short, applying a clear nail varnish. Then my three new friends lead me to the ship's crew shop. I was provided with the promised white T-shirt with blue banding for formal nights, two blue T-shirts for workshops and day wear, a pair of shorts and white sneakers that were very comfy, at the chemist I bought a tiny tub of hair gel, lip gloss, moisturiser and the all-important painkillers. I had not had any lunch and was feeling tired, joining my three new friends at the ship's crew café, then went back to our cabin. I was feeling exhausted, I did not want dinner it was only 6pm, I said my goodnights, I don't remember them closing the cabin door.

CHAPTER 46

It was 2am when I woke, I found the cabin too hot, the girls were sound asleep, I left as quietly as I could making my way through the maze of corridors up onto the deck. There was no-one in sight, just me and the cold, biting wind. Sitting on a deckchair I gathered my thoughts; the past forty-eight hours had been a whirlwind just making sure I got here on time. I knew I had done the right thing, I was supposed to be here, smelling the salty sea air and watching seagulls fight for fish in the harbour waters. My phone beeped; it was Elsa, I was awake, so I rang her immediately, she was breathless with excitement – I was her most successful client yet. My signature was needed for more paper work once I had finished my cruise, I would have a month off then Elsa had booked me on a tour to Ako in Japan as an arts representative; once back from there I would have a two-week break, then she had booked into another magical opportunity writers retreat at Crom Castle in Ireland, where I was booked in tto be a guest speaker courtesy of a well-known publisher Serenity Press.. After that, I would have four months of my own time. I thought of my family waiting for me to come home and have a holiday with them, hopefully they would understand and have that holiday with or without me.

Elsa and I agreed to meet, I would text her a s soon as I knew our ETA. I was still sitting in my corner of the deck when the motors began to throb; it was deep, satisfying throb biting into my core. I knew that sound meant one thing; we were on our way. *Cast-off starboard*; *all clear*: the gangway was hauled in, and a flurry of commands were issued. My three sleepy cabin buddies had joined me, each one in their pyjamas and each one holding a flower to throw into the water as we left port. I looked puzzled; they said in unison that it was to make sure we would have a safe journey and will one day return.

The ship's lights were ablaze in the early dawn as we left the deck, a fairytale of lights leaving the harbour. The horn gave off three deep bellows in farewell to these cold Pacific waters. We all went back to our cabin, by 7am I was up, showered and dressed in my new uniform and ready for the day. The kitchen had come to life, the aroma of hot cheesy herbed bread was divine, even more so when I was offered it with bacon and eggs, or I could have a fruit and cheese dish, and a fruit and chocolate bar to die for. Around two hundred crew were in the room; I was to finish off the storeroom packing, put all the rubbish into the proper dispensers then find the art auction room, check with them they did not need help in hanging the artwork, a lunchbreak, finish off my duties, then I was allowed to wander this huge ship to find my sea legs so to speak. My first stop the theatre, to watch a stage show in rehearsal. My three cabin buddies had disappeared in different directions; onboard romances were already in bloom.

The sun shone brightly for the three days we were at sea; it was a happy holiday ship, everyone smiled. I took my portable studio apart, rechecking all the paraphernalia that goes with a stocked storeroom, this was my first time in this role, so it was learn as I go. I gave it a good clean then put in my order through to Geo.

I had plenty of time to wander around the decks, finding out where most of the corridors led to. I spent a lot of time in the library and wrote some more on my own book. I now knew some of the crew members, grateful we all wore name badges, it was getting easier. On day three, as the sun was about to set, we saw land. We would be in Sydney in hours. As we approached Circular Quay we were asked to take our stations to make sure the passengers were made welcome. I did not have a station and was preparing to go to my cabin when Geo saw me. She called me over and handed me a tray of long stem glasses to be filled with cold champagne, these were to be offered to the adult passengers as they boarded, "And, Tara, smile please, it's the beginning of a fabulous time, enjoy!" she added. As we sailed towards the Sydney Harbour Bridge everyone gazed in awe at the beautiful structure that has been an iconic element of this famous harbour for almost a century.

As we docked, the midday Sydney sun encouraging us all to enjoy our day,

I texted Elsa to say I was back in Australia, my heart sang. I was home, even for a very short time. I waited till the first intake of passengers had settled, the line seemed endless, there were two intakes, today we had the first-class passengers board, the champers and smiles were everywhere. Tomorrow was a really big day when all the other passengers boarded. I rang Rae. When she picked up the phone, I breathed a sigh of relief, I was so grateful to have that quiet time just to sit and explain to her where I was and what I was doing.

She was sad I was not coming home immediately. We talked for an hour or more, then she asked when I thought booking a motorhome would tie in with my travels. It was at that moment I had an epiphany, saying to my daughter, "Rae, when I make it back home, I will be completing a circle. I will be back to where it all began."

I heard her catch her breath. "Mum," the silence crept in, I felt tears sting my eyes as I remembered why and where my journey had begun, with a request from my deceased husband Russ to travel with him as he introduced me to the real Western Australia, *The one where the tourists don't go,* he'd said. Where, somewhere between the azure bluest of blue skies and the deep orange red dust that swirls around your feet, the heartbeat of this land enters your veins pulsing with your blood and captures your heart forever. To see and feel the oasis of life with another is binding in more ways than one.

My tears fell into the black water joining the ripples made by the wind, *Scribe* was whispered so softly against my cheek. Was it time to surrender to the word that kept haunting me, no matter where I was. Or say *No, I'm not ready, leave me alone.* Or find my way back to my home? What would happen once I had made the decision to scribe, I did not understand what was wanted of me, or whom I was to scribe for. It was a mystery that I did not understand my heart was torn in two, to return to family, or continue with the sea adventure I about to embark on. "I told you I would be with you, when you are ready to walk between the two worlds, only then can I help you," Tanby's form shimmered beside me. Her voice as clear as crystal, "So, what will it be, Tara? Do you come with me, or do you stay? I cannot force you as you have free will, as we all do; all I can say is you are sorely needed; you are one of the few chosen to listen to the wisdom of the old ones. Come with me, Tara, the messages left behind by the ancients are important to this world." There was an urgency to her voice; "This world is about to be shaken to the very core; you are needed more now than ever before." There was a deep sadness to her voice. "Tara. It's time," echoed in the air as her shadow lifted, fading into the blackness of the sky. Whatever my decision it was obvious there would be major consequences. One lone tear traced its way down my cheek, the wind whipping it away. My heart to me spoke the loudest.

My decision had been made.

THE END

I wish you all enough.

KEZ

OR SHALL WE CONTINUE?

Dear readers, I felt incredibly unfulfilled when the last chapter came to an end. So as the author I gave Tara the opportunity to answer the call of *Scribe* with a different ending. And once you have read this ending, please let me know if you would like to read more of Tara when she enters the world of shades, to listen and scribe their untold stories. We all have a story, some of those that passed over have yet to tell theirs. Shall we begin?

ENDING TWO

CHAPTER 47

As we docked, I texted Elsa to say I was back in Australia. My heart sang, I was home, even for a very short while. The day had been exceptionally busy, so many questions asked of me, and I did not have the answers, as I was still new to these surroundings myself. I waited until the passengers had settled, these were the first-class passengers that did not need to queue up, now it seemed that everyone was tucked up and asleep, no-one roamed the decks or dallied in the bar. Tomorrow was the big day when the majority passengers that had not already come aboard did so. I called Rae; it was late in Perth. When she sleepily answered the phone, I breathed a sigh of relief, I was so grateful to have that quiet time just to sit and explain to her where I was and what I was doing. She was sad I was not coming home in the too-near future.

"The kids and I were hoping to see you within the next few weeks!"

I felt hot tears sting my eyes. We talked for an hour or more, then she asked when I thought booking a motorhome for us all would tie in with my travel plans, I suggested she and Kane get out the maps I had stored away. I told her where I had stored them, then suggested they both mark where they wanted to go, she was very quiet when I said I could not give her an exact date of my return. I had memories of Gordi and I laying out the maps on the lounge floor, I saw them both doing the same thing. I asked her to think about the times when her father and I had removed her, much to her displeasure, from crawling all over the paper maps when she was a baby. "Make it a family thing, Rae, I promise it will be fun."

It was at that moment I had an epiphany. "Rae, when I make it home, I will be completing a circle. I will be back to where it all began."

I heard her breath catch, "Mum," the silence crept in, I felt a tear roll down my cheek it had all begun when Russ introduced me to the real Western Australia, where the red dust swirls around your feet and the blue sky goes on forever. My tears fell into the black water, joining the ripples made by the wind. They had been so patient with me insisting that I travel; even Gordi had been the first to say, *What are you chasing, you already have it all?*

I knew now what he meant. I did have it all. Was this what Tanby had meant when she had implied I was too intent on getting not giving? The wind had become cold, it was time for my bed, tomorrow was a big day, the start of my role as arts director on a cruise ship. "Be grateful, Tara" I said out loud as I walked back to my cabin, but the words sat like dust in my mouth. Why? I should have been rejoicing, not feeling like I had made a big mistake. This was my dream job, writing, travelling to new places, seeing new sights, having new adventures, teaching my passions in the arts.

Inside the cabin, I undressed quietly; my three lovely companions were asleep. I had just settled down when Gretel gave a big stretch and sat up.

"Tara, you're in late, where have you been? Have we got a lover?" What is it about that word; no sooner was it uttered than all three girls were awake. Looking like three sleepy owls, now they were all keen to know why I was up so late. What does one do in this situation?

So, as a mother would her children, I told them a story, about being in hospital in the South Island, about hearing the word *Scribe*. I told them I was feeling that I was being torn in two, my need to see my family and the cruise adventure ahead, plus there was a signed contract. Gretel and Lisa were soon telling me to jump ship, that they would help me. Monnie, who up until now had listened more quietly than the others, looked past me with her grey eyes.

"I don't think your travel has stopped, Tara. I feel it is time to do what you're being called to do – scribe – whatever that means for you right now."

I looked at the three young ladies. "So, I am to jump ship, it seems."

It was time to talk to Geo, I knocked on her cabin door, it was early morning, and she was not happy. I briefly told her that I was leaving the ship, my family in Perth needed me, I would not be available tomorrow. Her mouth hung open.

"You can't do that, Tara; you can't just give us the fingers and go! Go back to bed; and think carefully – consider the consequences." She shut the door in my face, muttering to herself. Back in the cabin my three cohorts had already packed up my gear and were ready to smuggle me off. I told them what Geo had said, perhaps she was right. Gretel, Monnie and Lisa stood with their mouths agape.

Gretel said, "You're not going to let her tell you what to do, are you?"

I could see them waiting for my answer, all three of them hyped up to be part of this getaway. "To hell with it! I want to be with my family in Perth; consequences be dammed."

I changed to my old clothing, leaving my name badge on the bedside drawer, then we four ladies quietly closed the cabin door behind us. As we walked down the passageway, I was sure every sound was amplified, Lisa got a fit of the giggles and had to cross her legs as she sputtered, "Stop, I'm going to pee myself," which caused a chain rection. The sea air whipped down the stairwell that led to the deck, shivering up and down my body. As I made my way to the gangway the girls took up their lookout positions on deck, using their hands to signal the coast was clear. It was comical and a tad over the top, more like *Mission Impossible.* I loved it. The gangplank had been slightly raised and gates put over the entry and exit. Monnie grabbed one of the attached chains given it a light shake. "Looks like you're stuck with us, there's no way we can get past this lot," pointing at the padlocks.

"May I help you, ladies?" was said from above us.

We all stared at the tall shadow that was standing on the stairwell that led to the bridge. He had obviously been watching us trying to figure out how to navigate the gangplank. All four of us began to speak at once. "Just getting some fresh air, sir." My roomies disappearing, leaving this lone possum to face the outcome. His eyes bored into mine.

"Hello, I'm the executive officer, Charles Francis, and you're the new arts supervisor, aren't you?" Now he was standing beside me, we were the same height, his hazel eyes looked into my hazel eyes, from what I could see in the shadows, he was my age, his skin around the eyes crinkled, his forehead deeply lined, his face cleanly shaved, and as he removed his cap tucking it under his arm, silver curls escaped.

"Trying for some onshore excitement before we leave, are we?"

I shrugged: "Not really, just couldn't sleep." What else do you say when you're caught red-handed about to bound off the ship? I excused myself saying, "Perhaps I should try to get a few winks."

However, this officer had different ideas. "May I?" He offered me his arm; "I'm officially off-duty, would you care to join me?" He began to stroll along the deck. I saw no harm; the adrenaline had kicked in, I was certainly not tired. "It would be nice to know your name, I can't address you as Miss Arts Supervisor while we walk, and as I'm off-duty, if you choose to you can call me Charles." So, with my arm lightly tucked into his, it seemed harmless enough as we strolled the deck. That night, Charles Francis, the ship's executive officer, became my friend and confident, as I did his.

Maybe it was our age, maybe it was the attraction, and maybe just two people who found a friend. My decision to leave the ship had led me to meeting Charles, and I was very grateful, we would meet whenever possible to discuss our day, maybe a light supper between us or an aperitif was shared. Often sharing a funny incident between the passengers and ourselves. More often than not were shared our thoughts on philosophy, books, movies and art, sometimes religion would come into it. Charles claimed he was an agnostic; I talked about my spiritual outlook. We both loved Nostradamus and his predictions and both of us adored the prayer boarder art in the eighteenth century scriptures. I treasured these times, two adults discussing so many elements in their lives, agreeing to disagree. How wonderful to have an adult conversation without the drama of jealousy or ego-based opinions. And if we did not agree with an opinion it was not met with hostility but with consideration.

CHAPTER 48

When the ship moored in Lombok, Charles invited me on a pony and trap ride to a small village in the hills to watch the villages make tall clay pots, I was delighted with the mountain ponies so small and strong, each pony harnessed to a brightly painted wagon, the top of the harness covered in bright flowers and ribbons, small tinkling bells adding to the magic, I felt like I was on carnival carriage, six people including Charles and myself climbed onboard.

A bumpy, jerking one-hour ride into the mountains, but so worthwhile. I was amazed as we watched the men cut huge slabs of clay from the hillside, women, men and kids all joining in the carrying of this sticky muddy parcel to the village where the art side of things began. First the base was made, then passed onto another artisan who formed the wide girth and middle of this container, then another took over who formed the neck and top, all the time the spinning clay never stopped. We did not have time to watch them putting them in kilns and drying them but the finished product of many weeks were on display, brightly painted vases and urns of all descriptions were packed in straw-lined boxes ready to be exported. There was a small tourist shop where you could make a personal purchase, I would have loved to but getting it transported back to Perth would have cost me a small fortune and the prices were astronomical; they were doing a great trade, and why not? That's the way this world ticks.

Charles had a timeslot to meet so we opted for heading back to the ship, the same driver of the horse and cart very willing to drive us back, we were onboard before the two thousand or so passengers came onboard. I was very happy to sit quietly in the afternoon and continue sorting out the art cupboard. My recent art order receiving an affirmative the same day Lombok said welcome. Lombok and Bali are extravagant in many ways, with very beautiful traditions one of them welcoming tourists to the land of the gods. I had experienced this all before and so had Charles, it was truly a beautiful island with generous-hearted people, but it was time to begin my arts supervisor position in earnest. The female passengers were the first to discover my small room beside the theatre, we had room for ten people but then the creative menfolk began to arrive. We expanded into the foyer of the theatre, twenty adults all keen to learn and ask questions, this was my nirvana. Each night thanking the universe for the pleasure of showing others how to create and write was pure pleasure for me, to see their faces light up when they had achieved a difficult art piece or an entry into their journals. And I had been so close to throwing this experience away. Thanks to budding friendships, and Charles, I was feeling quite at home.

Overnight we had docked in Bali itself, the noise of the Bali traditional band had died down, all the passengers had gone to explore, if there was any one left onboard apart from staff, I could not see them. Charles had gone ashore for a massage, inviting me to join him but I was happy to stay and play with my arts cupboard. When Geo arrived in the foyer looking very flustered I thought it was the heat, I offered her a seat and a bottle of water. "No, Tara," she wailed into my face, "you don't understand, I've made a terrible mistake, you see I ordered your itinerary but put the wrong amount of numbers in the wrong column," she had no sooner spoken when four of the crew arrived with trollies carrying boxes upon boxes of pencils, glue, crayons and paper, and they kept coming, all in all ten boxes were now sitting around the foyer, it was like Christmas-time. And it had to be stored out of view from passengers attending the theatre that night. The only thing I could think of was to quickly fill up the art cupboard, it was overflowing, but five large cardboard boxes remained. Charles to the rescue, he saw what Geo and I were trying to achieve with an hour to spare.

The first dinner service had started, passengers dressed in their best were sauntering through to the bar and the restaurant. Charles commandeered the photo booth, heaving the heavy carton behind the cubicle curtain announcing, "Problem solved till the show's over."

I was not having dinner with the crew tonight, I opted for a fresh coffee and a small piece of bacon and egg pie made by the café. The sea breeze was beautiful, I thought of the two men in my life that Bali had seduced into romantics, my grief for Russ had settled into a space that would always there for him. The disappointment in Gordi was slowly healing, I just wanted them both to be at piece wherever they were. Returning to the cabin which was heavy with the fug of perfume and hairspray, these young ones partied hard and as often as possible. I had promised them I would attend tonight's late cabaret show, however, dressing up was not an option as I had nothing to dress up in, I peeped into Gretel's side of the wardrobe, she had once said, "Help yourself if you're stuck, babe." I found a lovely cotton paisley dress that fitted well, it was a cross-over style, and a pair of summer jandals with a small wedge heel, also curtesy of Gretel, adding a little make-up, using what I found in the bathroom, eye liner, mascara, plus a little shimmer powder for the face.

I was ready to go and watch the show, hopefully the second show had some free seats, they were very popular, "Booked out every night," so Charles informed me.

The first person I saw was Charles, with two gorgeous young women half his age on each arm, his smile from ear to ear, our eyes met, he nodded in approval as I walked past and I smiled, this was his job and he was enjoying it, they cooed up at him adoringly. Gretel waved out to me as she saw me. "Oh, love the dress, hon, your colour!" inviting me to join them, I made my way to the bar, ordering a white wine spritz. The lights dimmed and two young male violinists made their way to centrestage. They blew me away with their talent; I could not stop applauding. The audience clapping and whistling, shouting for an encore. The music they choose gave me good bumps *Hotel California* – my favourite of all songs.

Too soon it was time to head off to bed, when my hand was grabbed leading me onto the dance floor, my roommates all a little tipsy singing loudly. "We're off to see Singapore, come on, Tara, join us." It fascinates me the weird jiggy dance people do when there tipsy and try to dance, still it was fun. The ship's engines began to throb, one long blast of the ship's horn signalled that Bali's lights would soon be a faint glow in the distance.

I made my excuses; it was definitely my bedtime. Charles was at the theatre door, his shift for the night at the helm was only beginning, "I'll walk you back to the elevator, it's on my way." Charles lightly brushed my cheek with his, a gentleman's goodnight kiss, as the lift door smoothly opened, he smiled looking into my eyes, there was nothing but warmth and friendship in his, "See you sometime tomorrow." *Singapore, here we come,* was my last thought as I drifted into sleep, my body tired, reminding me maybe I should have accepted the invite for a massage.

Today, according to my roster list I was assisting with the first art auction, time to wear a different name badge, this morning I was the arts auction supervisor. I loved the way I could segue into different rolls on this cruise. It was kept at a frantic pace, my job was to take the small card that was flapped in the air by the buyer, write down their details and pass them to the coordinator who took a deposit to hold till the auction was over, when full payment was expected from the buyer. I was amazed that everything was sold, every time an art piece was sold a bell was rung and champagne was offered to the buyer and friends. I could see quite a few getting a little tipsy, money was flowing freely, one passenger saying very loudly they had just won Lotto and to his wife, "You buy whatever you want, sweetie, you deserve the best," it seemed to fire up the first-class passengers to bid higher and buy more. I was quite happy to close the auction room doors at midday, take a well-earned lunchbreak. The energy in that room had been electric, I was ready for a nanna nap.

The hour's break for my lunch was needed, I enjoyed a beautiful fresh fruit salad with a light creamy sauce and a hot black tea, then time to go on deck and put my feet up and get some sun on my body. I had drifted off when Geo texted me, *Time to open the arts studio.* I felt like grumbling, *I don't want to,* but this was my job, on with my arts supervisor badge. There were perhaps five passengers waiting at the lone table that had a plastic sheet on it with the afternoon arts activities. A small sign announcing today's activity, *Journalling with a creative flair and alcohol ink printing,* was on the agenda. The line to participate grew, a young crewman assisted me in setting up two extra tables in the library foyer, ten chairs were bought in as I unpacked the arts cupboard. Soon many heads were all bent over the afternoon's project.

Tomorrow we had, *How to make your own book to journal in*, already there were signatures on the enrolment form. So apart from eating and sleeping and a chance meeting with Charles as we passed each other on deck, my few days at sea were filled. After dinner I would chat for perhaps a half hour with the crew at my table. A quick stretching walk around the deck, then bed. My three roomies were the same, almost dragging their feet once their shifts were finished; they would climb on their bunks and it was literally lights out. It seems that life onboard a cruise ship was not about the nightly romantic flings and or steamy encounters with passengers; it was extremly hard work.

Singapore – I love Singapore, always have, I adore the number of plants that are grown here, especially the orchids. I have never been able to grow a successful orchid, here they seemed to sprout everywhere you look. From beautifully potted plants with flair and creativity to the odd jam jar placed on a shelf in a room. They grew from the tiniest, daintiest of blooms to gigantic saucer-sized flowers in a riot of colours. I woke up smiling, feeling my body give a big cat-like stretch.

I had invited Charles to see some of Singapore with me, he declined as he was needed elsewhere. My intention was to catch a small local ferry know as a bumboat. These small boats had quite a reputation to them. Apparently in the late 1800s and early 1900s these boats, or types of boats, were once known to ferry women out to the crew of the old steamer and tall ships, to entertain the crew. Therefore the name bumboats had been born. Today it was a small comfy passenger ferry that made its living by taking passengers from all walks of life, that worked in the city or from cruise ships, to all the different jetties around the city, there were ten jetties on the map and I wanted to see them all. Each jetty had an icon or statue to visit.

Charles offered a dinner that night at the famous Raffles Hotel. I was happy with that; my roomies were all off in different directions as well. The day was steamy hot, I was really happy my little ferry had a thick bamboo canopy, I was the first one onboard, my skipper spoke broken English, but I have learnt through all my travels, sign language is universal. The other passengers had destinations; I was happy to see whatever the wind blew my way. The first terminal stop was Jetty One, where the statue of Merlion the Singapore city super icon that is shown worldwide was a short walk away.

A tour guide with a loudspeaker was guiding tourists along the jetty, so I tailed them to hear about how the Merlion captures the heart of Singapore, that once was a fishing village, the lion's head representing the symbol of energy of this magic city.

I had my photo taken in front of the white monolith; this place was loud and buzzing with tourists, time to get back on my bumboat. I had the same skipper, and he asked if I was hungry, again with sign language, I nodded enthusiastically so off we went to Jetty Two where I would find the Marina Bay Sands. I had not been here before; I love new places. I had no idea of what I was about to see. Marina Bay was like going to a serious shopper's heaven. Everything, and I mean everything, was on sale here; it was an experience in art, culture and food. I spent the next four hours wandering, buying small amounts of munchies from food vendors, I sat and watched solo musicals and traditional performances played out on beautifully decorated platforms, no matter where you went or what floor you went to. The outdoor lifts made of glass were a wonder to me, this was commercialism at the highest point you could think of as you did not have to leave, you could book a room overnight or for as long as you wanted to stay to have this experience. Once again forests of lush greenery spilled over banisters and cascaded into pools of clear water.

CHAPTER 49

As you ascended to the higher, more expensive shops, it got quieter. I noticed it was here the chauffers in their smart black uniforms carried the boxes and parcels. There were no children, no fanfares of concerts or musicals. Here a solo pianists played the old tunes, the carpet so thick your shoes sank into it. On the next four flours were apartments, the floor I was on was number fifteen. I smiled when I thought of what my family would say to this sort of luxury. I could almost hear Ray say, "This is unbelievable!" To the Singaporeans it was everyday life, to me, however I had to agree, it was unbelievable.

Time to head back to my cruise ship. Tonight it was dinner at the Raffles Hotel with Charles. I had been to a luncheon at Raffles many years ago with Russ, and it had been a lovely experience, the food beautiful. Waving goodbye to my happy little ferry man, I walked back to where the ship was moored. From far off she looked massive but now I was becoming used to her and her many corridors she was not as mysterious as when I first went onboard. Once in my cabin, I showered, gelled my hair hoping it sort of looked as smart as when I had had it first done, added some make-up as I did look a little tired, and once again borrowed Gretel's dress. I felt a little dowdy, as Raffles was a top-notch place to go, but there was not really a choice as I had not had the time to take my city clothes that I had bought in Christchurch to the staff laundry. I was happy. As I left the cabin, my three cabin buddies came around the corner, Mon saying "You can't go to Raffles looking like that!" I was dragged back in, sat down, while she applied more make-up and clothes from all three girls were hurled in my direction. A long white top with pleating down the front, tight black faux leather leggings, a thick gold chain around my neck, with earrings and bracelet to match. My hair once again sprayed and styled, Gretel flicked my white linen perfume at me. Her wedge sandals still on my feet, I stood and did not recognise myself I looked sexy and very attractive.

"Now you're ready for Raffles!" they chorused.

So, this was it, time to meet Charles at his cabin, where we had agreed to have an aperitif before we left. Charles opened his cabin door, he looked very relaxed dressed in black T-shirt and dress pants and freshly shaved. "Oh, you do look smart," was his reaction. I was bubbling over about where and what I had seen, Charles saying he had been in training all day, so his day was not as fun as mine, but tonight we would make up for it.

To my delight, Charles had ordered a rickshaw; this was not anything like the modern ones we see, which are motorised. This was a genuine old-fashioned one. The city had come alive; it pulsed with energy, the streets alive, full of families, each avenue was lit with soft lights. The Raffles Hotel has not changed since I was here many years ago, the tall palms out the front of the while building, its lighting soft and inviting. Charles offered me his hand as I climbed out the rickshaw; it was the beginning of a beautiful night. The menu was a wonderland of gustation; everything you could want was written there for you to order. We began with a tall, frosted glass of a drink called a Singapore Sling; oh how that bought back memories, and they tasted just as lovely. For the entrée we decided on the tray of three miniatures, so we could share the taste experience: a champagne lemon curd, a brandy chocolate raspberry mousse, plus a gin-infused coconut and caramel, each one in a small crystal glass dish on a carved bamboo board. A small cheese board was offered between our entrée-tasting and the main meal. We were offered a carafe of house wine or a drink of our choice, I stayed with my gin-sling; Charles ordered a brandy snifter. The music was gentle, kind to our ears. Everything came in bite-sizes, no huge plates overlapping with gravy and greasy chips; this was silver service dining at its best. Charles ordered the steak tartare, and I had the lobster salad with an egg mayonnaise. Then coffee was served, Charles asked for a Turkish coffee and looked at me for confirmation. I agreed, it was a nice way to top off our meal. Dessert came to us on a silver trolley, I was too full to want even a sliver. Charles quietly asked the maître d' for a quiet spot outside on the veranda to finish off our coffees, and with a snap of his fingers, sir and madam were immediately ushered to a double swing couch, the cushions so large and puffy, we sank into them, it was perfect.

"We leave in four hours, Tara. Ready for Cambodia?" I had one more request. I really wanted to experience the Gardens by the Bay, this was one experience I did not want to miss, a geothermal biodome that collected water for the whole of the botanical city – even the Marina Bay Sands centre was fed by this magnificent structure. Charles put his card under the cloth serviette; everything was done with discretion. I shivered under the coolness of the night, Charles put his jacket around my shoulders, again he crooked his elbow for me to take.

"It's not far from here, would you like to walk off your dinner or should I hail a taxi?" I opted to walk. On each side of the path were green shrubs; the perfume from these was so fresh. Charles paid for our passes and we entered a world I will never forget. It was park-like, everything was pristine although tourists were everywhere, but it was so quiet. Charles found us two concrete seats that were more like chaise lounges; as we settled back looking into the night sky, four majestic tall steel trees hundreds of feet high towered above us. I was about to ask what next, when Charles put his finger to his lips then pointed upwards.

First the solo beat of a drum and a small red light flickered at the very tip of the tower, then the tempo changed, laser lights began to climb up and down the hanging green foliage that dripped off these steel towers, accompanied by the Bohemian Rhapsody – a performance of lights and every sort of music. I was mesmerised. Then Queen began to play *Bohemian Rhapsody;* the light show was beautiful, my eyes stung with tears as I thought of my road trip with my grandson Jess, we had worn that song out trying to best each other as we drove down the highways and byways of Australia. I was suddenly very homesick. Charles picked up my emotion, "I think it's time we put Tara to bed." *Pardon? What did he mean by that?* The show was over; our seats ready to be filled by other tourists.

Charles hailed a water taxi. "Come on, sleepy, I'm not going to be the one to blame when you can't get up tomorrow." His words 'put Tara to bed' still rang in my ears. As the water taxi slowly ambled towards the ship, Charles assisting me off the bouncing little water ferry. Taking my arm, he walked me to the gangplank of our vessel. A rush of relief went through my body when he said, "Goodnight, my dear, sleep tight, I'll see you tomorrow." With a quick kiss on my cheek he walked off, hailing a shipmate who was going in the same direction, I heard the word *casino,* and backslapping went on as blokes do, both getting into a taxi disappearing into the night. I loved it, no emotional struggle of you're mine and I'm yours, no battering of emotions: *Should we? Or what's the outcome if we do sleep together?* I had been his dinner date, that's it and I felt so comfortable, I knew then that Charles was a friend – a good friend, one I could trust.

My roomies woke me with their yawing and stretching , they all began their day with the 6am breakfast shift. Once all the showering, make-up, clothes-swapping and giggling had floated out the door into the corridor, I got up. The bathroom was a jumble of pretty hairclips, make-up, wet towels, and undies. My shift as arts supervisor was not until 10am, so I snuggled back into my bunk bed, grabbed two pillows off their beds and stuffed them behind my back, the motion of the ship then the horn blasting, letting me know we had set sail – in two days we would be in Cambodia. For some reason I had always felt uncomfortable in Cambodia., I always had, it seemed under all the bright lights and beauty there was a darkness. One that had undertones of tragedy. Or maybe it was my writer's imagination taking over, I sat up and journalled for an hour putting my thoughts to paper. Time to get up, shower, breakfast and go to work.

Today I had prepared a project of making origami swans. Unbeknown to me the crew had seen my small advert for the mornings activities I had placed on the library door; I had six ladies in the class when two of the crew asked if they could show us how to make towel swans, of course I agreed! I was delighted; the little room filled fast, Charles making an appearance to move the activities to the ship's main foyer as so many people wanted to see the demonstration. By the time I got to the foyer there was no room at all, people were sitting on the two main staircases, other passengers filled up balconies, or stood too close to the demonstration table until crew had to ask them to step back. Then four of the cabin cleaners stepped into the centre and became the entertainment. Soon small elephants appeared made from white hand towels, along with parrots, swans, rats and puppies. An hour went buy, once they had finished it felt a bit silly to introduce how to make a tiny paper crane at the workshop. It was lunchtime for passengers, for which I was grateful.

CHAPTER 50

While I was packing up my boxes of paper, my roomies appeared. Lisa had a look on her face I did not understand, and Gretel was pushing her away from me, saying "Take no notice, Tara, she's being a bitch."

Lisa had these enormous blue eyes filled with fear when she squeaked, "Don't look now but here comes your boyfriend with another woman."

Well of course I looked up, Lisa was right, Charles was walking past us with a stunning redhead on his arm, and of course he had to address us as he passed. "Hello, ladies." I greeted him with a nod saying 'sir' and carried on packing my paper away. At least they waited till he was out of earshot.

"The dirty bugger; he can't do that!" came from Gretel.

"Tara, are you okay?" came from Lisa. A small giggle had begun in my throat; it was the last retort that caused it to escape, my eyes watered up as I laughed.

"Men, who friggin needs then, fancy parading his new bit of fluff when he's been seeing you, the whole ship sees you as a couple." Lisa began to flap her hands in my face ordering the others to, "get her some water; she hysterical, God she's really upset."

Now it was my turn to try and calm them down. "Girls, yes, I would love some water, thank you, and secondly, Charles is a friend, that's it; a lovely friend no more no less. There is no reason why he should not walk the decks with another women, there is no reason why he should not become involved – if that is what he wants. We are mates, as we call our close friends in Australia, that's all he is. Now go back to work and stop being daft, thank you, but I'm fine."

I smiled all afternoon and into the night, amused by my three roomies, Lisa, Gretel and Monnie, being so protective towards me and about my friendship with Charles – I was the lucky one. I had not set about to be friends with any one, yet, here I was being cared for by my young friends.

That night the entertainment was a comedian from the UK, he was the funniest man I had ever heard tell a story. He spoke about the Hunchback of Notra Dame, I loved the play on words, and I was in stitches as he pulled his red blazer over his head and proceeded to speak with a French accent, my face ached with smiling when he left the stage. I joined my roomies for a dance and a drink after the show, then we all wandered up to the pizza palace. It was packed out. We ordered a slice of pizza each while Monnie raced off to get us some cold beers. Meeting us back on the deck, we chatted about our day in Singapore and what they had bought, when I admitted I had bought nothing, I was too busy sightseeing, it was met with disapproval: "What about your grandkids? They will want presents, don't be so mean. We are taking you shopping in Cambodia, we know some fabulous shops there. And we are not taking no for an answer." Something told me not to argue with them just enjoy the friendship.

I never sleep well after eating pizza late at night, and that beer, although delicious, was repeating on me. I slipped out of the cabin and took a turn around the deck trying to walk off the feeling of too much heavy food. I had read that on every Princess cruise ship a bronze statue was placed by the helm. I had not known this till I was reading the ship's brochure of the whereabouts of the ship's entertainment rooms: the casino, theatre, the many bars and cafés. My favourite so far, an intimate café tucked away in a small corner. However, these statues sounded fascinating, I decided this was my goal for the night, while my pizza and beer worked its way through my digestive system.

I found the bronze statue, placed just under the helm, a couple in bronze looking out to sea, it seemed as though they were looking for the horizon, I stood alongside them, placing my hand on their cold chests: *See us safely home,* was my prayer, the sea wind chilly against my skin, it seems my sea legs were not as strong as I thought, I made a grab for the railing. There was no-one here, not a soul, only the sound of the sea as the ship sliced its way through the blackened water. I was in that space of stillness, a place of Zen when your senses are on hold and it's just you. *Scribe, now is your time,* slid past me on the wings of the wind, it felt like cold hands were clutching at my clothes and hair, I turned and ran.

I was intent on taking the stairs two at a time, my breath heaving as a hand reached out from the shadows and caught me, I screamed. It felt like I was fighting for my life, I kicked and slapped my way free to be caught and held again, I lunged at the shadowed face screaming, "No, leave me alone!" I was fighting for my life. I was released, once in the cabin I pushed the heavy door shut: no-one woke. Curling up on my bed I shook with terror. Sleep came in short bursts; each time I closed my eyes I saw that shadowed face.

Waking was not hard, I was the first one up and showered, it still trembled with fear, my roomies looking concerned at my tired pale face, the dark rings accentuated by the paleness. Monnie, putting aside her usual first thing in the morning sharp no-nonsense quips, was concerned.

"Shall I inform Geo you are ill and not able to work today?" I gave her a wavering smile and shook my head; work was what I needed, but her empathy was appreciated. I made myself swallow a fruit smoothie for breakfast along with some magnesium powder – anything to calm me down. I was wishing with all my heart that I had some of that hemp oil that had been freely administered in the South Island . Opening my crafts cupboard, I began to unpack the art gear. Techniques using stencils and pencils had been advertised for this morning's entertainment; my hands were still slightly trembling when one large brown hand covered mine. I looked up to see Charles, his eyes boring into mine.

"You're relieved for the day, Tara. This is official, you will report to the captains' quarters in one hour." I was surprised, and began to ask why, when suddenly I saw the deep scarlet scratches down his face and neck. Had he been in a fight? The crew member taking over from me kept her eyes down as I instructed her on the morning's art classes. Then I wandered back to my cabin; there was not much to do but wait for the hour in the privacy of the cabin, wondering what the problem was or if it was a one-on-one staff meeting with the captain, we had met in social occasions but not in a staff situation.

My knock on the captain's door was answered with a gruff announcement: "In!" Charles and another crew member both stood in the large cabin, their stark white uniforms a severe contrast to the plush surrounds. "Good morning, Tara, we have not met personally my name is Captain Thomas Beaumont, I have asked you to attend my office due to a formal complaint of drunk and disorderly behaviour causing physical harm to my First Officer, as witnessed by our security cameras." He had not even looked at me as he had spoken, which irked me. Tucking my temper away, I focused on letting my logic take over.

"Good morning, sir". I had no idea of how to address this complaint.

Charles stepped forward: "Please address the captain as his rank."

I could feel my face flame with embarrassment, so I repeated myself with, "Good morning, Captain, in my defence I was not drunk or disorderly, I could not sleep so I went for walk on the deck; as I returned to the cabin I was assaulted by someone." The captain placed his pen on the silver holder sitting on his desk. I could see he had been writing my response, as had the extra person in the cabin with us, my words were recorded on a tablet that glowed eerily onto his face. When the captain finally raised his eyes to meet mine, I could see nothing but dislike.

"Then how do you explain screaming like a banshee then attacking my First Officer? You had been seen drinking beer earlier on in the evening." The captain stood up from behind the desk. "Please don't deny it, Tara, we have footage of your behaviour, let alone Charles' facial injuries, and believe me it was one of our passengers, also taking a late-night stroll, who reported you hanging onto the statue – you were mumbling, unable to keep your footing, then you attacked Charles as he tried to assist you."

Now I was angry, how dare they accuse me without asking me for the details first? I began to stutter my reply when the captain said, "You are formally dismissed, I have written a report of complaint to the ship's agent, your duties as arts supervisor will finish immediately, you are to have no contact with any passengers or staff and once we dock in Cambodia, you will make your own arrangements to return home. Or, as an alternative you can book a cabin onboard this ship and enjoy your cruise, which I feel would be more suitable for a woman of your tastes."

What did he mean by *my tastes*? OMG, this upstart had just accused me of being drunk and disorderly, and insinuated I had certain tastes. I could feel my fists clench. How dare this person who called himself Captain neither show empathy, nor want to know the circumstances. I looked at Charles, he also looked surprised.

CHAPTER 51

The captain spoke to me once more, his eyes darting everywhere except in my direction. "I'm placing you under house arrest, the security of my staff and clients are of the utmost importance, after careful consideration, I have found your recent behaviour untenable. It is my duty to offer you medical assistance, however, the company has no available amenities on board for this irrational behaviour, except isolation, it is also my responsibility to offer counselling. As such I would suggest you seek anger management and AA counselling. I'm sure both may be of assistance once you are in a stable environment. Hence your employment with this company is terminated. Please stay in your cabin until we dock, you will be escorted off by security; if you refuse then we will have no option but to employ the Cambodian police to remove you. We dock at fifteen-hundred hours, please leave all the company's belongings in the cabin and have your personal belongings ready to disembark."

I left the captain's quarters, my head whirling with the accusations, gutted with humiliation; I was under house arrest? I was not guilty of any of those accusations. Charles caught up with me.

"Tara, what happened last night? I've seen the camera footage. You do look drunk, and you were mumbling. Then when you ran past me, I tried to stop you, to calm you, but you attacked me."

"We need to talk, Charles – right now." He began to lead me to his cabin, I objected pointing out that he had heard I was under ship's arrest.

Charles turned and spoke with the security that followed me, whatever was said was agreed to. "You're not the only one given a slap on the wrist, Tara, I'm being transferred to another ship till this mess is resolved," he said, pointing to his scratches. Closing the door to his cabin, Charles made a pot of Earl Grey tea, sitting beside me, his hand again covered mine.

"Okay, tell me, what is going on?"

We had a friendship, it was time I tested the waters, "Charles, I had one light ale with one slice of pizza, what they claim was mumbling," I explained, "I put my hand on the statue's heart, I was not hanging onto it, and prayed for a safe trip home. I was not mumbling or stumbling. Tell me, if I were a paying passenger, would I have been on report?"

He replied, "No, we always expect some weird things to happen while at sea."

I gratefully sipped my hot tea; it felt soothing, opening the gateway to the words I was about to say. I confided in him why I had scratched him, I confided about my biggest fear, I told him about *Scribe*. Charles remained silent throughout my story, his arm around my shoulders as I sobbed into his chest. He did not ask questions, he did not interrupt, all he did was hand me tissues and hug me even tighter. After I had finished speaking, all he could say was, "Jesus, no wonder you fought me off! I was having my nighttime pipe when you let loose, I was in the shadows because there is a *No Smoking* rule on this ship. I did not think my action would terrify you."

It took a while for the sobs to die down, washing my face in his bathroom, so neat and pristine was which was just the opposite of the cabin I just shared. Charles had made another pot of tea, as I raised the cup to my lips, it suddenly clicked: "You smoke a pipe?"

Charles chuckled, "Yup, oh I know, disgusting for your health, but I love a bedtime pipe, and it doesn't hurt anyone. My cabin is out of bounds so I sneak up on deck when duties are over and have a smoke; I'll also happy to imbibe when I'm not onboard."

It was time to discuss my options. "Okay, you've been sacked and have nowhere to stay in Cambodia, plus you claimed you don't like the place, so here's what we can do: book a room at the Sky Palace for two days – it's clean, has a pool and restaurant and is close to all the shops you could want. I've stayed as a guest there, and enjoyed it; we can see some of the sights, and we can book you a flight home. Or do you want to book a cabin as a passenger on the return to Sydney? You have a choice, but we don't have that long to decide."

I carefully considered both options. A nice studio apartment with just me in it, and more or less do as I want when I want, and a pool to stretch in sounded heavenly. Or, book a standard cabin onboard the ship which considered me to be a disorderly drunk. The choice was simple. I rinsed the cups out, leaving them on the draining tray. Charles was packing his case; he was on shore leave for two days after leaving this ship, then would go to another as its first officer. I began to help him fold and pack, when he suggested I best get my own gear packed.

"I'll meet you onshore at the taxi rank." We hugged closely and Charles murmured into my hair. "I'm so sorry it ended like this, Tara; they have lost someone very special. Let me take care of you for two days till I leave." Those words 'take care of you' causing me to pull back – was he suggesting we become a couple? I looked into his eyes, there was nothing there but friendship and honesty.

I agreed. "See you at the taxi rank."

I was escorted back to my cabin, where I packed my belongings and wrote my new friends a note telling my them I had left the ship, thanking them for being wonderful people, that they were fun and I wished them all the best with everything. As the ship docked I was ready, the knock on my cabin door told me it was time to go; my passport was handed to me, then I was escorted by two crewmen from the ship that had once been a lot of fun, where I had met many lovely people. Geo was in the corridor as I was ushered past; she held up her hand to stop us . One of the crewmen said, "Sorry, Geo, you know the ships rules, no communication is allowed."

The look on her face said it all: "Shut up both of you, and look the other way." She enveloped me in a huge hug. "I'm so sorry, Tara, this does not feel right, keep safe and well, I'll miss you." She stood back to let my three roomies say their goodbyes.

Elsa said "I hate this ship; I'm leaving when I'm back in Australia."

The other two had tears in their eyes as we shared a group hug. "Ma'am, please, time to leave," one of the guards said.

As I walked down the ships walkway to the outside world, a million cars honked their horns, vendors screamed, selling their wares, the city was full blast, the sun hurt my eyes as did the sudden noise. I saw Charles at the taxi rank, he waved, I smiled. This was not what I had imagined. I had been sacked, put under house arrest, escorted off the ship by security, labelled as drunk and dangerous. Plus had endangered Charles' position in the company. Emotions rolled in my chest. There was so much to consider once I found a room to lie down in and find some peace and quiet. The nausea and flashing bright lights that I had felt earlier had signalled a migraine coming on; I needed two things immediately – painkillers and a dark room. Charles saw my face; gently bundling me into the taxi he gave the address. He had rung and booked rooms while waiting for me. The migraine was taking over as my speech became slurred, my sight growing foggy, my stomach cramping with nausea, I had never been in so much pain so quickly.

Charles was wonderful, almost carrying me to the room, lying me down on the bed, pulling the curtains to block out the sunlight. I heard him say "My mother suffered with these, I'll let you sleep," and sleep I did; deep, troubled dreams. I was in a forest of dead trees, being followed, no matter where I ran to hide that voice would find me, not only the word *Scribe* was being chanted, but so many hands were trying to grab me. I was stuck in a nightmare, my head was pounding, my body was frozen to the bed; I could not move. Where was Tanby? I needed her help, where was Charles? He had also promised he would help me. Why do people say that, why do people promise to be of help, and they don't show up in my time of need? I wrenched myself awake and sat up, my back against the wall. The spinning room slowly settled down. My sobbing settled down; the nausea very slowly eased off.

I swallowed the painkillers Charles had left behind. I sat there, but could not make head nor tail of what had just happened. My sight was still a little weird, I spied a tray with cups and saucers plus a small jug, I decided a cup of tea would help. That one movement had the room spinning again; I threw up onto the pristine white quilt of the bed, then my bowel went into spasm, I only just made it to the bathroom in time. I had not had a migraine this severe for years. As I sat in the bathroom feeling like my insides were falling out, Charles decided to pop in and say hello. I heard the room door click then a soft, "Tara, you awake?" then a louder, "Bloody hell, what's going on here?" I called out to say I was okay, just an upset tum. Charles was having none of it, he came into the bathroom, blanching at the odour, ran the shower and ordered me to stand while he undressed me down to my underwear. When the hot water sluiced it was over my head and body, it was pure heaven.

My head began to clear. "If I let go of you, you're not going to fall?" he asked. I shook my head. Right, let's get this mess sorted, If I had been in a better condition, I would have hugged him. I slid to a sitting position in the small cubicle, the water running over my head down my spine. Time had no meaning; the constant heat was helping with the pain. I could hear Charles in the main room talking to someone.

CHAPTER 52

I sincerely hoped he was talking on the phone; I did not want other people anywhere near me. There was a knock on the bathroom door; Charles came through carrying the hotel dressing gown in his hand. Helping me to stand, then wrapping me in the dressing gown, he carried me to the clean bed. Towels had been placed everywhere, the soiled doona cover in the corner of the room.

"Do you need to see a doctor?" he asked. I knew I did not need any medication; I was in shock and deeply hurt at what had been said about me, which would now be on the ship's records, I knew from a previous conversation with a crew member about misconduct – if we were in the Royal Navy I would have been put in the brig. Cruise ships came under the merchant navy law, which meant if a person under house arrest or was put ashore, as I was, the crime or discrepancy was written on the company's records, permanently. As Charles towelled my feet dry, his face was full of concern. "Are you sure you don't need medical attention?"

I managed a weak smile. "I'm going to be okay, I let this one get away on me," which was true, I was so busy in my head thinking of the things I could say to prove myself innocent I had not taken notice of the clear warning sign I get – a flashing blue light in my eyes. That cup of tea I had started to get before I became ill was now sitting in my hands, I took my first sip: heaven. Charles had bought some sweet spicy dumplings at a street market; he looked dubious when I accepted one. My first small bite into the sugar covered puffball of dough was divine; it settled my aching tum nicely.

"Now make yourself comfy, my friend, I have something to show you." Charles produced a thumb drive from his shirt pocket. "This is the damming evidence of you attacking me. I bribed Geo to speak nicely to one of her officer friends. This is a copy of last night's fiasco. Apparently, they were on your side and have given us both footage of what went on before and after." My attention was now seized by what I was about to see, which would hopefully prove my innocence. Charles plugged the thumb drive into his laptop, and my nightmares came true. On screen I was eating pizza and drinking a small glass of beer, laughing and talking to a group of crew members I had joined that night, along with my three roomies. We were all laughing, smiling, having fun, raising our glasses our toast was, *Here's to Cambodia.*

The screen went fuzzy for maybe ten seconds, then I was back on-screen walking towards the statues. I stopped to have a good look at them, placing my hands on their chests and wished the crew and ship a safe journey home. I had steadied myself as the bow rose a little over a wave, but I was not lurching or disorderly. That's when I saw the look of terror cross my face – hearing *Scribe,* I ran. We watched as Charles reached out to me, it showed me clawing and scratching him, his hand holding his face calling my name: "Tara, stop."

He turned to me. "So, there you have it, Tara, that's what was reported, and that's what the captain saw. It does look damming I know, but here's the proof." We had left the film running, as I was about to defend myself, I saw the cowled shadow behind him.

"Charles, look!" My finger was shaking as I pointed out the greyish image on the screen.

It was his turn to be shocked: "What is that?" He enlarged it, but could not make sense of it. I knew what and who it was; I had seen it before, in dreams and nightmares: it was Tanby, waiting for me to decide when I would become her *Scribe.* I knew she walked between our two worlds, she had told me that, I also knew she would not wait forever, I was the one she had chosen, why? I had no idea.

Charles began to talk but I had made up my mind it was time to meet my catalyst in this life. I wished him a goodnight, saying I was feeling better, but tired. Wishing me a goodnight with a light kiss on the forehead, Charles left. All I had to do was sit quietly. The room was small and dark, nightfall casting shadows in its corners. I had no fear; this was a meeting that had been prearranged.

Tanby walked from the dark night into my room, her cloak of green billowing around her. She looked older, her eyes that had always been a golden colour now had a bruised look to them. She held out her hands which I in turn clasped in the deepest of friendship. The perfume of fresh air and ancient forests clung to her, there was no fear between us, during our time together we had built sisterhood bond no-one could break, one of trust and empathy.

"It's time, my friend. We can no longer look away, the world is in turmoil, those that have not spoken cry out to speak through you. Tara, you will be tested and your journey on this planet questioned, only then will they permit you to *Scribe. I'll come for you soon, be prepared.*" So be it, it was time to head home and begin a new path in this life. I had no idea if I were to become as Tanby, a conduit between two worlds, or as she had claimed many moons ago, a catalyst, for what or who I had no idea. I only knew in my heart that trembled with fear, it was time.

Saying goodbye to Charles was hard, he had become like a brother to me. Our hug at the airport was quick and short, I was not one for long goodbyes, neither was he. "You'll be alright from here? Remember me." We reached the queue for the escalator to customs. Charles had a purchased a first-class ticket in my name online. At the check-in desk, I collected my boarding pass, tucking it into my passport, Charles and I took one long last look at each other, he kissed my forehead, we both knew it was goodbye, he turned and walked away.

"Thank you my friend. No, I will never forget you, you showed me a friendship I was yearning for, a meeting of the minds."

I was travelling first class, all I wanted to do was sleep. I felt drained of any energy. Behind my eyes a nagging small headache had persisted, my body felt drained. I had no idea if the flight was smooth or not, I simply boarded, buckled up my seatbelt, accepted a small plate of crackers and cheese with a glass of sparkling water with ice, my seat reclined, pressing a button the divider between the seats was raised, I has complete privacy, perfect. I slept for the six-hour flight .

I relished in the gold sunrise that burnished the wings as we touched down. When the captain announced, "Ladies and Gentlemen, we are now in Perth, Australia," it was music to my ears. Once through customs, first locating my bag on the carousel, I wanted to run through the doors that said EXIT. I felt the stress leave my shoulders; it was time to find a hire car company. A small two-door Getz was on offer, I booked it, made out the papers, the keys placed in my hand. The sun now well and truly up, galahs and fruit parrots were squabbling amongst themselves, the noise raucous, I loved it. Finally, I found my way to where they had stored the cars, throwing my bag onto the passenger's seat, I began my drive to Rockingham, at this time in the morning there was not a lot of traffic heading south. The tiredness had lifted a little, the headache still sitting behind my eyes.

The drive home was the most beautiful I had ever witnessed, everything was green, spring was on its way, gold and pink layered clouds were scattered across an azure blue. The house never looked so good, I heard Rae yell with delight as I pulled into the driveway.

"Oh my God! Gang, guess who just drove up! Mum's home." Her happiness at seeing me was music to my ears. Tears mixed with hugs, kisses and laughter. "Why didn't you call us and say you were coming home?" my daughter asked, I simply held out my arms to hold Shauna my beautiful granddaughter. She put her hands on my face welcoming me home with her pretty smile. So much chatter of when, why, who.

When I told them about my enforced hasty retreat from the ship; Kane, always the sensible one surprised me as he bent over with laughter: "Only you, Tara!"

Work, playschool and college were put on hold for the morning while we all caught up. I had spied brochures of the Pilbara region in north Western Australia sitting on the table. Kane's eyes met mine. "We going?" he asked.

"How long will it take you to make arrangements?" I asked. Kane stood; his arms going around Rae, my daughter, and Shauna, their baby girl, asking me to give him a day to sort it out.

Jess had made me a cup of tea, his arms slipping around me, "Don't go away too soon, Nana, I have so much to tell you," he had grown into a lovely young man. Once I could tuck this boy under an arm, today he stood under my chin. Jess my first grandchild was now a young man.

Jess carried my cup of tea into the fernery; making sure I was comfortable in a garden chair. If it all worked out, in a week or so I would be back where it all began in the outback of Western Australia. Laying my head back, that annoying headache still throbbed behind closed eyes, I could hear the muted sounds of family plans being made. At this very moment I knew deep down I had made the right choice. I was at last in the right place at the right time. The strangest feeling swept over me, I felt my time here stop.

CHAPTER 53

My spirit began to lift from my body, I walking in that twilight world of dreams; Tanby was beside me, my heart was light she held out her hand, "Welcome, *Scribe*," a breeze as soft as a summer wind, light and caressing curled around me, I felt myself lifting, drifting with it.

"Mum, Mum wake up, Kane call an ambulance. Oh God NO!! Mum …"

I walked in a different world now, my time as *Scribe* had begun; I was now part of this world of shadows, to listen to the stories of those who could not leave their words behind.

Gently, slowly, I passed through soft layers of silky clouds, no longer with shape or form, but a small kernel of light, still with the senses of sight and sound, I lingered on the fringe of a storm, the grey clouds swirling around me like a crone's cape of dark mystery, and watched in awe as a blinding blue green and orange light flicked its angry tongue across the sky, its voice a sizzling crackle, ending in a deep booming roar. I watched a rainbow form, its colours so vibrant it stained the sky with a mauve fingerprint of a promise once given in a holy testament. I watched as the dawn sun spread its tangerine petticoat over the earth, its yellowed fingers painting the tops of snow-capped mountains with gold. I felt part of all I witnessed, for me, there was no time, no limit, no demands, I was simply allowed *to be*. In wonder I watched as the sky turned the deepest ink blue, the cosmos of planets soaring above and beyond. The aurora wrapped around me, a multicoloured shawl, its colours of green, yellow and mauve, lifting me up in its billowing waves, leading me onwards. Earth below shimmered in deep greens and azure blues; I was amongst an essay of colour so vibrant that it is beyond description.

A feeling of being called shivered through me, on I travelled, who I once was had melted away, the timeless silence surrounding me, my spirit soared free of all claims to what I had once been, free of any trauma or earthly hindrances we all share on earth, free of any human traits. As I rose above and beyond, to the blackness of the universe, I felt others surround me, gently guiding me to a sliver of pale light as I passed through, I felt a shiver of emotion towards me. Who could forget the ties of those gone before? I knew deep down in my very core there was much more to experience than what I had already seen and felt. It started slowly; the feeling of harmony filled me with its glory, a universal song of reverence, as it summoned my essence before a presence I had known before time began. Becoming one with the tribal heartbeat, the beat that rules the entire universe, before creation. I was not asked; 'were you successful with your life on earth?' but asked; 'did you experience what you desired? Are you ready to become who you were meant to be?'

THE END

Acknowledgments

There are only so many times you can say thank you to the many that have shared their stories with me in our travels.

First to Lou, my husband and my friend, for his major role in letting me get on with storytelling, while he made sure life ticked over as it should, and who also drove me to so many destinations when I was not up to it, so I could write about the adventures and people I meet. Life's been an adventure, Lou, may there be many more ahead for us both. Thank you also to my friends and colleagues for sharing their ideas and stories.

A huge thank you to all the campfires, no matter in what form, where or why, to be invited to join in swapping yarns is a dream come true for any a storyteller. The places I have been to and people I have met, listened to their stories. Especially on those addictive cruise ships around Asia, South Pacific and Australia. As I travelled around Europe, UK, Ireland and Spain plus the South Pacific Islands, New Zealand and Australia, I am honoured to be able to be your storyteller. To my family, related or not, your many and varied senses of humour have always made me smile, thank you. To my friends and readers who ask, "When's the next book out?" thank you, all authors need encouragement, for without your encouragement I would not be known as an author.

Last but not least, thanks to my author tribe, I would be lost without you. Since meeting most of you at Crom Castle in Ireland, light and laughter has been with me nearly every day. And to my publisher, MMH Press, who believed in me and had faith that I would spin a good yarn, thank you.

Until next time when we once meet around my campfire, my heartfelt thank you to all.

Kez

POSTSCRIPT

Life, who would have foreseen my journey, from a tubby child with very short straight auburn hair, knock-kneed and pigeon-toed, my two front teeth protruding. A chubby, painfully shy, awkward child. My one saving grace, my wide with wonder hazel green eyes that saw the magic in this world. I had no idea then the power of the imagination. Bullied by my peers left a deep sadness inside my heart. I only hoped deep down one day people would say my name with a smile. I hoped someone would love me, no matter how I looked. The hows and whys of how this would happen I did not know. All I knew was how to put one foot in front of another day after day. As grew up I began to recognise the power of the word. Today as I recognise the magi around me, I'm grateful to still able to look at my world with wonder. So, to those who have rocked my boat and those that have helped me row my boat. You have all been intrinsic in my life in some way or another. I have always had the opinion that families are such weird and wonderful combinations of personalities, a mismatched source of humans we call 'our family'. Yet somewhere, somehow, we all meet up in the middle, not always as promised in the storybooks, 'a happy ever after'. There are families who rejoice in the difference of one another, accepting each other's character traits, the gifts and differences they bring into this world. Then, there are dysfunctional families that thrive and encourage dislike. My belief is each individual personality has a choice, it is called free will, and what we do with our choice, decides how we live this life. I also believe, we are all spirit beings having an experience in a human body, when we do return to spirit, hopefully it is a place where we all coexist in harmony. They once accused me of being a dreamer, a free spirit, one who did not fit in, expecting me to hang my head in fear and shame. Instead, with the biggest of smiles, I would now have to agree, I love every lungful of this life.

This novel is a reminder for those whom in their own ways have taught me so much. Life is what you make of it, it's not a practise run, or is it? I simply wish you all enough.

KEZ

ABOUT THE AUTHOR

We are all unique walking stories just waiting to be told.
   Kez Wickham St George is the driver of her own creativity, and her passion is to inspire and nurture others to tell their stories. Her values are simple; when you touch a heart with your story you can change another's life.

Travelling extensively including the length and breath of Australia, she has collecting stories and experiences. Now with ten novels published, the first three; *Adventures in the Outback* published internationally, three paranormal books published nationally. Also, two children's books that now reside in many different countries and with the two Royal families of UK and Denmark. Beginning of 2019 her first book of poetry, *Entwined* was published, forming a corridor between the City of Rockingham and Ako Japan, its sister city, bringing the poets and artists of these two cities together. In 2020, Kez co-authored a reciprocal book from Ako Japan *Entwined two*. Late 2019 an invitation to be a guest speaker at a writer's retreat at Crom Castle Dublin Ireland, this placed Kez on a global stage as a speaker and international Author.

In 2020 and 2021 her recently published trilogy *Metal Mermaid, Cuppa Tree* and *Scribe* became a number one bestseller and best read five-star in her category of adventure/caravanning

Kez is also a popular speaker, however, mentoring and consulting to assist others to tell their stories has become a large part of her life, running creative writing workshops, with a little bit of art included for those that have a story to tell. Encouraging people to do what they love has resulted in eight of her writing protégés to becoming published authors in the past two years.

Kez believes that writing has many roads, she now writes for magazines, and reviews many books on two radio stations including her own FB book review. Being a prolific author has many opportunities, from the book *Scribe* a short movie is being filmed, which will visit all the film festivals around Australia. Next year, 2022, is looking like a busy year for Kez as she introduces another anthology, publishers her own autobiography and will dip her toes into research as she finds out why her maternal grandparents left Kent, England, in 1900 to sail off to immigrate to New Zealand. Life is full of magic. But most of all Kez believes, *"You become what you believe."*

BOOKS BY
KEZ WICKHAM ST GEORGE

The Campfire Trilogy
published by MMH Press

I did not want the story to stop. These three books are the beginning of Tara's journey into the world of shades, where those that have passed over have not left their stories behind them. An exciting trilogy that takes you on adventures through Australia and New Zealand. They will wake your senses to the adventure of storytelling, which the author Kez does with inspired passion. Kez is what I would say is a reader's entertainer, once you open that first page, you dare not put it down, as you don't want the excitement or adventure to stop.
M Hodges – Hokitika, NZ

Kez is a master storyteller, her candid tales of adventure and travels encountering many different characters, including those of the underworld, left me wanting to know more. I found in this book, the third campfire trilogy's Scribe, *wanting to look over my shoulder at any shadows passing by. This author brings her lead character to us the truth and honesty about how relationships can be stretched to breaking point. I also enjoyed the humour*

Kez brings with her stories, encouraging you to see the funny side of life. When we suddenly take a twist into the paranormal, an encounter with a new acquaintance Tanby, it has Tara rattled emotionally, along with a near-death experience so close to joining those of the underworld, as Tara is unexpectedly summoned to scribe for those who have left this mortal coil. I loved the tricky double ending. I found this book to be a real page-turner – once you start, you don't want to put it down. Scribe *is a mix of adventure, fun, humour, thrills and spills, and I, for one, can't wait for the anthology* The Book of Shadows *to be published in 2022.*
S Beardsley – Perth, WA

Anthology – The Colours of Me
Co-authored by Kez Wickham St George & Michelle Weitering
published by MMH Press

So many authors joined us in this beautiful book of heartwarming personal stories of their lives. Each story adding to the beauty of living a life with compassion, forgiveness and empathy. To assist in funding our chosen charity Careers Australia please visit **www.mmhpress.com** to purchase.

Scribe Chronicles

This was the beginning of many adventures for author Kez Wickham St George as she travels between the two countries she calls her home. As Kez, ever the storyteller, excites you with a fast-paced adventure, only to put the brakes on suddenly when she meet up with her spiritual muse Tanby. Be sure to wear your seatbelt – it's a fascinating exciting, bumpy ride.
A Acmond – Auckland, NZ

Poetry & Short Stories

Entwined

In conjunction with Ako City Japan & Interntional Friendship Committee Rockingham City, WA.

Children's Stories

Sea Pea | Peli the Pelican

The author Kez Wickham St George has captured the characters in these two books beautifully, both very different but delightful sea adventures to read to my grandchildren. I felt they were aimed at teaching small children to read and write their own stories. It was a delight to learn that they were in the libraries of the Royal Children of Denmark and UK.
M Taylor – Perth, WA

Coming 2022

Anthology – The Book of Shadows

www.ingramcontent.com/pod-product-compliance
Lightning Source LLC
Chambersburg PA
CBHW030253010526
44107CB00053B/1693